D0859698

Virginia at War, 1862

VIRGINIA AT WAR 1862

Edited by William C. Davis
and James I. Robertson Jr.
for the Virginia Center for Civil War Studies

THE UNIVERSITY PRESS OF KENTUCKY

Publication of this volume was made possible in part by a grant
from the National Endowment for the Humanities.

Editorial and Sales Offices: The University Press of Kentucky
663 South Limestone Street, Lexington, Kentucky 40508-4008
ISBN-13: 978-0-8131-2428-5
ISBN-10: 0-8131-2428-X

Manufactured in the United States of America.

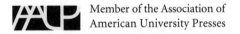 Member of the Association of
American University Presses

Book Club Edition

Contents

Preface

Virginians emerged from the year 1861 in much the same state of uncertainty and mild confusion as the rest of the Confederacy. One major battle at Manassas or Bull Run and a smaller affair at Ball's Bluff in October had both been crushing Southern victories, and humiliating defeats for the Union. Except for for Ball's Bluff, the last five months of the year had been a time of inaction and waiting, a "phony war" in later terms. While the North was known to be rebuilding its army, and building it up to epic proportions, still no one could be sure if the Northern people and government were willing to continue to prosecute a war. Even from the western Confederacy, west of the Appalachians extending to the Mississippi, there had been little real activity, and certainly nothing that could be interpreted as decisive.

And so Virginians had cause to hope for the best, side by side with reason for apprehension. Their expectations for the coming new year did not prepare them for what was really coming, however, for quickly the war became earnest and real, and the Old Dominion itself became then and thereafter the major battleground of the war in the East. The landscape and the people of the state were a part of that battleground, and as the essays comprising this second volume of *Virginia at War* attest, no individual and no aspect of Virginia life escaped the impact of the contest. As was stated in the preface to *Virginia at War, 1861*, this series will largely stay off the actual battlefield itself. Military accounts of the generals and campaigns and battles in Virginia are almost innumerable, and every year more and better ones appear. There is simply no point in trying to compress that vast story into yet another synthesis of it in these pages. Consequently, while each volume of the series contains an essay providing a succinct military overview of that year's action, it is solely for background and context to illuminate the essays that will follow. Nevertheless, because of the special circumstances of the topics at hand and the year 1862 itself, this current volume does offer rather more in the military line than the other volumes preceding and to come.

The essay outlining the movements of the armies in Virginia in 1862 comes from John S. Salmon, for many years an archivist at the Library of Virginia, and then staff historian for the Virginia Department of Historic Resources. He is the author of *The Official Virginia Civil War Battlefield Guide,* and currently creates the roadside marker texts and driving guides for Virginia Civil War Trails, Inc. His comprehensive survey of military activities in 1862 provides a backdrop and reference point for all of the essays to follow in this volume.

Harold S. Wilson is a professor of history at Old Dominion University in Norfolk, Virginia. His book *Confederate Industry: Manufacturers and Quartermasters in the Civil War,* published in 2002, is the definitive work on the South's uphill struggle to harness its limited manufacturing capabilities to the voracious appetites of war. Virginia was the major center of Confederate industrial activity throughout the war, and his essay demonstrates how the demands on, and limitations of, the state's factories first emerged and rapidly rose to a dramatic extent in 1862.

The history department at Roanoke College in Salem, Virginia, is host to Dr. John G. Selby, author of the essay on the dramatic and traumatic initial encounter of the state's civilian population with full-scale warfare on their own soil. Indeed, no Confederate citizens would experience as prolonged an enemy presence within their borders as Virginians, and Selby, author of *Virginians at War: The Civil War Experiences of Seven Young Confederates,* ably demonstrates the strains and challenges faced by all.

One of those challenges was the problem of being an invaded and occupied people. From an early date in 1862, Virginia began to see more and more of its territory come under the temporary or permanent occupation of Yankee troops, and as in all wars, such a change in circumstances and relations for both occupier and occupied led to serious confrontations in which the occupied rarely came out ahead. Thomas P. Lowry, the author of several recent works on Union military justice, and the landmark *The Story the Soldiers Wouldn't Tell* dealing with sex in the Civil War, has explored the responses of the occupying army's military justice system in dealing with federal soldiers' offenses against Virginians.

Not only did Virginia find itself playing host to occupying Yankees as well as its own Confederate forces, but it also had to deal with another new population that placed equal demands on the Old Dominion's financial and emotional resources. Large armies meant large numbers of sick soldiers, and battles meant even more wounded men. Richmond in particular became virtually a hospital city, placing serious strains on the community and its people. David J. Coles, professor of history at Longwood University in Farmville, is the acknowledged authority on Confederate hospitals in this area, and he aptly reveals the ingenuity demonstrated by medical authorities in addressing the pressing problem of a sudden population of invalids almost as great as the prewar population of the city itself.

Harold Holzer is well known to the Civil War and Lincoln community as the author or editor of a number of outstanding works on the pictorial iconography of the era. He is also the Lincoln Prize–winning author of *Lincoln at Cooper Union: The Speech That Made Abraham Lincoln President.* A vice president at the Metropolitan Museum of Art in New York, Holzer is also cochairman of the Lincoln Bicentennial Commission established by Congress to observe the 200th anniversary of Lincoln's birth. His essay on the pictorial depictions of the war that Virginians were able to view in 1862 gives us a perspective on how they lived with the conflict between the idealized version on the printed page, and what they could see in their own communities and fields.

Virginia was really multiple "states" then, as it is today, each separated and its culture and political outlook defined by geography. In the 1861 volume we looked at the Shenandoah Valley and its immediate military and logistical importance to the Confederacy. Here Brian Steel Wills examines the special circumstances of that deeply divided and equally forgotten backwater of the state. Indeed, since its importance to the state and the Confederacy was so heavily tied to its strategic location and geography, this essay of needs concentrates more on the military story than others in this volume. Wills, author of *A Battle from the Start: The Life of Nathan Bedford Forrest,* is professor of history at the University of Virginia's College at Wise in the far southwestern tip of the state.

The final essay of this volume also addresses another reality of that war for Virginians. For them, as for the Confederacy itself, the cause lived in its armies. There might be a president and a congress in Richmond, governors and legislators in state houses, and all the host of minor officials in the counties, but without its armies the Confederacy would die, and instantly. East of the Appalachians that meant Robert E. Lee and the newly christened Army of Northern Virginia. Anywhere that army moved, it constituted de facto the largest population center or "city" in the Old Dominion, and with it came all of the concerns and problems of a major city. Keeping the Confederacy alive meant keeping that army alive, and not just on the battlefield. Dennis E. Frye, historian at Harpers Ferry National Historical Park, is a longtime student of Lee's army. In addition to two regimental histories of Virginia Confederate units, he is the author of *Antietam Revealed: The Battle of Antietam and the Maryland Campaign as You Have Never Seen It Before.* His concluding essay in this volume addresses Lee's efforts to keep his army together after its first defeat, and to prepare it for its next victory in the struggle to keep Virginia inviolate and prolong the cause.

One Virginian spoke extensively in the first volume of this series, Judith Brockenbrough McGuire. Her diary published shortly after the war is an invaluable source for the personal experiences and observations of an intelligent and well-informed Virginian. Until now, however, it has never been properly edited and annotated. James I. Robertson Jr., coeditor of this volume and director of the Virginia Center for Civil War Studies at Virginia Tech in Blacksburg, has continued the task of doing that editing and annotation, thus making the McGuire diary vastly more useful and informative. To maintain balance among the several volumes of this series, and because the 1862–1864 portion of McGuire's diary is much longer than that for 1861 and 1865, only the first seven months of her 1862 diary are included here. The balance, along with much of the 1863 diary, will appear in the subsequent volume.

As before, the editors themselves and the Virginia Center for Civil War Studies are indebted to the William E. Jamerson family of Appomattox for their sustained and generous support of this series. The volume appears on the eve of the 2007 celebrations of the 400th anniversary of the founding of Virginia, and the Jamersons' commitment to the history of their state is in the finest tradition of the people of the Old Dominion for four centuries past, and a fifth one now opening. Acknowledgment is also due to the continuing commitment of the University Press of Kentucky to this project, and especially to editors Joyce Harrison and Ann Malcolm, and director Stephen M. Wrinn. They have been delightful to work with, and the result of our joint efforts has gratified every expectation.

Virginia at War, 1862

Land Operations in Virginia in 1862

John S. Salmon

During the Virginia campaigns of 1862, two men made their military reputations: Robert E. Lee and Thomas J. "Stonewall" Jackson. Three other men saw theirs demolished: George B. McClellan, John Pope, and Ambrose E. Burnside. McClellan had the distinction of rising phoenixlike from the ashes of the Peninsula Campaign only to fall from favor following his almost accidental victory on Antietam Creek in Maryland. Pope became the victim of his own bluster as well as of the successful melding of Confederate generalship at Manassas Junction. Burnside's fortunes declined after the debacle at Fredericksburg, and then he finished himself off with the infamous Mud March in January 1863. Clearly, in Virginia the year 1862 belonged to the two Confederate generals. But that is the verdict of hindsight—at the time, there seemed to be plenty of command confusion, badly crafted orders, poor teamwork, inexplicable hesitation, logistical snafus, and needless slaughter to go around.

The distance from Washington, D.C., the Union capital, to the Confederate capital of Richmond, Virginia, is about a hundred miles. In between the land is watered by rivers that range from free flowing to sluggish and swampy: Potomac, Rappahannock, York, Mattaponi, Pamunkey, Chickahominy, James. The land is flat between the Chesapeake Bay and the fall line that extends southwest from Washington through Fredericksburg to Richmond and Petersburg. Westward, in the Piedmont region, the terrain becomes more rolling until it reaches the Blue Ridge Mountains with their strategic gaps. Beyond, the Shenandoah Valley drains the Shenandoah River and its tributaries northwest into the Potomac. The Valley, a particularly fertile "breadbasket," provided Confederate forces with a back door to Washington and Federal armies with a back door to the Piedmont and Richmond. Great Union and Confederate armies would contend over this landscape until the end of the war.

Virginia's historically execrable road networks were improved during the antebellum period with several hard-surfaced turnpikes such as the Valley Turnpike in the Shenandoah. Canals, such as the Chesapeake & Ohio Canal west of Washington and the James River & Kanawha Canal that originated in Richmond, enabled barges to get around the rapids and rocks at the fall line and transport goods to and from the west. A network of newly constructed rail lines supplemented the rivers, turnpikes, and canals for the rapid transportation of armies and supplies. Railroad intersections, such as Manassas Junction, became strategically important supply depots. Civilian authorities and military commanders had to factor the speed of movement by rail into their planning.

During the winter of 1861–1862, the leaders on both sides had much else to ponder. For Abraham Lincoln, the first campaign season in Virginia had been a nightmare from the opening battle to the closing one. Brig. Gen. Irvin McDowell's raw army was trounced at the First Battle of Manassas on July 21, 1861. Exactly three months later, on October 21, a smaller Federal force was all but wiped out at Ball's Bluff on the Potomac River and Col. Edward D. Baker, a U.S. senator, was killed. Soldiers' bodies washed up in Washington for days thereafter, and Northern morale plummeted. In between the two debacles, Lincoln replaced McDowell with Maj. Gen. George B. McClellan, a superb organizer who reinvigorated the soldiers and created the Army of the Potomac. Unfortunately, McClellan refused to take the army into the field, frustrating Lincoln, who desperately wanted some good news. The popular refrain "All quiet along the Potomac" took on a sarcastic tone.[1]

Despite Confederate victories in Virginia, the prickly Jefferson Davis likewise had problems with his equally prickly generals, in particular the heroes of Manassas, Gen. P. G. T. Beauregard and Gen. Joseph E. Johnston. Quarrels erupted over who outranked whom, an irritated Davis muddied the waters further with confusing explanations, and then Beauregard published an account of the Manassas battle that seemed to slight Davis. The president packed Beauregard off to the Kentucky-Tennessee theater and decided to tolerate Johnston for the time being. At least Johnston was maintaining a presence in northern Virginia that worried Lincoln, limited access to Washington with a Potomac River blockade, and kept the cautious McClellan inside the capital's defenses.[2]

Elsewhere, the news soon improved for Lincoln. The Union Navy's blockade of Southern ports slowly grew more effective. In the West, as winter eased into spring, Forts Henry and Donelson in Tennessee would fall in February, followed by Nashville. The Battle of Shiloh on April 6–7 went down as a costly Union victory and a foretaste of carnage yet to come. On the Mississippi River, Federal forces captured Island No. 10 near New Madrid on April 8, New Orleans on April 25, and Memphis on June 6, while Vicksburg held out for another year.

Lincoln's immediate concern in Virginia, however, was to ensure that Washington was adequately defended while the Federal armies destroyed the Confederate army. His commanding general, on the other hand, seemed more eager to capture territory than to fight a decisive battle. McClellan developed a plan over the winter to transport his army down the Chesapeake Bay to the mouth of the Rappahannock River, thence up the river to interpose his force between Johnston and Richmond. He would find a good defensive position and await Johnston's attack in response to the threat to the Confederate capital. Lincoln was dismayed, noting that McClellan's plan left Johnston between McClellan and the Federal capital. Johnston himself inadvertently resolved the impasse for Lincoln when he withdrew his army south of the Rappahannock in March 1862. When McClellan marched his army to Manassas, he and Lincoln were embarrassed to find that Johnston's "formidable" defenses contained many "Quaker guns"—logs painted black to resemble cannons. Lincoln preferred that McClellan drive south in an overland campaign (such as Lt. Gen. Ulysses S. Grant would execute two years later), but the general wanted to transport his army to Fort Monroe in Hampton Roads and then march up the peninsula between the York and James rivers to Richmond. Lincoln reluctantly concurred.[3]

In Richmond, meanwhile, Davis spent the winter laying out the Confederacy's plans. He and his cabinet conferred with Johnston in Richmond on February 19, agreeing that Johnston would withdraw below the Rappahannock and bring most of the supplies from Manassas Junction. When Johnston moved, however, he did so without notifying Davis in advance and he also destroyed vast quantities of stores, irritating the president. In Johnston's defense, the rail lines south from Manassas were inadequate to the task, but Davis felt that decisions agreed to at the February meeting had not been executed and that he had been kept insufficiently informed.[4]

Both Davis and Lincoln were hands-on—even meddlesome—managers. Of the two, Davis (a Mexican War veteran) was vastly more knowledgeable about military strategy. Lincoln sought to make up the deficit by reading books on the subject. Davis did not hesitate to visit his generals in the field and offer advice, whereas Lincoln mostly wanted his generals to be in the field themselves and acting aggressively. Davis required special handling that the reticent and touchy Johnston could not supply; Robert E. Lee, on the other hand, quickly acquired the knack.[5]

Lee was one of the brightest stars in the U.S. Army when he resigned after Virginia seceded in April 1861, a protégé of Gen. Winfield Scott who was offered command of the Federal army but declined. Lee's reputation suffered when, after accepting command of Virginia forces and then a commission as a Confederate general, he led a lackluster campaign in western Virginia in the fall of 1861. He spent the winter in Savannah, Georgia, assigned to strengthen the South Atlantic coastal defenses—a hopeless task, given limited resources and the Union Navy's ability to attack wherever it wanted. Davis recalled him to Richmond in March 1862 as his principal military advisor, knowing that Lee's talents were being wasted and sensing that here was a man with whom he could converse. Lee's military experience, optimistic demeanor, and innate tact reassured Davis. Lee learned quickly that Davis was a high-maintenance commander in chief who needed to be kept informed. Davis, unlike Lincoln, had found his ideal general.

As Davis and Lee conferred, McClellan began embarking his army on March 17 to sail to Hampton Roads, the shipping channel that linked the James River with the Chesapeake Bay. The area was in Union hands despite a fright on March 8–9, when CSS *Virginia* (formerly USS *Merrimack*, transformed into a Confederate ironclad), savaged the wooden Federal fleet before dueling to a draw with USS *Monitor*, the Union entry in the ironclad arms race. It took McClellan until early in April to get his 100,000-man force in place.

McClellan would have had an even larger army were it not for Lincoln's detaching or withholding some elements to guard Washington and confront a new threat to the west. The general had assured Lincoln that some 70,000 troops protected the capital but Lincoln counted fewer than 30,000 (McClellan had counted some twice), withheld a corps, and detached other troops.

This enraged McClellan, who was convinced that he was being set up to take the blame if his campaign failed. He had, as was his habit, persuaded himself that he faced a vastly larger Confederate force that he in fact outnumbered by two or three to one. Lincoln was undermining him, McClellan claimed.[6]

Lincoln was perhaps overly worried about the threat to Washington, but he had a legitimate concern about recent events in the Shenandoah Valley, where one of the Confederate heroes of Manassas, Maj. Gen. Thomas J. "Stonewall" Jackson, was ranging freely. So many legends have accrued to Jackson, both in his own time and later, that the facts are sometimes difficult to discern. He was by all accounts a peculiar man, but his quirks and tics have been exaggerated (he may have liked lemons, but he loved all fruit, especially peaches). His famous ability to fall asleep at any time may have been the product of exhaustion, for he drove himself as relentlessly as he drove his men. There is no question, however, that Jackson was lucky: lucky in the opponents he faced, in his subordinates, in having good maps while his opponents had poor ones, and in leading men who would fight for him with unmatched zeal. But his was the luck born of an iron will, strict discipline, the ability to learn and adapt, and the confidence that success breeds. His victories also brought him good press, with the Southern papers declaring him the Confederacy's first great hero and the Northern papers creating a fearsome image of Jackson the will-o'-the-wisp, here, there, and everywhere. In the public's eye, his star eclipsed Lee's until Jackson's death in 1863.[7]

Jackson first surfaced in Lincoln's consciousness as a serious threat immediately after March 23, 1862, when the general launched an attack at Kernstown, just south of Winchester near the northern end of the Shenandoah Valley. The Union commander, Maj. Gen. Nathaniel P. Banks, had about 28,000 men and orders from McClellan to clear the Valley of Confederates, occupy Winchester, leave a small force there to guard the turnpikes and railroads, and then proceed to Manassas Junction to help protect the capital. Jackson, whose Valley army numbered about 4,600, retreated from Winchester to Mount Jackson as Banks approached and then pursued him. When Banks began to withdraw to Winchester on March 21, however, Jackson followed, then attacked at Kernstown two days later. The attack failed, and Jackson suffered the only defeat of his career, when the center of his line collapsed; Brig. Gen. Richard Garnett had ordered his men to fall back as they ran out of ammunition. Jackson later sought to court-martial

Garnett for cowardice but conditions prevented it, and Garnett continued his service until he was killed at Gettysburg.[8]

Despite Jackson's defeat, his attack put a scare into Lincoln, who ordered Banks to stay in the Valley and Maj. Gen. Irvin McDowell to remain in northern Virginia with his corps instead of joining McClellan. He also assigned Brig. Gen. Louis Blenker's 10,000-man division and Maj. Gen. John C. Frémont's similar-sized Mountain Department army to reinforce Banks. McClellan was thus immediately denied the use of about 50,000 troops thanks to Jackson.[9]

As Banks's reinforcements inched toward the Valley, his and Jackson's forces sparred with each other for the remainder of March and almost all of April. In the Tidewater, meanwhile, McClellan began his slow crawl up the peninsula on April 4. His massive army faced about 17,000 Confederate troops under Col. John Bankhead Magruder. The colorful "Prince John," as he was known, had constructed two lines of earthworks across the peninsula from Yorktown south to the James River. When McClellan probed the works in present-day Newport News in what is called the Battle of Dam No. 1 on April 16, the stiff little fight that resulted convinced him that he faced 100,000 men in impossibly strong positions. He decided to besiege the Yorktown lines and pound them flat with mortars. The delay allowed Johnston time to reinforce Magruder and bring the total number of Confederates to about 50,000, so that McClellan's actual numerical superiority shrank from almost six-to-one to two-to-one. When he launched his grand assault on May 4, he was shocked to find the lines empty and the works relatively weak. Johnston and Magruder were falling back toward Richmond. After a twelve-hour pause, McClellan set off in pursuit.[10]

The Federal advance caught up with the Confederate rear guard on May 5 at Williamsburg, in the first major clash of the Peninsula Campaign. Earthworks prepared earlier by Magruder protected the Southerners, who were under Maj. Gen. James Longstreet. Union Brig. Gens. Joseph Hooker and William F. Smith attacked the works directly while Brig. Gen. Winfield S. Hancock led a brigade around the Confederate left flank. Longstreet counterattacked Hooker but Brig. Gen. Philip Kearny's division held him off, while Confederate Brig. Gen. Jubal A. Early struck back at Hancock. Early's counterattack failed for lack of reconnaissance and coordination, and Early was wounded. Under cover of darkness, the Confederates withdrew.[11]

Two days after the battle, on May 7, a brief engagement took place south of Eltham's Landing on the Pamunkey River, after Brig. Gen. William B. Franklin's division disembarked from transport vessels and entrenched. Maj. Gen. Gustavus W. Smith, guarding the Confederate wagon train nearby, ordered Brig. Gen. W. H. C. Whiting to attack. After some fighting, and learning that Confederate artillery could not protect Whiting from gunboats out of range in the river, Smith broke off the engagement. The losses were light on both sides.[12]

As McClellan marched, other Federal troops in Hampton Roads occupied Norfolk and sent gunboats up the James River to attack Richmond by water. The way opened when Confederate authorities blew up the CSS *Virginia* because it was too heavy to escape. Soon, Union gunboats steamed upriver as far as Fort Darling, or Drewry's Bluff, where sunken vessels blocked the channel and Confederate gunners deployed their cannons. On May 15, the Federals suffered defeat when the artillerists fired with remarkable accuracy and the gunboats could not elevate their pieces enough to respond effectively. The Union Navy never again seriously threatened the Confederate capital.[13]

The York River forks at West Point, near Eltham's Landing, and the north branch is called the Mattaponi while the south branch is the Pamunkey. South of the Pamunkey, the Chickahominy River flows southeast to the James River, roughly paralleling the Pamunkey for several miles. McClellan pursued Johnston as he withdrew between the Pamunkey and the Chickahominy, until the Confederates crossed over the latter river and entered earthworks north and east of Richmond, destroying bridges as they went. Eventually, near the end of May, McClellan also began crossing his army over the Chickahominy on rebuilt bridges, corps by corps. On May 27, one of his corps commanders, Brig. Gen. Fitz John Porter, defeated a Confederate brigade near Hanover Court House, and within a couple of days two of McClellan's five corps had crossed the Chickahominy.[14]

Johnston's opportunity came on the evening of May 30, when a thunderstorm washed out bridges and turned the sluggish Chickahominy into a swampy lake. He attacked McClellan's divided army the next day at Seven Pines (Fair Oaks), but garbled orders, confusion on the roads, and an "acoustic shadow" that kept him from hearing nearby gunfire, resulted in mistimed and piecemeal Confederate assaults. Johnston himself was wounded that evening, and Gustavus Smith took command. Smith only lasted a day, launching an uncoordinated attack on June 1 and then suffering an emotional collapse under the pressure. Jefferson Davis ordered Lee to take his place. Lee, in turn, ordered the Confederates into their earthworks, and for the next several weeks he had them strengthening the fortifications. The Southern press criticized him, but Lee reasoned that stronger works would free more men for combat. McClellan cooperated by stopping his army within sight of Richmond's church steeples and spending the next several weeks complaining to his wife and Washington about the lack of reinforcements.[15]

In the Shenandoah Valley, meanwhile, Stonewall Jackson had been busy. Just after the engagement at Kernstown in March, he ordered amateur cartographer Jedediah Hotchkiss to make him a detailed map of the Valley. The elegant and accurate result gave Jackson a large advantage over his opponents, whose maps were outdated and sketchy. In April, as McClellan began his march up the peninsula, Lee ordered Jackson to shift from defense to offense, hoping thereby to keep Federal troops tied up in the Valley. On April 29, Jackson sent a plan to Richmond and put his army in motion without waiting for a response. His force had grown to about 14,500 with the addition of Maj. Gen. Richard S. Ewell's division. He marched his men eastward from Port Republic and out of the Valley, as though his objective was Richmond, then had them board trains and ride back into the Valley and disembark at Staunton. Jackson's great Valley Campaign was under way.[16]

"God blessed our arms with victory at McDowell yesterday," Jackson wired Richmond on May 9, after defeating Frémont's advance force in a fierce engagement atop Sitlington's Hill in Highland County. He pursued Frémont for a few days, then turned back to the Valley and marched north against Banks. Jackson concealed his movements from the Federals in the Luray or Page Valley, then overran the Union garrison at Front Royal on May 23 to expose Banks's right flank. At the First Battle of Winchester two days later, Jackson turned the Federal flank again and chased Banks into Maryland.[17]

Lincoln dispatched more troops to the Valley under Brig. Gen. James Shields. Jackson marched south up the Valley Turnpike ahead of Frémont, and Shields gave chase up the Luray Valley. On June 8, Frémont caught Jackson napping at Cross Keys but Ewell halted Frémont's advance. The next day, when Shields's vanguard emerged from the Luray Valley northeast of Port Republic, Jackson attacked and drove it back. Shields and Frémont retreated northward, leaving Jackson in control of the upper Valley. The Valley Campaign had ended, and Lee ordered Jackson to Richmond.[18]

During a period of about five weeks, Jackson and his 17,000-man "foot cavalry" defeated three Federal armies totaling 52,000 troops. He inflicted about 7,000 casualties while suffering about 2,500. He and his men marched roughly 650 miles and fought several battles. Jackson upset Lincoln's and McClellan's plans, made his name famous throughout the country, and aided the Confederate defensive effort at Richmond. Luck and skill had combined to give him a brilliant strategic victory. He would not fare so well at first under Lee's direct command.[19]

As Jackson's force proceeded with uncharacteristic slowness toward Richmond (probably because of exhaustion and poor logistical planning), Lee was about to take the offensive against McClellan. On June 12, he sent Brig. Gen. J. E. B. Stuart and his cavalrymen on a reconnaissance that became known as the "Ride around McClellan" and revealed that the Federal right flank was "in the air"—not secured by a natural or manmade feature. Lee decided to strike that flank on June 26, but the day before he did so, McClellan launched an attack of his own at Oak Grove, a probe of the Confederate lines. It amounted to little, and Lee attacked as planned the next morning. His army, which he had renamed the Army of Northern Virginia, crossed the Chickahominy River and hit Fitz John Porter's corps near Mechanicsville. Jackson was supposed to join in from the north but never arrived on the battlefield, having gotten lost in the unfamiliar and heavily wooded terrain. The attack stalled until Maj. Gen. A. P. Hill, frustrated by the delay, sent his division across Beaver Dam Creek near Ellerson's Mill east of Mechanicsville. The Federals were well dug in, and the result was a bloody Confederate defeat. Porter withdrew east in the night to a new position near Gaines's Mill.[20]

Lee struck Porter again the next day, June 27, in the bloodiest battle thus far in Virginia. Porter's corps held high ground, and Lee's commanders— A. P. Hill, D. H. Hill, Longstreet, and Jackson—attacked piecemeal until launching a concerted effort late in the day. Porter's line caved in at last, and he withdrew after suffering about 6,800 casualties; the Confederates lost about 8,700. South of the Chickahominy, meanwhile, a two-day action began on the Garnett and Golding (Gouldin) farms as John Magruder demonstrated against the Federal line.[21]

The attacks alarmed McClellan, who decided to "change his base" from the Pamunkey River to the James. In May he had established his supply base at White House, the home of one of Lee's sons, Col. W. H. F. "Rooney" Lee, on the south bank of the Pamunkey. There his army was supplied both by ship and by rail, using the Richmond & York River Railroad from West Point. Fearing that his supply line might be threatened, McClellan ordered his base shifted to the James River, ultimately to Harrison's Landing at Berkeley Plantation. Critics called it "the great skedaddle." From this point on, McClellan's actions were purely defensive, designed to cover the withdrawal.[22]

As the Federals moved south, Lee pursued. McClellan, ironically, had thought Lee would be overly cautious in the field; now he would learn how wrong he was. On June 29, Magruder struck again, this time at Savage's Station on the Richmond & York River Railroad, where he assaulted McClellan's rear guard under Maj. Gen. Edwin V. Sumner. McClellan had to order the combative Sumner repeatedly to break off the action and continue the march south. When the Confederates occupied the station, they found some 2,500 wounded and sick Union soldiers abandoned there.[23]

The next day, at Frayser's Farm near present-day Glendale, Lee launched a coordinated attack against the Federal army that succeeded briefly in penetrating the Union center. Jackson, marching to attack the Federal right flank, was delayed at White Oak Swamp, while Maj. Gen. Theophilus H. Holmes failed to turn the Union left near Malvern Hill. Lee thus lost his best opportunity to bag McClellan's force, which that evening took up a strong position on Malvern Hill.[24]

On July 1, the last of the Seven Days' Battles took place at Malvern Hill. It was a sad and bloody ending to Lee's relentless pursuit of McClellan, when everything that could go wrong for the Confederate general did. The massed Federal cannons atop the height silenced Lee's artillery; Magruder, commanding the Confederate center, marched and countermarched to no avail; other units arrived on the battlefield piecemeal; and Lee sent one attacking force after another up the middle, where the Union guns slaughtered them. D. H. Hill later observed, "It was not war—it was murder." McClellan, fortunately for the Confederates, insisted on continuing his retreat against the advice of his generals, who saw a golden opportunity to counterattack. Instead, the army marched to Harrison's Landing, where by July 4 it rested in a solid defensive position and for the next month Lee kept a wary eye on it.[25]

As the Army of the Potomac endured the heat and humidity of summer on the James River, in Washington Lincoln was forming a new army—the Army of Virginia—from Banks's, Frémont's, and McDowell's forces in north-central Virginia. He summoned Maj. Gen. John Pope, a pompous blowhard, from the west to command it. And he ordered McClellan to evacuate Harrison's Landing and join Pope in a new campaign against Richmond. McClellan angrily complied with the first part of the order, and on August 16 the last of his army marched away to Fort Monroe, leaving Quaker guns in the works to decoy the Confederates—with doubtless unintended irony.[26]

In Richmond, the Confederate government and people sang Lee's praises as they rejoiced over their deliverance and treated the thousands of wounded flooding the city. As Southern morale soared, Northern confidence plummeted at first as the public absorbed the news of McClellan's defeat. Soon, however, a grim resolve followed, as well as a massive recruitment campaign and an ominous shift toward the concept of total war. Congress passed a confiscation act in July, and its principal enforcer in Virginia was John Pope. He responded enthusiastically, seizing Confederate property and threatening to execute partisans and expel civilians who refused to take a loyalty oath. Although Pope did not carry out the latter threats, Confederate leaders branded him a savage and threatened retaliation.[27]

Lee shifted most of his army north in July to counter the strategic problem posed by Pope's forces. He ordered Jackson and 12,000 men to Gordonsville, an important rail junction, and then reinforced him with A. P. Hill and 13,000 more men. On August 9, Jackson (once again his aggressive self) fought Pope's advance divisions under Banks at Cedar Mountain in Culpeper County. Soon, the two armies faced each other across the Rappahannock River, where Pope planned to remain until McClellan reinforced him. Lee countered by sending Jackson around Pope's right flank and into his rear to strike the great Union supply depot at Manassas Junction. After creating havoc, Jackson took up a position on a wooded ridge just west of the old battlefield while Pope dispatched forces to find him. On August 28, as Lee, Longstreet, and the remainder of the Army of Northern Virginia marched through Thoroughfare Gap to join Jackson, one of Pope's divisions stumbled across Jackson and the Second Battle of Manassas began.[28]

Pope rushed his army to the field and attacked Jackson piecemeal the next day. Lee and Longstreet arrived in the afternoon, but Longstreet convinced Lee that then was not the time for his corps to attack. On August 30, as Pope sent his force to pursue a supposedly retreating Jackson, Longstreet fell on the Federal left flank and almost crushed it. Pope's men withdrew to Henry Hill, where they made a stand and then retreated to the Washington defenses. Jackson hit them again at Chantilly or Ox Hill the next day, in a vicious rearguard action fought during a thunderstorm, but the Federals escaped.[29]

McClellan, meanwhile, had remained with most of his army near Washington, where he essentially rooted for Lee against Pope, whom he regarded as a usurper of his rightful position as army commander. Although most members of Lincoln's cabinet wanted McClellan dismissed, the president understood that the soldiers still favored him. Lincoln sacked Pope and installed McClellan, who seemingly in a few days had his delighted men ready for the field.[30]

Haste was necessary, for Lee had lost no time in leading his weary but spirited men into Maryland on September 4 for his first invasion of the North. Lee and Davis hoped that the army could resupply itself there, urge an uprising of Confederate sympathizers, encourage foreign recognition of the Confederacy, and convince the demoralized North to give up the fight. None of these goals was achieved. The Confederate army found little but green corn and apples in the fields, the population of western Maryland proved largely loyal to the Union, and McClellan's bloody strategic victory at Antietam Creek on September 17 forestalled any possibility of foreign recognition or intervention. It also reinvigorated the Union war effort. In Washington, Lincoln found in the victory the opportunity he sought to issue a preliminary Emancipation Proclamation on September 22. Emancipation sentiment had been growing all year as most Northern politicians came to understand that slavery was the root cause of secession and the war. Now Lincoln was changing the nature of the conflict in Northern eyes, from a war for the Union to a war for Union and freedom.[31]

McClellan, meanwhile, exulted in his victory, but soon Lincoln was prodding him to cross the Potomac River and pursue and crush Lee. Both armies were battered, Lincoln understood, but surely the Army of Northern Virginia was in worse shape and could be destroyed by a decisive blow? McClellan, however, would not be moved and only crossed the river on October 26, more than a month after Lee. Jackson was posted in the Shenandoah Valley, on McClellan's right flank, and Longstreet blocked the way to Richmond. McClellan encamped his army around Rectortown and refused to budge. Lincoln decided enough was enough and replaced him on November 7 with Maj. Gen. Ambrose E. Burnside. McClellan gave up command of his beloved army with surprising graciousness, and spent the next two years nursing his ambition to be president.[32]

Burnside, who did not consider himself qualified to command the army (he would prove himself correct), acted quickly. Within ten days he had marched two of his corps to the eastern side of the Rappahannock River across from Fredericksburg. He planned to cross the river on pontoon bridges and conduct an overland campaign to Richmond. Unfortunately, the pontoons went astray and Burnside had to wait—a delay that Lee employed to entrench his army on the high ground across the river. When the pontoons finally arrived, Burnside's engineers laid the bridges under intense Confederate sniper fire on December 11. Union infantry then crossed over, looted the town, and prepared to attack. On December 13, the assault came. Jackson held firm on the Confederate right, while Longstreet occupied Marye's Heights on the left, overlooking Fredericksburg. Here the Federals ran into a meat grinder; Longstreet's massed artillery and infantry fire cut them down by the thousands. As bloody for the Union army as Antietam had been, the Battle of Fredericksburg would forever be remembered for its concentrated carnage. Burnside wanted to attack again the next day, but his horrified lieutenants talked him out of it.[33]

With this battle, the fighting in Virginia ended for the year. Burnside remained in command of the Army of the Potomac, but not for much longer. Lee's men guarded the Rappahannock River fords and settled in for the winter. Jefferson Davis traveled west to rally his generals there. Lincoln prepared to issue the final Emancipation Proclamation, which also permitted the enlistment of African American soldiers, thereby changing the course of the war and giving captive peoples a hand in their own liberation. And, finally, the truth dawned on the civilians of both sides: 1862 had been a turning point. This would be a war to the death, and a bloodletting unprecedented in American history. No one knew how it would end, but the old Union was dead and gone, whether the country reunited or not. The question was what would take its place. Both sides looked to the new year with some hope—and much fear—of what was to come.

Notes

1. David Herbert Donald, *Lincoln* (New York: Simon & Schuster, 1995), 318–20; John S. Salmon, *The Official Virginia Civil War Battlefield Guide* (Mechanicsburg, Pa.: Stackpole Books, 2001), 58.

2. William J. Cooper Jr., *Jefferson Davis, American* (New York: Alfred A. Knopf, 2000), 363–65.

3. James M. McPherson, *Battle Cry of Freedom: The Civil War Era* (New York: Oxford University Press, 1988), 423–25; Stephen W. Sears, *To the Gates of Richmond: The Peninsula Campaign* (New York: Ticknor and Fields, 1992), 5–11; Salmon, *Battlefield Guide*, 58–59.

4. Cooper, *Davis*, 374.

5. Donald, *Lincoln*, 329; Cooper, *Davis*, 342, 346–47; Emory M. Thomas, *Robert E. Lee: A Biography* (New York: W. W. Norton, 1995), 198, 227.

6. McPherson, *Battle Cry*, 425; Salmon, *Battlefield Guide*, 61; Donald, *Lincoln*, 352; Sears, *Gates of Richmond*, 32–34.

7. James I. Robertson Jr., *Stonewall Jackson: The Man, the Soldier, the Legend* (New York: Macmillan, 1997), 143, for his preferences in fruit, and 517, for one example among many of his sleeping habits; Salmon, *Battlefield Guide*, 27–30.

8. Salmon, *Battlefield Guide*, 33–35.

9. McPherson, *Battle Cry*, 425.

10. Salmon, *Battlefield Guide*, 76–80; McPherson, *Battle Cry*, 426–27; Sears, *Gates of Richmond*, 42–62.

11. Salmon, *Battlefield Guide*, 80–83; Sears, *Gates of Richmond*, 70–82.

12. Salmon, *Battlefield Guide*, 83–85; Sears, *Gates of Richmond*, 84–86.

13. Salmon, *Battlefield Guide*, 86–87; Sears, *Gates of Richmond*, 91–94.

14. Salmon, *Battlefield Guide*, 88–91; McPherson, *Battle Cry*, 461; Sears, *Gates of Richmond*, 112–17.

15. Salmon, *Battlefield Guide*, 91–95; McPherson, *Battle Cry*, 461–62; Sears, *Gates of Richmond*, 117–45.

16. McPherson, *Battle Cry*, 454–55; Salmon, *Battlefield Guide*, 31; Robertson, *Jackson*, 363–70.

17. Salmon, *Battlefield Guide*, 35–44; Robertson, *Jackson*, 371–410.

18. Salmon, *Battlefield Guide*, 45–54; Robertson, *Jackson*, 435–47; for a thorough treatment of the Battles of Cross Keys and Port Republic, see Robert K. Krick, *Conquering the Valley: Stonewall Jackson at Port Republic* (New York: William Morrow, 1996).

19. Salmon, *Battlefield Guide*, 32.

20. Robertson, *Jackson*, 467–68; Sears, *Gates of Richmond*, 167–74, 183–209; Salmon, *Battlefield Guide*, 95–101.

21. Salmon, *Battlefield Guide*, 102–9; Sears, *Gates of Richmond*, 210–48.

22. Sears, *Gates of Richmond*, 210–11.

23. Sears, *Gates of Richmond*, 57, 265–74; Salmon, *Battlefield Guide*, 109–12.

24. Sears, *Gates of Richmond,* 277–307; Salmon, *Battlefield Guide,* 113–19.

25. Sears, *Gates of Richmond,* 308–36; Salmon, *Battlefield Guide,* 119–24.

26. McPherson, *Battle Cry,* 488–89; Sears, *Gates of Richmond,* 355–56.

27. McPherson, *Battle Cry,* 490–92; Cooper, *Davis,* 393; Thomas, *Lee,* 248–49.

28. Thomas, *Lee,* 249–53; Salmon, *Battlefield Guide,* 125–45; see Robert K. Krick, *Stonewall Jackson at Cedar Mountain* (Chapel Hill: University of North Carolina Press, 1990), for the definitive study of that battle.

29. Salmon, *Battlefield Guide,* 145–54; for a detailed account of the campaign and battle, see John J. Hennessy, *Return to Bull Run: The Campaign and Battle of Second Manassas* (New York: Simon & Schuster, 1993).

30. McPherson, *Battle Cry,* 528, 533.

31. McPherson, *Battle Cry,* 534–36, 545, 557–58.

32. Thomas, *Lee,* 265; McPherson, *Battle Cry,* 568–70.

33. Salmon, *Battlefield Guide,* 161–65; Thomas, *Lee,* 269–72; McPherson, *Battle Cry,* 570–72.

Virginia's Industry and the Conduct of War in 1862

Harold S. Wilson

In the second year of the war Confederate troops in Virginia endured both the enemy at the front and the inefficiency of the Confederate War Department at the rear. Sometimes there were more supplies to be obtained from the enemy on the battlefield than from the Confederacy's rear depots.[1] Battlefield literati wrote that planters took better care of common slaves than the Confederate government did its soldiers. Deliveries of military supplies were sporadic; but there were both peaks and valleys. Confederate bureau chiefs in the War Department, Abraham C. Myers in the Quartermaster's Bureau, Josiah Gorgas in Ordnance, and Lucius Northrop in Commissary, faced enormous problems. They had to work with a parsimonious government and a limited military budget. At this stage of the war they had only limited influence over privately owned factories, foundries, and railroads. The demands of the Navy Department, the surgeon general, and state agencies added to the confusion of procurement. Confederate civilians, themselves, were very reluctant to surrender control of the marketplace to military necessity, and a revolutionary government in Richmond was reluctant to force public rationing of scarce supplies. A still larger shortcoming, at all levels, was a general lack of knowledge about what military resources Virginia and the South really possessed, and no agency was charged with securing such information. In the great evolution toward modern war, the War Department in Richmond struggled mightily to overcome its greatest deficiency, a want of method and organization; however, by the fall of 1862 a permanent military supply system began to take shape and prepare armies for the great campaigns ahead.

The classic writers on warfare, such as Henri Jomini, called for armies to gather supplies for a great battle or short campaign, to build depots on lines easily adjacent to the main forces, and to fight the decisive battle. If there were more battles, then this ritual would be repeated until a victory was achieved or defeat ensued. This is much the way the Confederate army went to war in 1861, with men mostly equipped from the store shelves of the South. For many Virginians the battle of Manassas in July 1861 was the great decisive battle of the war and an excusable reason for the government's general lethargy through the ensuring months.

The actual extent of Virginia's material resources for war was unclear as early as the secession convention of 1861. In that gathering, usually in closeted sessions and muted tones, a number of delegates showed a general awareness that the South was the fourth- or fifth-most developed region in the world, that Virginia was easily the most developed state in the South, and that the urban areas of Richmond and Petersburg held the core of Virginia's manufacturing. These premises underlay much of the confidence of the ultra secessionists, although they saw the need for imports. The state clearly led the South in the production of critical metals and minerals such as iron, lead, salt, and coal. In 1853 Virginia had twenty-nine blast furnaces, which consumed 1.5 million bushels of coke and charcoal and 114,000 tons of coal to produce 43,000 tons of pig iron.[2] By 1860 many of these mills were idle, but sixteen furnaces in the west successfully competed with Pittsburgh and Great Britain to produce 23,000 tons of pig a year. With war practically all went into service. About half of the twenty establishments across the state engaged in rolling, casting, and milling were located near Richmond and Petersburg. Joseph R. Anderson, West Point graduate and former chief engineer of the Valley Turnpike, was the chief proprietor of Tredegar Iron Works, the premier iron works of the South, which had a rolling mill, locomotive shop, and cannon foundry. The Bellona Foundry, in Chesterfield County, cast the cannons installed at Fort Monroe. Others, such as the Union Manufacturing Company, made sewing machines and factory findings. In 1860 Virginia also produced 3.4 million bushels of salt, mostly from Saltville, and quantities of lead at Wytheville.

In the Virginia convention not all delegates agreed with the delegate who boasted that with secession, "our noble waterfalls would whistle with machinery, and the spindles of the North would be transferred to the Potomac, the Rappahannock, and the James," but few Virginians doubted that the Old Dominion could raise, equip, and maintain an army of 125,000, enough to defend a northern military frontier before Washington.[3] George Wythe Randolph, subsequently secretary of war, advised pointedly on the issue of state preparedness.

He explained that the state in 1850 produced a surplus of 5 million bushels of wheat, enough to bread a large army. By secession Virginia harvested 63 million bushels of wheat, rye, corn, and oats, which were processed by over 1,300 mills, making the state the fourth-largest flour exporter state in the union. Two of the three largest flour mills in the country, the ten-storied Gallego Mills and the Haxall Company, were in Richmond and produced over 1 million bushels of flour a year.[4] The offal from these mills alone was sufficient to provide short fodder for a small cavalry arm. As secretary of war, Randolph's subsequent exclusive and lucrative contracts with the Haxall Company proved quite controversial. Virginia held nearly three hundred thousand horses. By 1862 over 10 percent of this number were in military service in Virginia, and, by regulation, eating three or four quarts of oats or corn a day.

The state wool clip amounted in peacetime to 2.8 million pounds, a sufficiency to uniform a large army. To fabricate this product, 121 woolen mills were available.[5] Most of these mills held no more than a half-dozen looms, but two of the largest woolen mills in the South were located near Richmond, the James River Manufacturing Company, operated by Effort B. Bentley, and the Crenshaw Woolen Mills, owned by Joseph H. Crenshaw and brothers. Jacob Bonsack at Salem, Granville J. Kelly and John E. Tackett at Fredericksburg, and Benjamin Crawford at Staunton operated other large and productive woolen factories. There were two dozen productive factories lying near the wool district in the Lower Valley.

Virginia also had thirty cotton mills processing almost twenty thousand bales a year, and again the larger ones lay adjacent to the James and Appomattox rivers. The leader of Virginia's wartime cotton manufacturing was a unionist, Archibald G. McIlwaine, of Petersburg. A native of Londonderry, Ireland, McIlwaine was the principal owner of the Merchant's Manufacturing Company, as well as three other large Petersburg mills, Ettrick, Matoaca, and Battersea, serving as president for each on occasion. The Virginia mills employed 3,000 workers and produced over 15 million yards of duck, sheeting, and shirting in 1860 along with 1.8 million pounds of yarns, twine, and ropes.[6] These factories provided a sufficiency of rags and waste cotton to support a dozen paper mills, two at Richmond. The Southern paper mills produced on average about 5,000 pounds of paper a day, and in 1862 the Belvidere paper mill at Richmond earned $172,000 on a capital investment of $41,000.[7]

Virginia's transportation facilities tied producers and manufacturers to their markets, often in the North, and provided easy access to the anticipated fronts in northern Virginia. Possessing 652 miles of rails in 1851 in such stellar lines as Orange & Alexandria, Richmond & Danville, Southside, Manassas Gap, Central, Norfolk & Petersburg, Virginia & Tennessee, and the Seaboard & Roanoke, Virginia's total track mileage by 1860 rose to 1,771, or one in every fifteen miles in the United States. Highly competent Northern firms manufactured most of the engines and rolling stock. Mileage of telegraph lines linking major cities was more than double that of railroads. The James River & Kanawha Canal, a venture that cost the state over $6 million, followed the James River through the Blue Ridge Mountains at Balcony Fall and tapped an extensive river network of producers and markets along a 147-mile route. Mostly free from ice, in 1860 the canal carried $12 million of merchandise. An interior network of smaller canals and roads served such cities such as Alexandria, Norfolk, and Charlottesville.

In going to war, Virginia's political leaders carefully considered the advantages of seizing important federal installations such as the arsenal at Harpers Ferry with over twenty thousand rifles, Fort Norfolk with three thousand barrels of powder, and the Gosport Navy Yard with its dry dock and vast array of cannons, naval stores, and machine tools. The state arsenal in Richmond, built after John Brown's raid, was a valuable asset quickly conveyed to the Confederacy, and expanded under the direction of James H. Burton with the addition of a set of rifle-musket machinery taken from Harpers Ferry.

As Southern military forces assembled in Virginia after First Manassas, Confederate and state authorities attempted to forge instruments of war from these resources. Armies needed weapons, ammunition, food, uniforms, and tents. They also needed canteens, shoes, knapsacks, hats, wagons, blankets, horseshoes, and saddles. Soap, candles, and paper were important. The *Richmond Enquirer* boasted in June 1861 that "in every section we hear of new and extensive enterprises springing up; it is no sooner ascertained that we are deficient in a certain manufactory, than the ingenuity and energies of our people are enlisted to make the very article needed."[8] In villages and cities across the state local manufacturers were pressed into service to provide usable articles for the troops, but self-help of necessity gave way to a more systematic method of provisioning. Although costly, despite the loss of West Virginia and portions of northern Virginia along the Potomac by the late fall of 1861, the state still held substantial reserves of material resources for the conduct of war.

The movement of the Confederate government to Richmond and Confederate military forces to Virginia's northern frontier created an opportunity to rationalize and organize a system of procurement. Virginians who had some acquaintance with state resources were layered into the critical bureaus of the military departments. Professor Albert Taylor Bledsoe, from the University of Virginia, became an assistant secretary of war in charge of the Bureau of War. William B. B. Cross, a son-in-law of Thomas Ritchie, editor of the *Enquirer,* became Abraham Myers's chief assistant in the Quartermaster's Bureau, and Larkin Smith, a native Virginian, was appointed manager of the Richmond depot. In the Commissary Bureau Lucius Northrop chose Francis "Frank" G. Ruffin as his chief aide. Ruffin, a member of an illustrious secessionist family, was well connected with planters, having previously edited the *Farmer's Register.* James H. Burton from Harpers Ferry worked under Gorgas, and French Forrest served as an assistant secretary of the Navy Department.

These men were in a position to mediate between centralized Confederate authorities and the local business leaders. Burton, at the arsenal, developed a close working relationship with Anderson's Tredegar Iron Works, Frank Ruffin patronized the Haxall and Gallego mills, French Forrest played a leading role in exploiting the assets of the Gosport Navy Yard, while Cross and Smith developed a network of contacts beginning with William Crenshaw and his woolen mill. These were arrangements full of good potential.

However, Confederate military policy was based on the premise of a short war or the decisive battle doctrine with the war being waged by a citizen militia. Until its repeal on October 8, 1862, the commutation statute required volunteers to rely on self-help whereby they equipped themselves in return for a monetary stipend, initially $25, every six months, "the government in no way making itself responsible to the party furnishing the clothing for the amount due."[9] There was some rationality in the policy. Merchants and manufacturers were dispersed across the South, and as militia units were mustered into service, they could be prepared locally. Soldiers were equipped either individually or through company and regimental quartermasters, and Confederate authorities paid the commutation money. Through local agents, particularly near rail junctions such as Staunton and Lynchburg, the War Department purchased leather and metal ware for army use. The onset of the winter of 1861–1862 forced a modification in these rules. After noting that "the war existing between this Government and that at Washington will probably be prolonged during the coming winter," Myers charged the individual governors "to have made up at an early day, to the extent of your ability, woolen clothing to supply the needs of the Army, to be charged to this Government."[10] The governors called upon local aid societies to fill the breach. For good reasons many soldiers said it was the women of the Confederacy who saved the army that winter. Bundles of quilts, blankets, comforters, cut-up woolen carpets, socks, soaps, and condiments found their way through the aid societies to the front.

Virginia was singled out as an exception to Myers's new rule. The quartermaster composed a special response for Governor John Letcher: "As the resources of the State of Virginia are entirely taken up by the Quarter Master's Department of the Confederate States, I respectfully suggest they remain so, and that the Governor be informed to that effect. This will render it unnecessary for him to cooperate with the Department in procuring supplies."[11] Of course, the governor could not entirely abandon the markets of the state. The inmates of the prisons and asylums, patients at hospitals, impressed slaves, the indigent, soldiers' widows, and state troops came under his purview. Letcher found it necessary to order Charles Dimmock, the state ordnance officer, to establish a manufacturing facility at Lynchburg to provide for these commonwealth responsibilities. Nor could the state neglect the Provisional Army. While North Carolina, South Carolina, Georgia, and Alabama provided basic camp equipage and a clothing supply for their troops in Virginia in 1861–1862, Virginia could do no less.[12] A subsequent report by the state quartermaster itemized expenditures of $2 million on behalf of the Provisional Army and the State Line troops, or about $60,000 a month throughout 1862.[13]

Other active agencies also sought supplies in the Virginia market. Michael G. Harman, a business leader and quartermaster at Staunton, especially promoted the interests of Maj. Gen. Thomas J. "Stonewall" Jackson and the Army of the Valley; James L. Corley, a South Carolinian, served as an aggressive staff quartermaster to Lee throughout the war; and Alfred M. Barbour, earlier a member of the Virginia secession convention, was a vigorous, strong-minded chief quartermaster for Gen. Joseph E. Johnston's Army of the Potomac. Johnston himself had been chief quartermaster of the old army. The public represented another important interest in the commonwealth. Planters were persistently advised from press, hustings, and pulpit to break out the old wooden looms and manufacture homespun in the manner of Virginians during the War of 1812, and many did so. A British visitor noted "that nearly all the planters find some difficulty in buying clothing for their slaves, and they have therefore resorted to the common spinning-wheel and hand-loom for the manufacture of woolen and cotton."[14] Several patterns of handmade looms were on the market. John Scott of Fredericksburg sold modern, mechanical twill looms at $100 each. However, many planters, especially those that needed cotton warps for weaving, chose not to follow this advice, but rather besieged the mills in droves looking for goods. Many patronized the black market established by shops that dealt with smuggled, imported, and "surplus" war goods.

The prospects of a short war and the competitiveness for limited resources contributed to an early hiatus in planning at the center. After arriving in Virginia, Myers conducted a perfunctory "inquiry among intelligent merchants" and concluded "that the resources of the Southern States cannot supply the necessities of the Army of the Confederate States with the essential articles of cloth for uniform clothing, blankets, shoes, stockings, and flannel."[15] Other bureau heads, Gorgas and Northrop, came to similar conclusions. It is unlikely that Myers conducted a very thorough investigation of Virginia's resources, although he had easy access to the state's merchant and manufacturing elite. Larkin Smith queried William Crenshaw, whose new woolen factory was on the James River a few blocks away: "Will you do me the favor to advise me of the location of any blanket manufactory in Virginia, or North Carolina?"[16] Crenshaw himself had the best set of double-width looms for making blankets in the state. Factory agents for the seven local textile factories were easily available for advice, men such as John Lemoine, the agent for the Mechanics Manufacturing Company; Richmond merchants James Lynch and David Callendar, who represented three mills at Petersburg (Ettrick, Matoaca, and Battersea); and Effort B. Bentley, the proprietor of the James River Manufacturing Company. In Richmond George W. Randolph had already publicized the fact that over half of the ready-made clothing, shoes, and hats sold in the city came from the North, and he believed "it is in vain that we struggle to make ourselves a manufacturing State, while we have adversaries so powerful . . . as the manufacturers of the Northern States."[17]

Although Myers quickly contracted for woolens with Crenshaw as well as Kelly, Tackett, Ford, and Company in Fredericksburg, he readily embraced a strategy calling for dependency upon foreign supply, should the campaigns last into 1862. In October 1861, he repeatedly urged the secretary of war to turn to Europe for materials, "if the war is to continue for any length of time."[18] Myers's preferred foreign appointment was James B. Ferguson, the senior proprietor of a local import house. After lengthy lobbying, Myers secured approval to dispatch Ferguson to England in 1862 with $1 million in cotton bonds. Agents from the Ordnance Bureau, such as Caleb Huse, were already on the foreign scene cooperating with Trenholm, Frasier, and Company. In the meantime, Myers contracted with private firms for substantial imports to supply the army in 1862; some of these companies were French firms operating through New Orleans. However, by the summer of 1862, with the exception of the cargoes of the *Bermuda* and the *Fingal,* the latter brought into Savannah by James Bulloch, practically no foreign supplies reached Richmond.

To meet miscellaneous requests from the troops, Myers established a clothing manufacturing establishment under Larkin Smith and Richard Waller, then, later, a shoe fabrication workshop managed by Ferguson's brother, William. In one transaction, he bought sixty thousand yards of duck from Scott and Green at Fredericksburg, and, probably, other cottons from local mills, but Lee's maneuvers in western Virginia in the fall of 1861 and Johnston's needs at Manassas quickly drained the department of all its shoes and woolens. Myers's procedure, he wrote Lee in western Virginia, was to await requisitions from the army quartermasters before having the necessary articles made up. Buying on the local markets of the state and undertaking small-scale manufacturing seemed sufficient.

In the late fall of 1861 Andrew Hunter from Harpers Ferry visited Richmond, called on Jefferson Davis and Secretary of War Judah P. Benjamin, and brought news of important resources in the Valley totally neglected by the War Department. In his district Hunter counted "twenty-three considerable woolen factories pouring out daily from 6,000 to 8,000 yards of army cloth." A distant relation of Union Gen. David Hunter, Andrew Hunter was the state attorney who prosecuted John Brown. As well as beef and wheat, he pointed out the Lower Valley held a plentiful supply of mountain wool and in fifty days could manufacture about as much clothing as Myers proposed to purchase abroad. "Should the war be prolonged," he advocated military action "to uncover these rich resources of both food and clothing." Hunter later wrote that the product of these Valley mills, probably manufactured in large part at Staunton, "contributed largely toward clothing the [Virginia] army last winter [1861–1862]."[19]

Michael Harman, Jackson's regional quartermaster at Staunton, identified these mills and quickly began the manufacture of army clothing. On December 30, 1861, Myers found it necessary to warn him: "You will issue immediate orders to agents who are seeking in different parts of the state, to make contracts with different factories to furnish cloth for the Staunton manufactory, that they will discontinue their operations. The clothing establishment at Richmond had engaged the supplies of all the factories, and no competition with them can be allowed."[20] It is unlikely that Myers had such binding contracts with all mills. Duff Green's Falmouth Cotton Mill at Fredericksburg sold the Clothing Bureau between two thousand and five thousand yards of duck a week through the fall and winter, an allotment that was only a portion of its total product.[21] Myers had token contracts with some mills, but with many Virginia mills no contracts at all.

Like Myers, other bureaus of the War Department concentrated manufacturing in Richmond: Gorgas expanded the armories, arsenals, and laboratories to downtown tobacco warehouses. In June 1861, the Sloat Sewing Machine Company began the production of machines to make percussion caps.[22] A month later 370 women and girls commenced the manufacture of cartridges on Bird Island.[23] By October, five hundred women and three hundred men produced two hundred thousand cartridges a day.[24] A visitor proclaimed, "Richmond is invaluable as a manufactory of arms and munitions of war. We make nearly everything here important to service."[25] At regional cities, particularly Staunton, Lynchburg, and Fredericksburg, Lucius Northrop established local depots for fodder and meal, even those staples gleaned from the front. He and Ruffin established a large pork packing facility at Charlottesville for the exclusive use of the army. Confederate officers on the front often complained about supply trains loaded with fodder and food leaving northern Virginia for Richmond while troops and animals on the line were in great need. In the Quartermaster's Department Myers not only bought goods and distributed them, but commenced the manufacture of uniforms and shoes in the Clothing Bureau.

The number of military issues of articles of clothing, tents, and camp and garrison equipage during the winter of 1861–1862 gave evidence of the inadequacy of Myers's planned system of supply. Between October 11, 1861, and March 29, 1862, a period of almost six months, the Quartermaster's Bureau delivered the following to Gen. Joseph E. Johnston's Army of the Potomac:

Overcoats	11,475	Shoes	26,214
Coats	15,546	Boots	1,056
Pants	14,604	Hatchets	347
Shirts	17,584	Picks	2,192
Drawers	15,587	Spades	1,084
Caps	7,174	Pans	3,520
Socks	6,407	Kettles	1,318
Blankets	27,747	Skillets	500[26]
Tents	8,265		

The most conspicuous items issued were the overcoats, blankets, and shoes, many of which were either fabricated in the lower South or manufactured in the Richmond Clothing Bureau from materials provided by Georgia mills. A contract with Kelly, Tackett, Ford and Company provided for ten thousand blankets, but a portion were from the cargo of Bulloch's *Fingal;* the remainder were probably manufactured by William Crenshaw. Cotton was plentiful, but wool was increasingly scarce. Once the stocks of the larger city merchants were exhausted, hatchets, skillets, and pans had to be fabricated by local whitesmiths or blacksmiths and sold to quartermasters or else manufactured in Richmond shops under contracts with the depot. Overall these returns reveal little effort to tap into Virginia's rich prewar resources outside of the Richmond area. Rather than seek wool in the Valley and contested western Virginia, Myers rather placed contracts to purchase two hundred thousand pounds on the Mexican-Texan border. When field commanders complained about the scarcity of items, the bureau enjoined them to be more provident.

Behind the lines an impressive array of wartime manufactures appeared by the spring of 1862. The April issue of *DeBow's Review* gave a glowing review of Virginia's newly found industrial progress. New iron forges, button factories, tanneries, and soap factories abounded across the state. Old blast furnaces were rekindled. Artisans at Lynchburg and Richmond launched new enterprises in making lucifer matches, envelopes, felt hats, and caps. Salt production at Saltville, mostly controlled by Confederate authorities, rose first to two thousand bushels a day, then, with numerous deep wells dug, three thousand bushels daily. Wytheville's lead and new chemical compounds fueled weapons production in Richmond, as Duck River copper and tin flowed to Virginia. In Richmond, Staunton, and Madison County there were new shoe factories under military contract. A new large wagon factory was in operation at Staunton. At Charlottesville there were new manufacturers of swords, oil cloth, harnesses, and saddles, while at Hampton Roads the Union Car Works turned to the production of gun carriages, wagons, wheelbarrows, camp stools, tent poles, and pins, saber bayonets, and bowie knives.[27]

In competition for these goods perhaps no field quartermaster created a greater challenge for Myers in Virginia than Alfred M. Barbour of Johnston's Army of the Potomac. Major Barbour, a native of Jefferson County, superintended the armory at Harpers Ferry at the time of John Brown's raid. Along with Henry Wise and George Wythe Randolph, he was an outspoken ultra at Virginia's secession convention and personally participated in the seizure of the federal facility. He aided the War Department in securing the machinery of the arsenal and transporting it to Richmond, where he helped establish the first percussion cap facility. As Gen. Joseph E. Johnston's chief quartermaster, at times, Barbour's operations in Virginia rivaled those of the large Richmond depot, for he leased numerous warehouses in the city, maintained a fleet of 104 four-horse wagons and teams, and established at Richmond his own quartermaster staff.[28] His transactions, sometimes amounting to hundreds of thousand of dollars, were legendary, and he left little paper trail. Barbour personally contracted with cotton mills through Petersburg agents Lynch and Callendar for 16,680 cloth sacks, and hired his own staff of blacksmiths, forage agents, teamsters, and free black laborers. He expended $6.3 million, or about one-half million a month, from secession through September 1862. Probably for political reasons, Myers approved these vouchers without a formal review, a tacit acknowledgement of the limitations of his own bureau.

By the spring of 1862 the short-war doctrine was in decline. The passage of the first Confederate Conscription Act of April 16, 1862, exempted certain critical categories of workers from the draft, and control of these exemptions was delegated to the respective bureaus. In Virginia, Myers granted exemptions to workers at only six woolen mills, apparently the only mills with which he was contracting. These were Manchester, Scottsville Manufacturing Company at Charlottesville, Keath and Chilton at Waterloo, and three mills at Fredericksburg: Granville Kelley, Green and Scott, and Washington Mills. The latter produced blankets, and the bureau regarded it as "the largest mill in the country & [it] is running exclusively for the Government."[29] Other major woolen mills were inexplicably excluded: William Crenshaw at Richmond, John Bonsack at Salem, and Benjamin Crawford at Staunton. The mills may not have had wool, or else the mills employed substitutes or slave workers. A British visitor at the Richmond mills found a common sight, "slaves both men and women, engaged in weaving by power, in the card room, at the throstles, mules, winding and warping, and [he] heard upon inquiry that they made tolerably good hands," and produced a good quality of sturdy cloth.[30] The new Confederate Conscription Act gave the War Department considerable leverage over owners, their families, and their hands.

In other ways, the mills evolved into a dependency on the War Department. By spring 1862 a number of woolen factories that traditionally relied on Baltimore merchants for pickers, shuttles, reeds, card clothing, dyes, and warps were in short supply, and James B. Ferguson responded by establishing something of an exchange facility for these orphans. Ferguson called on Francis Fries, a spinner at Old Salem, North Carolina, to forward regularly ten to twelve bales of warps a week, number ten thread, with 1,200 ends, for distribution.[31] Among the grateful recipients were John G. Martin of the Scottsville factory at Charlottesville, Samuel Pursel at Circleville in Loudoun County, Thomas B. Wood at Morgan Mills in Strasburg, James Watson at the Millville factory in Jefferson County, and Duff Green in Fredericksburg. The small mills needed warps, while the larger mills near Richmond needed wool. Necessity gradually moved the War Department into acting as both central supplier and purchaser of goods.

If the movement toward centralization needed any further impetus, it was the Federal invasion in the spring of 1862 that exposed gross weaknesses in the improvised supply system. In anticipation of the great events to come, Myers wrote George Randolph, then secretary of war:

It sometimes happens that regiments, after receiving the regulation allowance of clothing in kind, or drawing commutation money, with which to supply themselves, have lost without fault on their part, in the casualties of the campaign, all, or a portion of their clothing, application is then made for a new issue; and the question arises, whether the value thereof is to [be] charged to the soldier; or the government. . . . I have not felt at liberty to order re-issues, even under the peculiar circumstances stated, without directing that stoppages be entered against the men.[32]

With the armies of Gens. John C. Frémont, Nathaniel Banks, James Shields, Irvin McDowell, George B. McClellan, and Ambrose Burnside poised around the periphery of the state, the loss of resources seemed likely. The surrender of Gen. Henry Wise's entire command on Roanoke Island to General Burnside was only the beginning of a spring filled with disasters as the Confederate defensive perimeter in Virginia contracted.

Unaware until the last moment of McClellan's seaborne movement from northern Virginia to the peninsula, on March 7 Johnston ordered a precipitate withdrawal of Confederate forces from Manassas Junction to Gordonsville. An Alabama officer, William C. Oates, described a scene verified by many others: "We were marched by the Junction in splashing mud, where we saw huge piles of baggage and stores of various kinds ready for the consuming flames. Vast supplies which our army soon sorely needed were destroyed. . . . Johnston's retreat from Centerville [Centreville] and Manassas was precipitate and with unnecessary haste, which sacrificed vast stores and supplies of all kinds. Among them vast quantities of clothing which the people at home had sent to the soldiers in trunks and boxes were unnecessarily given to the flames."[33] Federal soldiers soon arrived on the scene and found debris littering a front of several miles. McClellan wrote, "This movement from here was very sudden. They left many wagons, some caissons, clothing, ammunition, personal baggage, etc. Their winter quarters were admirably constructed, many not yet quite finished."[34]

A much longer and incriminating catalog of abandoned Confederate materials was assimilated by the hearings of the Federal Joint Committee on the Conduct of the War. Other theaters were similarly threatened. On March 18 Myers requested that Johnston immediately evacuate 7.5 million pounds of quartermaster and commissary stores from Fredericksburg and direct the supplies to a new depot; Richmond controlled no rolling stock on the Fredericksburg railroad and the storehouses along the line were full. The large flouring, textile, and manufacturing enterprises at Fredericksburg were also endangered, as well as facilities at Norfolk and Portsmouth.

Responding to Andrew Hunter's persistent pleas about Valley mills, on June 16 Myers wrote General Jackson, soliciting his aid in garnering supplies,

> Your successful movements in the Valley . . . afford the substantial results of opening to us resources from which we have been cut off. Among these is the opportunity of securing fine supplies of cloth from the various mills which have already been brought within lines. I therefore, request, that you will detail an officer of the Q. M. Department for the purpose of procuring all the cloth to be obtained in the Valley, and also purchase shoes or leather if either can be obtained. . . . Messrs. Wood & Brother of the Morgan Mills near Winchester [Strasburg] have on hand from fifteen to twenty thousands yards of cloth, part of a supply contracted to be furnished by them. So soon as you reach Winchester, it is desirable that this stock should be secured.[35]

Myers wanted the goods delivered either to Smith in the Clothing Bureau at Richmond or Harman at Staunton for fabrication. He little knew that Jackson, who rarely neglected to sequester available military supplies, had placed his entire army between the Federals and the small mill at Port Republic in a battle only a few days previous.

McClellan's advance up the peninsula compelled Confederate authorities to fight an intensive series of defensive battles to secure the administrative and manufacturing base at Richmond. To compound the confusion of the spring, General Lee ordered the military evacuation of the city. Larkin Smith promptly discharged the employees of the Clothing Bureau and dispatched almost one thousand packages of goods and equipment to the Danville depot. The military calls for men, both white and black, in the local factories further acerbated the situation. As the battles opened, Barbour presented requisitions for a complete outfit of 40,000 men in the Army of the Potomac, and Myers exploded in anger to Secretary Randolph. Vast stores had been lost in the retreats, new supplies were totally inadequate, there was a want of economy on the part of the troops, and the Conscript Bureau seized skilled men from factories working on the Quartermaster's account. Unless rectified, "the inability to fill requisitions for the different species of Quartermasters stores must be indefinitely continued and the resources of the country cannot be made available for the important requirements of the service," Myers wrote.[36] When Lee requested tents for the entire army a few weeks later, Myers replied that no tents or tent flies would be issued over the summer. The Army of Northern Virginia was practically bereft of tents. While soldiers employed the principle of self-help on the battlefield, Myers renewed his demands to provision the army from foreign sources. "Every exertion has been made to render all the resources of the country available," Smith wrote Randolph, "but if, in the matter of clothing and shoes, there were ample supplies of the raw material[,] the capacity to manufacture them is wanting, thereby rendering it certain that a reliance upon our own sources of supply will be in vain."[37] However, with the tightening of the Federal blockade, reliance on local resources seemed the only way to keep the army in the field through the fall.

With only modest resupply over the summer, Lee's army that invaded Maryland on September 5 presented a very bedraggled appearance. A Georgia reporter widely cited across the Confederacy and in Europe, Peter Wellington Alexander, described a force in which "a fifth of the troops are barefooted; half of them are in rags, and the whole of them insufficiently supplied with food."[38] About the only way soldiers could get soap or combs was to make them or buy them. Lee's official correspondence after the Antietam campaign noted 6,648 men without shoes alone in Longstreet's corps, exclusive of Ransom's brigades. On September 21 Lee wrote Myers:

> I desire to call your attention to the great deficiency of clothing in this army (particularly under-clothing and shoes), for the want of which there is much suffering. When in Maryland, I am informed by Colonel Corley, there were purchased, through individuals privately, by the Quartermaster's Department, for distribution, some 4,000 or 5,000 pairs of shoes. This was by no means sufficient to supply the men without them, there being at this time at Winchester a camp of 900 men who are not effective because barefooted, and a great many more likewise with the army. The near approach of cold

weather renders it all the more necessary that clothes, and especially underclothing should be supplied.[39]

Lee's letter was based on the certain knowledge that the Richmond factories produced millions of yards of cotton cloth suitable for underclothing and that over one hundred Virginia tanneries had no binding contract with the War Department for leather. He ordered that all supplies within the lines of his army within the Valley and northern Virginia be directed to Major Harman at Staunton, where one factory produced four hundred pairs of shoes each week for Jackson's command. Richard Waller in the Clothing Bureau shared this frustration. Four hundred bales of woolens from Mexico were arrested at the Mississippi River by a military commander, blockade-runners brought in little of value, and Virginia wool supplies were either exhausted or inaccessible. On November 7, he wrote Smith, "If this depot keeps going, I must have competent men and money *at my command* to go South for wool. I state as my deliberate judgment, that the alternatives are to get wool at the south, or virtually, to *stop*. To think of stopping in the midst of a snow storm to day with a great army in the field without overcoats, so far as my knowledge extends and many other comforts in the way of clothing, appalls me."[40]

With four inches of snow in Richmond and more in the mountains, on November 8 Alexander, the Savannah journalist, heaped coals on the heads of the War Department personnel: "A brigade, composed for the most part, if not entirely, of South Carolinians, passed through this city yesterday, many of the men in which were badly clothed and destitute of shoes. Their feet was as naked as when they first came into the world, and yet they marched over the frozen streets through a furious snow storm, and right under the eye of the Government officers by whom they have been so cruelly and shamefully neglected!"[41] While this scene transpired, Waller in the Clothing Bureau held contracts with a half dozen Virginia woolen mills for minimal supplies: Crenshaw for twenty-five thousand yards of blanket material, Scottsville Mills for fifty thousand yards, Manchester for ten thousand yards, Danville Mill for between five thousand and twenty thousand yards, and with two or three small mills for a few thousand yards each. There were two outstanding contracts with Petersburg mills for cotton goods for shirts and drawers.

In October and November Alexander and the editor of the *Richmond Whig* toured the Clothing Depot and found 58 tailors and 2,700 seamstresses manufacturing 2,500 garments a day for Virginia troops. The establishment,

William Ferguson explained, turned out eight thousand to ten thousand suits of pants and jackets each week, but less if the force also worked on drawers, shirts, and overcoats. The scraps of woolens left from the cuttings were made into quilts at the state prison; cotton scraps went to the paper mills. Ferguson wrote the *Richmond Whig* in November that contracts were outstanding for shoes, blankets, and uniforms to outfit 1 million men and that issues during the previous twelve months included "153,347 blankets and 320,000 pairs of shoes and boots" as well as "a proportionate amount of other clothing," but Alexander disputed these figures.[42] By his own estimation, in twenty days from mid-September to mid-October, the army received only thirty-three thousand garments, an outfit for fourteen thousand soldiers, which "will afford very great relief as far as it goes; yet it will fall far short of the necessaries of the army."[43]

The press, the Virginia legislature, and the Confederate Congress demanded an accounting for any shortcomings. Public clamor, while acknowledging the failures of an errant government, was chiefly directed at speculators and manufacturers who seemed to be extortionists. The resulting legislation effectively established the War Department on a path toward the centralization of authority. On October 8, 1862, Congress ended the commutation system. On October 9, a congressional act permitted up to two thousand cobblers to be detailed to government shops to manufacture shoes. Within this authority William Ferguson contracted with 159 tanneries, secured 200 detailed men for the Richmond Shoe Depot, and raised the manufacture of shoes to 600 pairs a day. On October 11 the Second Confederate Conscription Act authorized the quartermaster general to delimit the profits of all contracting mills to 75 percent on costs through the control of exempt or detailed workers. With this act the lower South mills were effectively bought under Myers's control, and their products with greater facility brought to the Virginia theater. A New York newspaper noted, "the government shows a determination to do the best for the army, and let the people take care of themselves in the way of necessities."[44]

As the armies of Lee and Burnside faced each other across the Rappahannock River at Fredericksburg in the winter of 1862, the *New York Herald* puzzled, "How are we to account for these great Southern armies?"

The loyal Union man of the North, who is aware of the hundreds of millions and immense manufacturing labors which have been required to arm and equip forces of the Union in the field, will be embarrassed to account for these multitudinous armies of the South, raised by a spurious government, without money or credit, and from a combination of States hitherto almost wholly dependent upon the North and upon foreign nations for all their manufactured articles, from their hats to their shoes, and from their carriages and harness to the very hoes with which they cultivate their cotton.[45]

Surprised that armies of over three hundred thousand men had been raised and equipped, the newspaper noted that in Virginia cobblers, tailors, and seamstresses at cities such as Lynchburg and Richmond produced "large quantities of boots, shoes, clothing, and supplies" for Lee's army, and shoes were "more plentiful among the people now than at any time since the blockade" while cloth was "also more plentiful and cheaper."[46] This industrial base in Virginia, consisting of skilled personnel, natural resources, and manufacturing establishments, provided the great bulwark for the forces that successfully resisted the Federal invasions in 1862.

Notes

1. Useful studies of Virginia's war industries include Charles B. Dew, *Ironmaker to the Confederacy: Joseph R. Anderson and the Tredegar Iron Works*, 2nd ed. (Richmond: Library of Virginia, 1999); Frank E. Vandiver, *Ploughshares into Swords: Josiah Gorgas and Confederate Ordnance* (Austin: University of Texas Press, 1952); Angus J. Johnston, *Virginia Railroads in the Civil War* (Chapel Hill: University of North Carolina Press, 1961); James H. Brewer, *The Confederate Negro: Virginia's Craftsmen and the Military Laborers, 1861–1865* (Durham, N.C.: Duke University Press, 1969); and Harold S. Wilson, *Confederate Industry: Manufacturers and Quartermasters in the Civil War* (Jackson: University Press of Mississippi, 2002). The author expresses his appreciation to the Vicki Betts Archive, http://www.uttyl.edu/vbetts/.

2. Richard Swainton Fisher, *A New and Complete Statistical Gazetteer of the United States of America Founded and Compiled from Official Federal and State Returns, and the Seventh National Census* (New York: J. H. Colton, 1853), 887.

3. Virginia, *Proceedings of the Virginia State Convention of 1861* (Richmond: Virginia State Library, 1965), I, 178, 200.

4. Ibid., II, 740; Joseph C. G. Kennedy, *Preliminary Report on the Eighth Census, 1860* (Washington, D.C.: Government Printing Office, 1862), 64.

5. Fisher, *Statistical Gazetteer,* 886–87.

6. Edward Pollock, *Historical and Industrial Guide to Petersburg, Virginia* (Petersburg, Va.: T. S. Beckwith, 1884), 34; Book of Wills, January 1, 1878, Va.-Petersburg Courthouse, 310–15; U.S. Ms. Census-1860, Pop., Va.-Dinwiddie, 294/2,879.

7. *Savannah (Ga.) Republican,* March 27, 1863; *Austin (Tex.) State Gazette,* July 22, 1861.

8. *Richmond (Va.) Enquirer,* June 4, 1861.

9. A. C. Myers to James Glover, May 30, 1862, War Department Collection of Confederate Records, T-131, reel 8, National Archives, Washington, D.C. (hereafter cited as T-131).

10. Leroy P. Walker, circular to governors, August 7, 1861, *War of the Rebellion: Official Records of the Union and Confederate Armies* (Washington, D.C.: Government Printing Office, 1880–1901), series IV, vol. 1, 534 (hereafter cited as *OR*).

11. A. C. Myers to L. P. Walker, August 12, 1861, Letters Sent to the Confederate Secretary of War, April 1861–January 1864, Quartermaster General's Office Ms. chap. V, vol. 157, RG 109, National Archives.

12. Thomas G. Pickens to Francis W. Pickens, September 20, 1861, Governor F. W. Pickens Papers, South Carolina Archives; Thomas O. Moore to Judah P. Benjamin, September 29, 1861, *OR*, series II, vol. 1, 707.

13. Virginia, *Messages of the Governor of Virginia, and Accompanying Documents,* doc. no. VIII, "Report of the Quartermaster General of the State of Virginia, 1864" (Richmond, Va., 1864).

14. *Richmond (Va.) Whig,* June 9, 1864.

15. *OR*, series IV, vol. 1, 314–15.

16. Larkin Smith to Crenshaw & Co., May 17, 1861, T-131, reel 7.

17. *Proceedings of the Virginia State Convention of 1861,* I, 750.

18. A. C. Myers to J. P. Benjamin, October 10, 1861, *OR*, series IV, vol. 1, 688.

19. Andrew Hunter to George W. Randolph, July 5, 1862, *OR*, series I, vol. 51, pt. 2, 587–88.

20. A. C. Myers to M. G. Harman, December 30, 1861, T-131, reel 8.

21. "Falmouth Cotton Mill—Letterpress Book—1859–1867," July–October, 1861, Duff Green Papers, Duke University, Durham, N.C.

22. *Memphis (Tenn.) Daily Appeal,* June 8, 1861.

23. *Memphis (Tenn.) Daily Appeal,* July 25, 1861.

24. *Natchez (Miss.) Courier,* October 25, 1861.

25. *Clarksville (Tex.) Standard,* September 13, 1862.

26. Quartermaster General's Report to Honorable L[ucius J.] Dupree, Confederate House of Representatives, March 29, 1862, T-131, reel 8.

27. *Charleston (S.C.) Mercury,* April 29, 1862.

28. Wilson, *Confederate Industry,* 70, 316n.

29. Exempts in Woolen Mills, March 1, 1862, Letters Received by Confederate Quartermaster General, 1861–1865, M-469, reel 1, National Archives.

30. *Richmond (Va.) Whig,* June 9, 1864.

31. F. & H. Fries to John L. Martin, April 29, 1862, Fries Ms., Moravian Historical Society, Old Salem, N.C.

32. A. C. Myers to George W. Randolph, April 5, 1862, Confederate States of America, Quartermaster Department Papers, National Archives.

33. William C. Oates, *The War between the Union and the Confederacy, and Its Lost Opportunities* (New York: Neale, 1905), 88–89.

34. Cited in ibid., 88.

35. A. C. Myers to T. J. Jackson, June 16, 1862, T-131, reel 8.

36. A. C. Myers to G. W. Randolph, May 23, 1862, T-131, reel 8.

37. Larkin Smith to G. W. Randolph, July 31, 1862, *OR,* series IV, vol. 2, 30.

38. *Savannah (Ga.) Republican,* October 1, 1862.

39. R. E. Lee to A. C. Myers, September 21, 1862, *OR,* series I, vol. 19, pt. 2, 614.

40. Richard Waller to Larkin Smith, November 7, 1862, Compiled Service Records of Confederate Generals and Staff Officers, and Non-regimental Enlisted Men, M-331, reel 258, National Archives (hereafter cited as M-331).

41. *Savannah (Ga.) Republican,* November 14, 1862.

42. William G. Ferguson to McDonald, editor of *Richmond (Va.) Whig,* November 18, 1862, M-331, reel 92.

43. *Richmond (Va.) Whig,* October 18, 1862.

44. *New York Herald,* November 10, 1862.

45. *New York Herald,* September 21, 1862.

46. *New York Herald,* November 10, 1862.

Virginia's Civilians at War in 1862

John G. Selby

When the new year of 1862 dawned, Virginians could look forward with a mixture of relief and trepidation. The enormous state had lost 24,000 square miles in October 1861, when forty-eight counties in the northwestern sector seceded from the state, coming under Federal protection. Given that the sentiment in most of those counties was decidedly Unionist, there was little sense of loss in Confederate Virginia. Two battles had been fought on Virginia's soil, Manassas in July and Ball's Bluff in October 1861, both ending in Confederate victories. Virginia's armies were in winter quarters now, resting and training in anticipation of battles to come. Taxes were up, enlistments down, and spot shortages of provisions were occurring, but on the whole Virginia's citizens had weathered the first year of war quite well. With the Federals steadily building a large army near Washington, however, Virginians knew that the spring would bring fresh battles and occupying armies. How Virginia's civilians reacted to the tragedy and privations of the second year of the war would set the tone for the rest of the war.

The first test came from Richmond. Disappointed by the lagging number of reenlistments and new enlistments, Governor John Letcher encouraged the General Assembly to pass a law requiring all white males between eighteen and forty-five years of age to enroll for county militia service. That was soon followed by authorization for Letcher to use militiamen in volunteer levies, should that be necessary. As he told the representatives on February 17, "We are too apathetic, too insensible to the wants and necessities of the times. . . . Now is the day and now is the hour." Across the state enlistments soon rose, and some disbanded companies reformed. Ranks swelled, however, in the spring, when the Union armies pushed out of their winter camps and began marching through the Old Dominion.[1]

One of the first towns to come under Union army domination was Warrenton. The rituals of Sunday worship were rudely disturbed on April 6, when churchgoers left their pews to observe the approaching soldiers "as far the eye could see." For young Amanda "Tee" Edmonds of Fauquier County, war arrived when Union troops set up tents in the hills around her village of Paris on April 10. The thud of boots could be heard on the streets of Front Royal later that month, when Lucy Buck watched Union troops go by, "a file of infantry with their bayonets glistening and arms flashing in the morning sun."[2]

By late May 1862, Union troops occupied or had occupied large swaths of Virginia, from Fauquier County in the west, through Manassas, down to City Point and even Norfolk and Suffolk in the east. Though civilians had been afraid of plunder and pillage on a colossal scale, little of that had actually occurred in this early stage of the war. Actually, more random acts of kindness probably showed rather than overt displays of hostility, as the Northern soldiers and Southern civilians tested the boundaries of a new, forced relationship. In Suffolk, for instance, a Union lieutenant threatened to shoot an unidentified soldier accused of stealing property. At the Buck home in Front Royal, a Union corporal took it upon himself to serve as a guard for the Buck's house, and Susan Caldwell of Warrenton had a visit from Union Lt. William J. Mackey, a former lodger in her parent's boarding house in Charleston.[3]

Matching the fear and uncertainty of Union occupation was the un-bridled joy of liberation by Confederate forces. When Maj. Gen. Stonewall Jackson's army chased Maj. Gen. Nathaniel Banks's army out of Middleton in May, Pvt. Robert T. Barton recalled, "Everything in Middleton turned out to greet us, men, women, girls, children, dogs, cats, and chickens, and nobody corrected the frequently repeated mistakes when some pretty girl would take some young man for her brother." Similar scenes occurred in Stephens City and Winchester as Jackson concluded his grand Valley Campaign.[4]

It took the massive movement of huge armies and the fierce fighting of the Peninsula Campaign to bring the full impact of the war to many Virginians. Beginning in March the 100,000-strong Army of the Potomac slowly and relentlessly advanced from Yorktown northeast up the peninsula, capturing Williamsburg after a hard fight on May 5 and edging within seven miles of Richmond in the weeks following the Battle of Seven Pines on May 31–June 1. Nearly 5,000 Confederate soldiers were wounded at this battle (triple the number wounded at the Battle of Manassas), and the sheer numbers overwhelmed the military and private hospitals. Hundreds of wounded men were sent to private homes, and the people of Richmond, led by its women, "cooked and sent refreshments, beds, pillows, and blankets, water, soap, and all that could for the time relieve the helpless sufferers." Richmond resident Sallie Putnam further recalled: "The daily routines at the hospitals, from dawn till night were performed by the ladies of Richmond, to whom these sad duties, though so painful, were the chief delight."[5]

As the difficult tasks of comforting the wounded and burying the dead proceeded throughout June, the two large armies jockeyed for position along the Chickahominy River. In a week of hard fighting, Lee sent portions of his 72,000-man army against perceived weak spots in McClellan's Army of the Potomac. Just as the long casualty list at the Battle of Shiloh in April had brought the full import of this civil war to citizens of the West, the staggering numbers of dead, wounded, captured, and missing sent shock waves to those living in the East. It was left to the families of the more than 35,000 total casualties to absorb the complete impact of war's horrors. And the burden fell heavier on Southern families, whose 20,000 casualties exceeded Northern casualties by over 4,000 men (reflecting the greater toll that offensive maneuver almost always exacted).[6]

As always in great campaigns, some units suffered tremendous losses, while others had light losses, or may not even have seen combat. The four regiments from the Virginia counties of Nansemond, Southampton, and Isle of Wight had twenty-eight casualties at the Battle of Malvern Hill alone. One Southampton mother wrote her daughter, "Frank Crocker is mortally wounded[,] Captain Vermillion is killed. . . . Joe Whitehead[,] Bob Whitehead, and Euclid Borland all shot in the arm and ball still in the arm of Bob. . . . Col. Eley's son had both feet shot off." In sharp contrast stood the activities and results in Pvt. Henry Robinson Berkeley's Hanover Artillery. A three-hour artillery duel at the Battle of White Oak Swamp on June 30 produced no casualties for his unit, which then sat out the Battle of Malvern Hill.[7]

Meanwhile, the residents of Richmond braced for another flood of dead and wounded. Sallie Putnam wrote: "We lived in one immense hospital, and breathed the vapors of the charnel house." Though Richmond had been saved, "there were no bells rung, no cannon fired, no illuminations, no indecent manifestations of exulting victory over our enemies." Instead, people tended to the wounded and buried the dead. While the "mournful strains of the 'Dead March'" echoed through the streets when officers were laid to rest, others were buried without ceremony in burgeoning cemeteries. As a gravedigger later told Putnam: "We could not dig graves fast enough to bury the soldiers."[8]

As the Confederates of Richmond counted their losses and breathed a collective sigh of relief for the survival of their city, another group of Virginians, its large population of black slaves (490,000 at the start of the war), found nothing to cheer as the Army of the Potomac retreated to the safety of Harrison's Landing on the James River. The slow trickle of runaway slaves (called "contrabands" by the Federal government) that reached Union lines around Fort Monroe in 1861 had swelled to a river of humanity in the spring of 1862, with numbers increasing daily as McClellan's army moved up the peninsula. By mid-summer 1862 the thousands of slaves who had fled to Union lines overwhelmed Federal authorities, who assigned most to residence in ramshackle "contraband camps." The largest camp was established on Craney Island, in the Elizabeth River. There two thousand Afro-Virginians attempted to scrape out gardens on one and a half acres of land per family, while needing government rations to survive day to day. Many adults sought work as "stevedores, laundresses, cooks, and common laborers," often working for the Union army. They also sought education for themselves and their children, with over 1,200 pupils in schools run by fifteen teachers in Norfolk by the end of 1862.[9]

The treatment of the escaped slaves ran the gamut from paternalistic to patently cruel. With their legal status in limbo and the government unwilling to take full responsibility for their well-being, the former slaves truly depended on "the kindness of strangers." While some white missionaries labored to teach and preach to their new charges, other whites sought profit from their misery. Some Army quartermasters sold supplies designated for the runaways, a few paymasters withheld wages due black laborers, and worst of all, the Ninety-ninth New York Infantry allegedly sold escaped slaves back to their masters. The Ninety-ninth New York was also involved in a race riot with the contrabands, provoked by the death of a white cook. Several blacks were killed and dozens wounded in retaliation.[10]

Despite the mistreatment, uncertain legal status, and diseases rampant in the squalid camps, the lure of freedom proved irresistible to thousands of black Virginians. Israel Lafayette Butt, a prominent presiding elder in the African Methodist Episcopal Church after the war, recalled in detail the night he, his father, and a neighbor girl escaped to freedom. After walking nearly fifteen miles at night, Israel's father fell ill, and the runaways had to be hidden by Israel's grandfather for three days. Finally, his great-uncle rowed them across the Elizabeth River to the freedom of the Union lines. When fourteen-year-old Israel saw his first Union guards, "he fell in love with them, admired their beautiful uniforms, guns, bayonets, swords, and the bright buttons on their clothes, and wished he was a soldier."[11]

Few were more surprised and disturbed by the boldness of slaves than their masters. Jim, the trusted servant of Henry A. Wise, former governor of Virginia, helped his master's family pack up their belongings at Rolleston, the Wise estate near Norfolk; then he ran off. John Wise, the youngest son of Henry Wise, later wrote, "We never saw him again. The prospect of freedom overcame a lifetime of love and loyalty." Obviously, the Wises did not know Jim's true feelings as well as they thought.[12]

To the perpetual anxiety of slave owners, the flight of one slave not only reduced the labor force, it also increased suspicions toward the remaining slaves. When Cinda left the Caldwells of Warrenton in June 1862, Susan Caldwell wrote her husband, Lycurgus, "Since Cinda has left we begin to distrust Aunt Lucy. Altho she speaks well and has behaved well, Sister wants to know if it will not be best to give her *freedom* and *hire* her." If distrust grew, so did the power of remaining slaves in some households. When William Johnson's master and four sons left for the war, he found himself appointed "houseman," a critical position he held until his master took him to the front in January 1863. Others may have used their new leverage to obtain better treatment, while a few slaves were shipped south or to the interior to prevent them from running away.[13]

Another group of Virginians, usually quiet and discreet early in the war, had also been "liberated" (or perhaps "uncovered") by Union occupation: the white Unionists. Many of the Unionists in Portsmouth cheered when Union troops arrived in 1862, and approved resolutions condemning secession and its adherents. In Culpeper, Unionists offered food and information to the Union army in the summer of 1862. And in the old northwest of Virginia, Unionists were busy establishing a government and a constitution for a new state that would officially come into being the next year, the state of West Virginia.[14]

The war took a decided turn for the worse for civilians in July 1862. The three Union armies scattered across Virginia were consolidated (on paper) into one new army, the Army of Virginia, under the command of a bombastic general from the western theater, John Pope. With the complete support of President Lincoln, Pope issued several infamous general orders that significantly altered the policy and perhaps the outcome of the war. Instead of treating civilians and their property with respect, General Order No. 5 instructed the Union soldiers to "subsist upon the country." General Order No. 7 declared that anyone caught attacking Union troops would be treated as a prisoner of war, and his house burned. General Order No. 11 commanded Union officers to "arrest all disloyal male citizens within their lines or within their reach." Those willing to take an oath of allegiance to the Union would be left alone. If one violated his oath by participating in illegal activities, he would be "shot, and his property (including slaves) seized and applied to the public use."

The new orders so outraged President Davis and Gen. Robert E. Lee that the latter sent a letter of protest to the new general-in-chief of the Union armies, Henry W. Halleck. He said that Pope and his subordinates would be treated as "robbers and murderers," and if any unarmed Virginian were killed by Pope's men, the Confederates would execute an equivalent number of commissioned Union officers.[15]

The brutal war of soldiers had become an expanded war against civilians. Faced with a determined and obdurate foe, stung by the "half-defeat" of the Seven Days, and besieged by criticism that he was too "soft" toward the "Rebels," Lincoln had decided to pressure the civilians directly. His new policies gave a harsh edge to Union occupation which, as many feared, would lead to equally cold and vengeful conduct by Confederates when in Union territory. A devil was loosed in 1862, and though temporarily restrained in 1863, it would be unleashed in full fury in the latter half of 1864.

For the citizens of Culpeper, the apocalypse had come now, in July 1862. Soldiers moved through towns and villages like biblical locusts, unchecked by their officers or their mores. Furniture was broken, windows smashed, doors ripped off their hinges, and buildings burned to the ground. Lucy Thom watched soldiers take her horses and clothes, then destroy her corn. One Confederate officer found out he had lost his slaves, his livestock, and his entire farm through a deliberately set fire. Soldiers even tore up a church.[16]

Pope's orders, however, were not always followed so zealously. From Warrenton Susan Caldwell wrote her husband: "During the sojourn of Genl. Pope's army in our town and county I must say we were treated kindly and they were all respectful and gentlemanly." They paid "silver and gold" for vegetables and milk, never dug up her corn or gardens, and even seemed "mortified" by Pope's orders. She was not sure why she was treated better than some other citizens of Warrenton, though having one's father-in-law in charge of the local commissary (that did business with whatever army was in town) may have played a role.[17]

The Union soldiers encamped in Front Royal did not feel as kindly toward their Confederate hosts. They arrested some men from the nearby town of Nineveh who had confiscated groceries from an overturned wagon. Even worse, to Lucy Buck, was Pope's order that the oath of allegiance be administered to all, and that those who did not take the oath would be banished and lose all their property. She wrote: "This is what I have all the time been dreading and now it had come in a more hideous shape than I ever anticipated."[18]

The heavy hand of Federal authority was acutely felt in Winchester. On July 30, Gen. Julien White ordered that only those who had taken the oath of allegiance could leave the city. When the Twelfth Virginia Cavalry embarrassed White by raiding a Union-guarded train in late August, White retaliated by arresting all men who had refused to take the oath of allegiance. He then rewrote the oath for the men of Frederick County, offering them a bit of an escape clause; if they swore not to take any action against the Federal government or aid someone who did, they could remain in town. Some men took the oath, while others did not. White sent a few men away, but never arrested the prominent men who refused to sign the oath.[19]

For another group of Virginians who supported the Confederacy, those living on the periphery of Virginia in places like Alexandria, Fairfax, Norfolk, Hampton, and Suffolk, the burden of occupation became endemic. Anne S. Frobel of Fairfax had Union troops on her property, Wilton Hill, for virtually every day of the war. From March to September 1862 she had to feed two "Yankee friends" who lived with them, as well as the guards assigned to protect their house. Little did she realize that life would be considerably worse after the unwanted guards left. One day men from the Twentieth Michigan Infantry descended upon Wilton Hill, stealing all the fruit from the trees and threatening to burn the house down. The next day, at the risk of heat prostration and incalculable social embarrassment, Anne Frobel went to headquarters to complain, and the general's aide promised her a guard would be appointed.[20]

For those living in Virginia's heartland, the fortunes of war quickly turned from terror to triumph in late summer. With bold victories at Cedar Mountain on August 9 and at Second Manassas on August 28–30, the Army of Northern Virginia regained control of the Piedmont and sent the despised Pope reeling back to Washington. General Lee maintained the strategic initiative by marching his army north into Maryland, taking the fighting out of Virginia.

When the Confederates first reappeared in Culpeper and other "liberated" towns, the citizens acted as if it were the Day of Jubilee. In Culpeper some women gave water or lemonade to thirsty soldiers, while others kissed battle flags. In Warrenton "the streets were thronged with all who could walk—and Secession flags were everywhere displayed." The Caldwell family offered supper to sixteen soldiers, and breakfast the next morning to another twenty hungry soldiers. In Winchester the joy actually began before the Confederate army arrived; the Union garrison left on September 2, destroying Fort Garibaldi as they left.[21]

Joy was soon tempered by the appearance of hundreds of wounded men in Winchester and other towns, fresh from the battlefields at Manassas. The townspeople could scarcely accommodate these wounded before a new, much larger batch arrived in late September. These men came by the thousands from the bloodiest single day of battle in the entire war, the Battle of Antietam on September 17. Lee's army was forced to retreat to the safety of Virginia, and his battered army set up camp between Winchester and Bunker Hill.[22]

As the conflicting news reports filtered out the story of the major battle in Maryland, Virginians also had to digest the impact of Lincoln's second most important political decision: his Preliminary Emancipation Proclamation freeing all slaves in rebellious areas by January 1, 1863. In Richmond John B. Jones wrote: "This [proclamation] will only intensify the war, and add largely to our numbers in the field." It led to a heated discussion in the Confederate Senate, with some senators advocating the "raising of the *black flag*, asking and giving no quarter hereafter." An editorial in the *Staunton Spectator* with the title "Lincoln's Fiendish Proclamation" stated the case with passion: "He invites the servile population of the South to enact the bloody scene of St.

Domingo throughout the limits of the Southern Confederacy." Even Susan Caldwell of Warrenton felt compelled to write about the implications of the proclamation in her weekly letter to her husband. "I feel much troubled in regard to Lincoln's proclamation in regard to the servants," she said. "I don't expect we will have one left any where in Va."[23]

The much feared rebellion and rapid exodus never occurred, however, nor did the state of Virginia accept President Lincoln's offer to return to the Union by January 1, 1863. Instead, life almost resumed a degree of normality for many Virginians, as farmers began to gather their harvests and sell them to local markets or to the army in the wartime capital of Richmond. In Culpeper, John Rixey sold his "wheat, corn, and cordwood" to the Army of Northern Virginia for $1,000. Lemuel Corbin sold ten beef cattle for $457.50. Even smaller perishable items sold well. Mary Foushee earned "$5.40 for fifteen gallons of milk, $6 for a dozen chickens, $2.50 for five dozen eggs, and $6.00 for twenty pounds of lard." Over in Winchester, David Barton reported to his brother that "every article here has got to be extravagantly high—potatoes $4 and $5 pr bushel. Flour $12 per bl. Oat $1.25 and corn $2. Hay $25–30 per ton, wool $10 pr ton and hard to get at all." Even after an initial flood of these products into the markets of Richmond, prices crept upward as cold weather approached. John B. Jones wrote in December that one could pay "$20 to $40 per bbl. for flour; $3.50 per bushel for meal; $2 per lb. for butter; $20 per cord for wood, etc."[24]

Who was to blame? The "extortionists," argued Jones. "Our patriotism is mainly in the army and among the ladies of the South," he complained. "The avarice and cupidity of the men at home, could only be excelled by ravenous wolves." Or maybe the fault lay with the government, which "monopolizes the railroads and canals." Or maybe it was much more innocent and common than Jones argued, or else why would the *Staunton Spectator* run a brief column in October 1862 exhorting farmers *not* to sell surplus crops to speculators? Wherever blame was placed, the simple fact remained: a Richmond family's grocery bill increased tenfold between 1860 and 1863, according to a market study by the *Richmond Dispatch*.[25]

While the central government seemed powerless to stop the inexorable price rises, it had proved more effective at refining its conscription laws. On September 27 the Confederate Congress expanded the draft of men from age thirty-five to age forty-five. The Congress revisited the issue the next month, when it increased the number of occupations open to exemption, and added an exemption for those who owned or supervised twenty or more slaves. While criticism of this new exemption rose quickly in the newspapers and on the streets, a focused study of the laws in action tells a different story. In three Piedmont Virginia counties, Albemarle, Campbell, and Augusta, 63 percent of the exemptions came from paid substitution, with skilled workers accounting for 16 percent. Out of 812 exemptions, only 47 (5.8 percent), resulted from the "twenty slave law." Substitution actually provided some essential income for the needy, with prices for substitutes rising from $1,000 in April 1862 to $2,000 by the end of the year. Yet there was an unintended consequence of the tough enforcement of the conscription acts in 1862, for desertion from Virginia units reached its peak in 1862. That level corresponded with the government's intense effort to force men to enlist or reenlist for three years.[26]

Given the logical emphasis on the hardships and suffering of this war, it is also important to note that despite the battles, deaths, wounds, and destruction caused by the war, the bulk of the state's territory remained untouched by fighting or invading armies. The war surely became the central topic of concern regardless of region, but from Staunton in the north to Abingdon in the southwest to Danville and Petersburg in the east, peace reigned. The normal rhythms of life continued, with a bountiful harvest in most areas that fall, insuring a comfortable winter for many. For wealthy Lucy Breckinridge of Grove Hill in Botetourt County, with autumn came the usual rounds of visitations with friends and family, church meetings, knitting at home, and playing games and singing songs with friends. The highlight of the season was a two-week visit to a friend's home, Avenel. Somehow soldiers found their way to Avenel as well, with four men visiting the estate for part of Lucy's stay. Meanwhile her father continued to run his large plantation, supervising the work of his fifty slaves. Except for news from the war or occasional military visitors, the closest the Breckinridges got to the war was in late October. They found out "Yankees were in Fincastle"—imprisoned in the courthouse.[27]

Residents in other sections of Virginia did not have the luxury of avoiding Union soldiers. By late October General McClellan finally had his Army of the Potomac on the move into Virginia, headed toward Warrenton. When Gen. James Longstreet's corps arrived at Culpeper Court House, effectively blocking McClellan's move toward Warrenton, President Lincoln had had enough. On November 7, he relieved McClellan of command, placing Maj.

Gen. Ambrose Burnside in his place. Burnside decided to shift toward Fredericksburg, setting into motion one of the most lopsided Confederate victories of the war.[28]

The Army of the Potomac camped for a time around Warrenton, and Susan Caldwell wrote her husband after the army left, "(they) took everything they could find from farmers and families." In Fauquier County Tee Edmonds went from feeding and entertaining Confederate soldiers in October to doing the same for Union soldiers in November. When she saw Union Gen. Winfield Scott Hancock she remarked that "he is certainly the finest looking man I have seen in either army, and very handsomely dressed." The Bucks of Front Royal were out of harm's way that late fall, and enjoyed the visit with Gen. James Longstreet and his staff on October 31. Lucy found the young officers to be "refined, polished gentlemen," and Longstreet a "very quiet, dignified old gentleman" (he was thirty-eight at the time). Meanwhile, in southeastern Virginia the civilian population found itself under the constant threat of foragers that autumn. When not beset by voracious soldiers, the civilians might find themselves in the midst of skirmishes that occurred weekly in the contested terrain between Suffolk and Blackwater.[29]

The last major battle of the year fought in Virginia, the Battle of Fredericksburg, produced not only a Confederate victory, but also the first instance of heavy shelling and major looting of a city. The shelling occurred on December 11, as Union guns tried to silence the Confederate sharpshooters who occupied the city. In time, five bridges were constructed across the Rappahannock River and Union forces captured the city. They then began an extensive period of looting, which had no precedent in the war. Maj. F. E. Pierce of the 108th New York wrote to a friend, "Finest cut glassware goblets were hurled at nice plate glass windows, beautifully embroidered window curtains torn down, rosewood pianos piled in the streets and burned." Yet the mania would not last long. On December 13 General Burnside threw wave upon wave of troops at fortified Confederate defenses, only to have them repulsed at a terrible cost of life. He withdrew his army from the city and across the Rappahannock on Sunday evening, December 14.[30]

Between the unusual number of snowfalls—twenty-seven that winter in Richmond alone—and the fallout from the Battle of Fredericksburg, Christmas celebrations in Virginia seemed muted from past years. In Richmond John B. Jones had to sell a silver watch to pay for his family's Christmas dinner, while Lycurgus Caldwell probably spent a lonely day in the same city, pining for his family back in Warrenton. His children received "candy, cake, and apples," because not a "book or toy" could be found in Warrenton. The women of Warrenton prepared a huge Christmas meal for the wounded soldiers in town, with "turkeys, hams, meats of all kinds, cakes—custards, pies, jellies and every nicety." The Bucks of Front Royal had a quiet holiday, with treats and toys for the children. In Fauquier County the Edmonds family reunited and enjoyed "glasses of nog and cake." Still, Tee wrote in her diary, "Christmas, but not of old. The merry holidays that once were have given place to sad and gloomy pleasures."[31]

As December inexorably gave way to the new year, civilians in Virginia could take stock of their losses, and quietly celebrate their achievements. Three major battles fought in Virginia, along with Jackson's Valley Campaign, the Battle of Cedar Mountain, and the huge battle fought just across the state line in Maryland, had brought nearly three thousand casualties to Virginia families.[32] Still, the Army of Northern Virginia remained intact, with its top leadership well-tested under fire, its recruitment up and desertion rates down after the initial shock of the 1862 conscription law, and its spirits high after saving Richmond and driving the Union army back across the Rappahannock. So while northwest Virginia was lost, and certain sections along Virginia's periphery were occupied for what might be the remainder of the war, the bulk of the state's agriculture, industry, commerce, and transportation lay safely in Confederate hands.

At the same time, the fighting near Richmond and throughout the Piedmont and Shenandoah Valley had fully exposed Virginia and the Confederacy's vulnerabilities. The largest and most populous Confederate state also sat closest to the North and the Union capital, thus insuring that Virginia would remain a battleground for the duration of the war. To win this war, Confederates would need not only to hold Richmond, but also the breadbasket Shenandoah Valley and the artery of Virginia, the Piedmont region. With Union forces ensconced in cities along the Tidewater, the danger to Richmond could come from the east by water or land, or from the north, on roads and rails. Similarly, the Union cavalry and infantry would need free movement through upper Virginia if any major move was made on the Shenandoah Valley, thus guaranteeing a constant wash of enemy soldiers across the fields of Fauquier and other northern counties.

Besides the horror and grief accompanying death or wounding of loved ones, civilians in Confederate Virginia either found hardship or opportunity as the war began to dominate all aspects of life. For those in permanently occupied Union areas such as Fairfax and Norfolk and Suffolk, the war would be one long period of Babylonian captivity. For those in between Confederate authority and Union forays, residents of Fauquier County or Winchester, the war meant constant threats of raids, looting, and frightening encounters with deserters. For those even closer to Washington, in places like Culpeper and Front Royal, the war could involve the hardships of occupation at the worst, or the belt-tightening of inflation and scarcity of goods at the least. And for those far from the battlefields, people in Staunton or Roanoke County or Danville, the war would mean new opportunities for trade and commerce, along with growing unease about the fortunes of the war (and one's potential vulnerability).

For slaves in Virginia, especially those living along the state's borders, the war brought freedom closer than ever before. Thousands took advantage of the opportunity, fleeing the certain harshness of slavery for the uncertain possibilities of freedom. The exodus of slaves from Confederate-controlled sections of Virginia began in earnest in 1862, and never appreciably slowed as the war continued.

As for governmental policies, the larger aims of both sides remained intact. The Confederate leadership still sought independence, and was pre- pared to fight on all fronts to maintain its tenuous freedom. Union leaders had shown an equal determination to force the Confederacy to surrender, relentlessly increasing the pressure through battle, emancipation of slaves, and, for a brief time, an experiment with a tough policy of occupation in the east and the west.

For the Confederates in Virginia, it would be fair to say they had held up well in the first full year of the war. Despite thousands of casualties, land loss, occupation, and privation, the bulk of them remained loyal to the Confederacy and hopeful that with a few more victories, the Union might actually leave them alone. They had experienced some of the worst this war would toss at them, save the systematic crop and property destruction in the Shenandoah Valley late in the war. And they continued to send their sons to fill the depleted ranks, and traded for goods with depreciating Confederate currency, seeing both sacrifices as necessary to their "cause."

But beneath the sturdy facade of Confederate unity, the people whose labor underpinned the entire Southern economic system—the black slaves—were individually and collectively destroying the very institution the Confederacy fought to save, slavery. Their escape from the bonds of Virginia slavery showed the irresistible attraction of freedom over slavery, and if enough slaves left the fields and houses of Virginia, the system would collapse.

So while the Confederates in Virginia gamely faced the uncertainties of another year of war in 1863, the very way of life they fought to defend was rapidly evaporating before their eyes. They needed to win the war quickly, or there would be nothing left to preserve.

Notes

1. *War of the Rebellion: Official Records of the Union and Confederate Armies* (Washington, D.C.: Government Printing Office, 1880–1901), series IV, vol. 1, 923–25 (hereafter cited as *OR*); Daniel Sutherland, *Seasons of War: The Ordeal of a Confederate Community, 1861–1865* (New York: Free Press, 1995), 92.

2. Susan Caldwell, *"My Heart Is So Rebellious": The Caldwell Letters, 1861–1865*, ed. J. Michael Welton (Warrenton, Va., n.d. [first available in 1990]), Susan Caldwell to Lycurgus Caldwell, April 10, 1862, 93–94 (hereafter cited as Caldwell, *Letters*); Amanda Virginia Edmonds, *Journals of Amanda Virginia Edmonds: Lass of the Mosby Confederacy, 1859–1867*, ed. Nancy Chapplear Baird (Stephens City, Va., 1984), April 11 and 12, 1862, 73–74 (hereafter cited as Edmonds, *Journals*); Lucy Buck, *Sad Earth, Sweet Heaven: The Diary of Lucy Buck during the War between the States, December 25, 1861–April 15, 1865*, 2nd ed., ed. William P. Buck (Birmingham, 1992), April 27, 1862, 54 (hereafter cited as Buck, *Diary*).

3. Brian Steel Wills, *The War Hits Home: The Civil War in Southeastern Virginia* (Charlottesville and London: University Press of Virginia, 2001), 53; Buck, *Diary*, May 14, 1862, 66–67; Caldwell, *Letters*, Susan Caldwell to Lycurgus Caldwell, April 10, 1862, 93–98.

4. Margaretta Barton Colt, *Defend the Valley: A Shenandoah Family in the Civil War* (New York: Crown, 1994; reprint, New York: Oxford University Press, 1999), 143, 151.

5. Stephen W. Sears, *To the Gates of Richmond: The Peninsula Campaign* (New York: Ticknor and Fields, 1992), 146; Sallie Putnam, *Richmond during the War: Four Years of Personal Observation* (New York: G. W. Carleton, 1867; reprint, Alexandria, Va.: Time-Life Books, 1983), 135–36.

6. Sears, *Gates of Richmond*, 343, 345.

7. Wills, *War Hits Home*, 59–60; Henry Robinson Berkeley, *Four Years*

in the Confederate Artillery: The Diary of Private Henry Robinson Berkeley, ed. William Runge (Richmond: Virginia Historical Society, 1991), 20–21 (hereafter cited as Berkeley, *Diary*).

8. Putnam, *Richmond during the War,* 154, 149, 151–52.

9. James Marten, "A Feeling of Restless Anxiety: Loyalty and Race in the Peninsula Campaign and Beyond," in Gary Gallagher, ed., *The Richmond Campaign of 1862: The Peninsula and the Seven Days* (Chapel Hill: University of North Carolina Press, 2000), 138, 141–42.

10. Ibid., 138–39.

11. Israel L. Butt, *History of African Methodism in Virginia; or, Four Decades in the Old Dominion* (Norfolk: Hampton Institute Press, 1908), 17–19. Butt's father immediately went to work unloading cargo for the Union troops, while Israel worked as a water boy for the men. In 1864 he got his wish: he enlisted in the United States Colored Infantry.

12. John S. Wise, *The End of an Era* (Boston and New York: Houghton, Mifflin, 1902), 210.

13. Caldwell, *Letters,* Susan Caldwell to Lycurgus Caldwell, June 9, 1862, 131; Charles Perdue Jr., Thomas E. Barden, and Robert K. Phillips, eds., *Weevils in the Wheat: Interviews with Virginia Ex-Slaves* (Charlottesville: University Press of Virginia, 1976), interview with William I. Johnson Jr., 167; Marten, "Feeling of Restless Anxiety," 135.

14. Marten, "Feeling of Restless Anxiety," 132; Sutherland, *Seasons of War,* 272; James M. McPherson, *Battle Cry of Freedom: The Civil War Era* (New York: Oxford University Press, 1980), 303–4.

15. *OR,* series I, vol. 11, pt. 3, 359; *OR,* series I, vol. 12, pt. 3, 500–501 (Lincoln's approval); *OR,* series I, vol. 12, pt. 2, 50 (General Order No. 5); *OR,* series I, vol. 12, pt. 2, 51 (General Order No. 7); *OR,* series I, vol. 12, pt. 2, 52 (General Order No. 11); *OR,* series I, vol. 12, pt. 3, 57 and 576 (Lee's letter).

16. Sutherland, *Seasons of War,* 123.

17. Caldwell, *Letters,* Susan Caldwell to Lycurgus Caldwell, August 18, 1862, 146–47.

18. Buck, *Diary,* July 26, 1862, 122.

19. Roger U. Delauter Jr., *Winchester in the Civil War* (Lynchburg: H. E. Howard, Inc., 1992), 39–40.

20. Anne S. Frobel, *The Civil War Diary of Anne S. Frobel of Wilton Hill in Virginia* (McLean, Va.: EPM Publications, Inc., 1992), 92–95.

21. Sutherland, *Seasons of War,* 178; Caldwell, *Letters,* Susan Caldwell to Lycurgus Caldwell, August 23, 1862, 147–48; Delauter, *Winchester in the Civil War,* 40–41.

22. Delauter, *Winchester in the Civil War,* 42.

23. John B. Jones, *A Rebel War Clerk's Diary,* ed. Earl Schenck Miers (New York: Sagamore Press, 1958), September 27, 1862, 100, and September 30, 1862, 101; *Staunton Spectator,* October 7, 1862, found in *Valley of the Shadow,* http://valley.vcdh.virgina.edu/; Caldwell, *Letters,* Susan Caldwell to Lycurgus Caldwell, October 6, 1862, 156.

24. Sutherland, *Seasons of War,* 197; Colt, *Defend the Valley,* David Barton to Bolling Barton, October 1862, 186; Jones, *Rebel War Clerk's Diary,* October 18, 1862, 108 and December 1, 1862, 126.

25. Jones, *Rebel War Clerk's Diary,* December 1, 1862, 126 and January 18, 1863, 152; *Staunton Spectator,* October 7, 1862, in *Valley of the Shadow,* http://valley.vcdh.virginia.edu/; Jones, *Rebel War Clerk's Diary,* January 30, 1863, 158–59.

26. E. B. Long, *The Civil War Day-by-Day: An Almanac, 1861–1865* (New York: Da Capo Press, 1971), 271, 278; Ernest B. Furgurson, *Ashes of Glory: Richmond at War* (New York: Knopf, 1996), 174; William Blair, *Virginia's Private War: Feeding Body and Soul in the Confederacy, 1861–1865* (New York: Oxford University Press, 1998), 58–62.

27. Mary D. Robertson, editor, *Lucy Breckinridge of Grove Hill: The Journal of a Virginia Girl, 1862–1864* (Columbia: University of South Carolina Press, 1994), September 11, 1862–December 19, 1862, 51–90, and October 20, 1862, 75–76.

28. Long, *Civil War Day-by-Day,* 281–85. Two excellent books on the Fredericksburg campaign have been published recently: George C. Rable, *Fredericksburg! Fredericksburg!* (Chapel Hill: The University of North Carolina Press, 2002) and Francis Augustin O'Reilly, *The Fredericksburg Campaign: Winter War on the Rappahannock* (Baton Rouge: Louisiana State University Press, 2003).

29. Caldwell, *Letters,* Susan Caldwell to Lycurgus Caldwell, November 29, 1862, 159; Edmonds, *Journals,* November 5, 1862, 125; Buck, *Diary,* October 31 and November 1, 1862, 146; Wills, *War Hits Home,* 74–85.

30. Rable, *Fredericksburg! Fredericksburg!,* 162–67 (bombardment), 177–84 (sack of the town), 249–56 (attacks on Confederate lines), 269–72, 281 (debates about further attacks); Pierce quoted in Mark Grimsley, *The Hard Hand of War: Union Military Policy toward Southern Civilians, 1861–1865* (Cambridge and New York: Cambridge University Press, 1995), 108.

31. Jones, *Rebel War Clerk's Diary,* 139–41; Caldwell, *Letters,* Susan Caldwell to Lycurgus Caldwell, December 28, 1862, 165–66; Buck, *Diary,* December 25, 1862, 157; Edmonds, *Journals,* December 25, 1862, 129.

32. Statistics compiled from William F. Fox, *Regimental Losses in the American Civil War, 1861–1865* (Albany, N.Y.: 1889), 560–65. It does not include Virginians serving in regiments from states other than Virginia.

The Trials of Military Occupation

Thomas P. Lowry

The process of going to war involves three beliefs. The first is that some external enemy is intolerable in his philosophies, policies, and actions. Whether the perceived enemy is a Bolshevik, a capitalist, an unbeliever, or an abolitionist, the process is the same. The second belief is that this enemy can be easily overcome, because he is evil, or undeserving, or of weak moral fiber, the corollary being that the person proposing war possesses some special quality, whether it be élan, or Bushido, or manifest destiny, or having been chosen by God.

The third essential belief on the road to war is that victory will be relatively painless. In the imagined triumph of arms, the enemy—who of course is cowardly—will flee before the gleaming swords of the righteous, who will return home covered in medals and glory, with perhaps a slight wound as a badge of manhood. Swooning womenfolk and admiring noncombatants will indeed hail the conquering hero. Perhaps no one embodied the concept of painless triumph more than South Carolinian Armisted L. Burt, who offered to personally drink all the blood spilled as a result of secession.[1] Not only was Burt 5 million pints wrong, but he also failed to predict the occupation of his beloved South by a Yankee army, with all the consequences inherent when women and children confront armed men, men whose opposing political values (and empty stomachs) imbue them with a sense of entitlement. In 1862 northern Virginia, pieces of the southeastern coast, and intermittently, places in the lower Shenandoah Valley took rank among the first portions of the Confederacy to suffer Union military occupation. Their inhabitants were to learn firsthand what lay in store for more and more of the Southern people as the war rolled on.

An army marches on its stomach, Napoleon remarked, and an army marching on hardtack, with its total absence of protein, fat, vitamins, and flavor, quickly seeks to supplement the government ration. In 1862 Virginians were to learn that hunger, the most immediate of soldier needs, was also to be the most easily remedied in an occupied country, and that civilian ownership and rights meant little or nothing to a Yankee with an empty belly. Nine soldiers of the Eighty-seventh New York slaked their hunger at a farm near Fort Monroe. William Van Voohes, William Ferdon, Augustus Van Grosbeck, David McConnell, William McCarty, and four other men returned to their camp with stolen hams, turkeys, ducks, chickens, and milk. One New York plunderer, perhaps of a more Sybaritic bent, returned bearing an armload of peacock feathers. At their court-martial, the keystone of their defense was that "a Negro told us the owner was a Rebel." Each soldier was fined $10, none of which went to the victimized farmer.[2]

Fort Monroe had space for only 1,400 soldiers. In May 1861, the garrison was increased to 6,000 men. The overflow went to the newly established Camp Hamilton, just north of the fort. There, two Union men made recorded mischief. Lewis Hickox, Eleventh Pennsylvania Cavalry, was raising hell at the store of Vorhies and Bell. He was drunk and obnoxious enough to be expelled. The next day, he reappeared, drunk and obnoxious, and armed, and shot at (but missed) a civilian, Henry Clark. Hickox pleaded for clemency, claiming to be "very feeble and very old [almost fifty] and a wounded veteran of the Mexican war." His feebleness seemed somewhat selective.[3] William Cunningham, Sixteenth Massachusetts, was less flamboyant. He stole a farmer's fence near Camp Hamilton and used it to cook his dinner, for which he was fined $10.[4]

Mutton was on the menu at Catlett's Station.[5] F. L. Melott, Twelfth Pennsylvania Reserves, was fined three months pay for killing a sheep.[6] John Pircall, Thirty-fifth New York, was a deserter who made his way to Catlett's Station, where he destroyed his uniform, donned civilian clothes, spent the night in a whorehouse, and stole three horses. He and his friends seemed to have become instantly unpopular, evidenced by what he told the court: "I was with Frank Pierce and a man named Curly, who was shot and killed by the citizens who arrested us."[7]

Near Camp Warren, three men of the Second U.S. Infantry had also killed a sheep, and John Kinney, William Boehing, and Elijah Burley were still skinning the animal when they were arrested.[8] At Camp Wilkes, where Peter Doyle of the Second Delaware had been posted as a sentry, instead of standing his post, he went to a nearby home where he made a nuisance of himself for two hours. Because of his "youth," the court was "lenient": half pay for ten months, fourteen days on bread and water, and sixty days of hard labor.[9] But such sentences would never curb the inclination of soldiers to scavenge off the enemy civilians in their reach.

Langley was the site of Camp Pierpont, where 1st Lt. William H. Hope, Ninth Pennsylvania Reserves, left his duty post—to steal a hog. The court-martial board, which contained Brig. Gen. George Meade, concluded that Hope's action reflected poorly upon the officer corps and dismissed him in disgrace.[10] Meanwhile another soldier from Camp Pierpont, Felix Mellon, Sixth Pennsylvania Reserves, inadvertently contributed to the evolving subject of black civil rights. Mr. E. McAnnery had lived in Langley for thirty years, and kept a store there. George Green, a "colored" man, had a carpetbag filled with valuable clothes, which he kept at the store. Mellon stole the carpetbag. The court called Green as a witness; Mellon objected to the testimony of a black man. The court passed the decision to the local commander, Brig. Gen. George McCall, who referred the decision back to the court. Green did not testify. Mellon was convicted and ordered to forfeit five dollars a month of his pay for five months. There was no restitution for Green.[11]

Camp McDowell was near Chatham, on the heights overlooking Fredericksburg. Four hooligans from the First New Jersey Cavalry—John Schrotts, Henry Chamberlain, William Anderson, and Joseph Schubert—left camp without permission and made life miserable at three Virginia homes. At one they stole clothing and a daguerreotype; at another they stole a telescope and cut up the mattresses; while at a third home, they stole jewelry. Schrotts got thirty months in prison and a dishonorable discharge. The others each did twenty days at hard labor and lost a month's pay.[12]

The army and its many stomachs continued to march. Two Dranesville hog hunters, members of the Eighth Pennsylvania Reserve, were court-martialed. J. C. Darnell blazed away at the hog until the gunfire attracted the wrath of his commanding general. George Wagner succeeded in killing the hog. Both men were fined three months' pay.[13] Farther along the way from Washington, D.C. to Fredericksburg sat Falmouth. At this way station,

Union men helped themselves to civilian property. Hiram Brady, Nineteenth Indiana, straggled from his regiment, but returned to it with a stolen mare. His captain's response was to admonish him that "If you're going to steal, you should steal a better horse than that." In spite of his captain's complicity, Brady got twenty days at hard labor.[14]

A far more shocking display of officer impropriety was seen in the cases of Capt. Thomas Strong, and Lts. John Fassett, William Battie, and Charles Pierson, all of the Twenty-second New York. They entered the Falmouth home of a Dr. Rose and stole a bottle of jelly, two pounds of sugar, a basket, cakes, biscuits, a box of tools, a decanter, a spoon, a butter knife, a pound of tobacco, three wine glasses, a bucket, and a pair of shoes. Each officer was suspended for thirty days from rank and pay, and was reprimanded.[15]

The First Pennsylvania Light Artillery contributed two Falmouth malfeasants. David Maynard and Oscar Larrabee broke into a house and stole a pistol, a dirk, spoons, forks, and table knives. They both pled guilty and were each fined five dollars.[16] A court-martial held at the Lacy House in Falmouth tried Nelson Ford, Twelfth Pennsylvania, who stole a horse from William Pollock and sold it, keeping the receipt! Ford lost half his pay for three months and was forced to stand on a barrel for two hours every day for ten days, wearing a placard that read, "Receiver of Stolen Goods."[17]

Far to the west, Winchester in the Shenandoah was to be the scene of many battles. It was also the scene of a scam by Guidon Chauncey Parker and Corp. Stephen Lockwood, both of the First New York Light Artillery. They went to the homes of several citizens and threatened to "press," or confiscate, their horses unless a bribe was paid. Parker was convicted, drummed out, and given six months of hard labor with a twenty-four-pound ball and chain, and no pay. Lockwood was acquitted.[18] Some soldiers went even further, to actually terrorize civilians. At Warrenton, Sgt. Michael McHugh of the Eighty-second New York was drunk and disorderly. He left his regiment and made his way to Rectortown, where he entered a private home, cursed the inhabitants, and smashed their furniture. When arrested, he "hooted" at his lieutenant and called him a "son of a bitch." He was sentenced to be shot, but Lincoln spared the life of this wretch.[19] Three more Yankee soldiers helped terrorize Rectortown. Troy Martin, Thirty-fourth New York, marched into a civilian home, threatened the family with death, smashed their furniture, and took what he pleased. He cursed the officer who told him to stop. For the latter crime, a violation of the Ninth Article of War, Martin was sentenced to die. Lincoln reprieved him on a technicality: the officer's badge of rank was concealed by his overcoat.[20] In the same village, Edwin Hoyt, Eighth Connecticut, stole two ducks, and John Cramer, Eighty-ninth New York, stole two chickens. Each man was fined a month's pay.[21] Ten men of the Thirty-second Massachusetts stole and killed a pig at Warrenton. The army was unable to identify the owner of the deceased, and was able to identify only two of the purloining porcucidal privates: George Gould and Cyrus Watson. Both men were fined five dollars.[22]

A few miles west of Warrenton is the village of Orlean. There, two men of the Tenth New Hampshire terrorized a Mrs. Marshall, smashing in her door, breaking her furniture, and carrying off portable valuables. R. B. Morris and Daniel Loftis each had his head shaved and was drummed out of the regiment. Each departed for the Rip Raps (a coastal breakwater) where each served six months at hard labor, carrying heavy rocks, while dragging a thirty-pound iron ball riveted around his ankle.[23]

No corner of Virginia was safe, it seemed. The men of Fort Ward, overlooking the District of Columbia, were given permission to get drunk on payday, but only if they stayed in camp. Naturally, not everyone followed this reasonable restriction. John Garnold, Second New York Heavy Artillery, left camp and beat up a civilian baker.[24] Alfred Stillwell, Third Pennsylvania Cavalry, stole a wagon at Station House.[25] Edward Cutler, Second Michigan, stole a silver watch from a "colored citizen" at Fredericksburg.[26] At Port Republic, Albert Molitor, Thirteenth New York Light Artillery, stole a trunk from a civilian.[27] In Frederick County, James Johnson, Third Delaware, shot and kept a civilian hog.[28] Maryland's Purnell Legion was home to William Brown, who kicked down a woman's door at Eastville, and insulted her.[29] Thomas Calihan, Fourteenth Indiana, shot at a civilian, John Stilly, at Webster. The bullet missed, but was close enough to leave powder burns on Stilly's face.[30] Myron Wordell, Sixty-first New York, stole a horse at Upperville.[31] George Wilde, Fourth Rhode Island, stole a pistol at Lovettsville.[32] At Cumberland, in New Kent County, 2nd Lt. Charles Woodruff, First New York Cavalry, was convicted of stealing five horses and a mule. Judge Advocate General Holt noted that the animals had immediately been turned over to the United States (in fact, confiscated for Federal use) and overturned the conviction.[33] As McClellan's stymied army cowered at Harrison's Landing in August 1862, the enterprising Jonathan White, a wagon master with the 104th Pennsylvania, stole three bags of corn from a local farmer. Most likely the horses appreciated this act more than did the farmer.[34]

Virginia's Haymarket, a town of only seventeen structures, got a special taste of the pillage that always threatened with the approach of occupiers. Hugo Ingelheim of the Fourth New York Cavalry and Capt. Kurd Veltheim of the Sixty-eighth New York were tried for burning fourteen of the buildings at Haymarket, leaving only St. Paul's Church and two homes still standing. They had been ordered to do so because searchers had found Confederate uniforms hidden in the homes; during the search shots had been fired from the window of one home. Veltheim told the court-martial board: "My orders were: 'Burn the damned rebel nest town,'" and added that in his native land he would have been punished if he had *not* burned the town. Veltheim was dismissed from the army; Ingelheim, who had struck a civilian with his saber, was sent to do three months of hard labor. These punishments were of scant comfort to Williama Newman, whose desperately ill son died in her arms as she stood near her blazing home.[35]

The even smaller village of Sperryville was also the scene of Yankee depredation.

John Waschow, Fifty-fourth New York, stole two calico dresses, a petticoat, a mantilla, and a collar. Whether they were for his personal use is unknown, but his theft did get him six months at hard labor with an iron ball chained to his ankle.[36] A Mrs. Holland went out into her Sperryville garden and found Herman Lammers and Benedict Emler, both of the Forty-fifth New York, pulling up her new potatoes and removing the stalks. She protested mightily. Both men pled guilty. They were each fined a month's pay and reprimanded.[37] Far more terrifying than Mrs. Holland's encounter was the experience of "the widow Swindler," who was confronted with two soldiers of Battery I, First New York Light Artillery, also known as Wiedrich's Battery, Louis Sorg and Louis Troest, aided and abetted by Wiedrich's African American servant, Jerry Spades. The threesome rode up to her isolated home and set about their business. First, they demanded cherries, bread, honey, and milk. Mrs. Swindler fed them, hoping that would satisfy them. It did not.

"Then they got up and went through the house, breaking locks and plundering what ever suited them. They pretended they were looking for a pistol. Then they turned my things upside down. They asked me a great many questions, and said there would be many men there presently to set my house on fire. I started to leave, but they ordered me back, so I set in the door. They robbed my house, my henhouse, my springhouse, and my garden. They went upstairs and through all my rooms and took coverlets, blankets, and other clothing, socks. . . . They put a silk dress and a coverlet on the floor, poured preserves on them and then trampled on them until they were spoiled."[38] Soldiers often excused their depredations on the basis of hunger, but this excuse seemed dubious for these three robbers. They killed Mrs. Swindler's chickens and ducks but did not eat or take away the victims. Preserves are for food, not for pouring onto silk dresses.

Then there was the issue of rape. Rape has long been associated with military conquest. Genghis Khan supposedly said that "the greatest pleasure a man can have is to kill his enemies, take their horses, and rape their weeping women." Whatever the great Khan actually said in his native Mongolian is hard to document, but this most sordid and callous crime is documented in several Virginia cases and Union court-martials for the year 1862, including an instance at the same widow Swindler's Sperryville home.

The victim was Polly Walker, a slave belonging to Swindler. In violation of longstanding Virginia law, she was later allowed to testify against the white soldiers who molested her. "I belong to the widow Swindler," she began:

> I saw him [Troest] the day he came to our house. . . . He said he wanted to do something with me. He took hold of me and laid me down on the floor. I told him I did not want to do it. I told him I had a husband, but he said that made no difference. I cried and struggled. He said if I did not give up he would kill me. . . . It was in my own room. . . . There were two beds in the room. I don't know why he used the floor. I guess he liked it. He pulled up my clothes. . . . When he was done, the black man came upstairs and began before the white man left."

Polly was cross-examined by Jerry Spades regarding the rape.
"I told him I did not want to do it," she said.
"What did he say to you?"
"He said he wanted to fuck me."

The nineteen-year old Sorg appeared as a defense witness for Spades, stating: "You asked the Negro woman to give you a fucking. She said she was willing if you kept the white man away. I saw you at it. . . . She did not cry out or seem troubled when you did it to her." Sorg, who was not charged with rape, got a year at hard labor. Spades got five years at hard labor and Troest, two years. After serving his time in prison, he rejoined his regiment and was soon locked up again, this time for stealing money from a sleeping comrade.[39]

At Camp Butler, near Newport News, Sgt. Henry Snow and his accomplice, John Gray, both of the Second New York, were charged with throwing down, "ravishing," and injuring "an old Negro woman, Harriet Lane." The trial was terminated when the only witness, the same Harriet Lane, died. There is no record of the two men's being tried for murder.[40] Charles C. Rogers, Third Vermont, attempted rape upon the body of an eighty-two-year-old woman, Pricey McCoy, at Warrenton. The court-martial, held in the victim's own home, convicted Rogers of beating and bruising her. He was acquitted of rape, because there had not been actual penetration. Rogers was sentenced to have his head shaved, be drummed through the regiment and spend the next five years of his life in prison. His appeal went to the Executive Mansion, where Lincoln approved the sentence.[41]

At York County's Crab Neck, William Lightfoot, "a free colored man and camp retainer," was tried by a military court for rape. The two women who testified against him were nineteen-year-old Mrs. Lucy E. Thomas and her aunt, Mrs. Mahaly Wright. Lightfoot had appeared at their doorstep at daybreak and told the two women that he had orders from General McClellan to bring them to the general's headquarters. Lucy provided most of the testimony. "When we started off, we thought he was a white man. He kept his head covered. He let [sic] us about three miles into a swamp, water up to our knees." At a spot deep enough in the swamp so that nobody could hear their cries for help, he tied Mrs. Wright to a tree and forced Lucy onward another hundred yards, where he told her he would blow her brains out if she did not "give up to him." Then, "he treated me as mean as a man could treat a woman."

The court queried her sharply:

"Did or did you not resist him?"
"I resisted him."
"Did he use force with you?"
"He used force."
"Did you lie down?"

"I did."

"Did you lift your clothing?"

"No, he did."

"Did he succeed in having sexual intercourse with you?"

"He did."

Mrs. Wright confirmed the story up to the point when she had been tied to the tree. The next events were out of her sight. Lightfoot claimed that he was back at camp, cleaning his captain's tent, at the time of the crime. He was hanged May 13, 1862.[42]

The court-martial route was not the only way to get rid of erring men and officers. Commanders—and the president—could choose direct dismissal for attempted or accomplished rape and assault. At Upperville, 1st Lt. Thomas Sullivan, Tenth New Hampshire, and several other men, appeared at the door of a Miss Taliaferro, perhaps a relative of Confederate Brig. Gen. William Booth Taliaferro. The men claimed they were searching for "rebel arms." Sullivan's unique method of searching began with instructing his comrades to remain in the parlor and play the piano, while he led Miss Taliaferro upstairs to "search." She vividly recalled the next moment: "[He] closed the door and threw his arms around me, trying to hold me. I escaped from his arms and rushed downstairs." Sullivan was dismissed by General Order No. 195, in November 1862.[43]

Sarah Ann Compton lived on Duke Street in Alexandria. She was walking across a field with several friends, one of them elderly, when she was accosted by James Hickman, Seventh Pennsylvania, and a small group of his comrades. Hickman asked the women if they had anything to sell. When told "No," the men continued to follow the women. "The accused caught the old lady by the mouth and set her bleeding. I hollered. He ran up and pushed me down with violence." He held her face in the snow as he described in the coarsest terms what he planned to do with her sexually. Sarah told the court, "I cannot say the words. They were of the most vulgar character." He threatened to kill her if she would not cooperate in gratifying his lust and performing those acts which so inflamed his imagination. When she still refused, he picked her up and was carrying her "into the swamp," when the provost guard arrived and saved her from being raped. Her injuries were a bleeding nose, a torn dress, and the loss of several clumps of hair. Hickman was sent to prison for three years.[44]

While Confederate soldiers would not conventionally be regarded as "oc-cupiers" in their own territory, still a few of them were also guilty of abusing their power over civilians by resorting to rape. Recorded cases are few, since virtually all Southern court-martial records were lost in the war, but a few references survive, enough to know that rape did happen to white women and to blacks alike. In 1862 Secretary of War Judah P. Benjamin responded to an inquiry from Virginia's governor John Letcher, advising him that rape was a civil matter not a military crime, and that the Virginia state authorities should catch and prosecute any Confederate soldiers who committed rape. That Letcher had asked about the question of jurisdiction in the first place is evidence that he had specific instances in mind, while soldier memoirs and diaries provide a few instances of Rebel rapists.[45]

A civilian's cash was always at risk. Near Alexandria was Hall's Hill and Camp Jamison. Several soldiers came for supper at the home of civilian Samuel Birch. William H. Lovejoy, Second Maine, pretended to feel ill. He went upstairs to "rest," and found $115 in cash ($3,000 in today's money), which he put in his pocket. On the way out the door, he boasted to a comrade that he had more money than any other soldier there. Lovejoy, a fool as well as a thief, was sent to hard labor for nine months, during which time he lost 60 percent of his pay, a sentence approved by Brig. Gen. Fitz John Porter.[46]

Among their most common offenses were gratuitous vandalism, which soldiers of all eras think only fitting and modest retribution on an enemy's people. Pohick Church, the place of worship of George Washington and the surrounding gentry, is now a place of beauty, with an active congregation and a lovingly restored interior, but it was not always so. In 1785, the U.S. Congress disestablished the Church of England and the loss of financial support led to partial abandonment and disrepair at Pohick. By 1837, owls, bats, and mice made revel in the empty pews. An 1840 effort by Martin Van Buren, John Quincy Adams, Daniel Webster, and others led to a restoration of much of its former glory. The record over the next twenty years is unclear; whether the building was still consecrated in 1860 seems uncertain. The Second Michigan arrived in November 1861. Lt. Charles B. Haydon of that regiment wrote:

Gen. Washington contributed and was a frequent attendant. It has a very ancient look & one would suppose that it was sacred enough to be secure. I have long known that the 2nd Michigan had no fear as a general thing for God or the places where he is worshipped but I had hoped the memory of Gen. Washington might protect almost anything with which it was [associated]. I believe our soldiers would have torn the church down in 2 days. They were all over it in less than 10 minutes tearing off the ornaments, splitting the woodwork and the pews, taking the bricks to pieces & everything else they could get at. They wanted pieces to carry away. A more absolute set of vandals than our men can not be found on the face of the earth. As true as I am living I believe they would steal Washington's coffin if they could get it.

The now-famous soldier-artist Robert Sneden visited the site in January 1862 and made sketches. In his journal he noted: "Now the church is in ruinous condition. Windows were all broken out, doors gone, pews nearly gone, being used for firewood by our pickets. The ceiling broken by the rain. . . . The mahogany pulpit was half cut away . . . for relics, while the cornerstones had been unearthed and carried away. . . . There was not much left for the relic hunters now."[47]

Near Pohick Church, Capt. Emory D. Bryant, Third Michigan, entered a private home, removed a six-pane window, and installed it in his winter shelter. One witness said the house was abandoned and already in ruins; another witness said the house was quite livable until the Union army arrived. Many people saw the captain's Christmas Day theft. Surprisingly, Bryant was acquitted.[48] George Washington and his sacred memory appeared again in an article in the *Richmond Dispatch* of September 25, 1862, which reported that Maj. William Atwood, First Michigan Cavalry, stole the famous Gilbert Stuart portrait of Washington, while his troops were ransacking the old estate at Mount Vernon.

Hundreds of thousands of soldiers wrote home about every aspect of army life, and many expressed shock at their comrades' behavior in occupied Virginia. Lafayette Bayard was a member of Company K, Sixty-seventh Ohio. In October 1862, he was at Suffolk and wrote a long letter to his parents, describing not only the weather and the usual gossip, but also a heartfelt protest against the evil acts of some of his mates. While his spelling is far from perfect, his message was clear:

Pore people, robed of all or nearly all they had to, and other thins committed toward them and on them to vulgur to mention. At the rich man's house you saw Sentinals stationed to protect them from being interrupted in the least, and the poor have to suffer. I can tell you, I cannot blame these poor much for arming themselves to protect their own property. . . . It makes me feel to the bottom of my Heart to see little Children of poor families . . . See the soldiers dig the last hill of potatoes they have. . . . Vile specimens of Bruit . . . Treated his young daughter worse than a bruit and made threats of shooting her if she resisted.[49]

William Hood, 148th New York, and a dozen comrades contributed to the general misery of civilians in the Suffolk area. They paid a visit to the home of Mrs. Nancy Redd, who lived near where the Petersburg Railroad Bridge crossed Nansemond Creek. Hood was charged with violation of General Order No. 6, and had stolen six geese from a citizen. He claimed that Mrs. Redd had told him that she had no geese to sell, that the geese she had were not fit to eat, and that the troops were welcome to take any geese that they could catch. Hood further asserted that the lieutenant said it was all right to go and take a sheep, and he and his friends had generalized this permission to include geese, and "I was thus thrown in the way of temptation."

In her deposition, Mrs. Redd gave a very different story. "They said nothing to me," she testified. "I gave them no permission. About 15 men came running into my yard, some through the gate, others over the paling. They caught seven of my geese and turned one loose. They caught them in their hands and on their bayonets . . . one of them shot a chicken. I told them to go away and let my things alone. . . . One of the men said to another, 'Shoot her calf.' I stood between the gun and the calf and told them to shoot me." Mrs. Redd's neighbor, Sophia Ann Rogers, also made a deposition on the outrage:

I saw the men coming. I called to a little colored boy of mine. I told him to run to see if he could get my geese back. The boy started and he went so slow I then called my two daughters and asked them to run and see if they couldn't get my geese back. They had got but a short distance before I saw some of the men mount the fence. The men commenced firing and my geese commenced flying. And the men commenced chasing the geese and still firing. They chased them until they got as many as they wanted. . . . I lost 10 geese that day. . . . The men never spoke to me.

Her daughter, Martha Rogers, confirmed the story, adding that the reason she and her sister and the "little colored boy" were unable to herd the geese to safety was that the Union soldiers were firing so wildly.[50]

At Fort Richardson, part of the defenses of Washington, D.C., in October 1862, 1st Lt. Albert Raymond was hardly a credit to the First Connecticut Heavy Artillery. Mrs. Charles Garrett returned from church one Sunday to find this lieutenant drunk in her kitchen. He insulted her, though his exact words are not in the record. Minutes later, Mr. Garrett returned home and ordered Raymond to depart. He refused. Garrett threw him out. Raymond returned with a piece of firewood and beat the door to pieces. A bloody encounter continued until the provost guard arrived. Raymond was dismissed in disgrace.[51]

There was nothing new in an occupying army, even one humane by historical standards, being a source of great mischief and even hardship for civilians. The Union never suffered a real "occupation" by Confederates, since most incursions into the North were brief raids with no intent of conquest. Nevertheless, a few actual events suggest that Confederates as occupiers would have behaved little differently. On the march to Gettysburg, Confederate troops seized free blacks and shipped them south into slavery. Confederate soldiers burned Chambersburg when the citizens refused to pay ransom, and Confederate soldiers robbed the banks in St. Albans, Vermont, killed one citizen, and escaped with their loot into Canada. Confederate agents attempted to set fire to twenty hotels in New York City, hoping to burn the entire city, and at Mount Sterling, Kentucky, Confederate raiders even robbed the local bank containing the deposits of citizens sympathetic to the Confederacy. A gentlemanly war was only a foolish dream.

Notes

1. William C. Davis, *The Cause Lost* (Lawrence: University Press of Kansas, 1996), 55.

2. Court-martial Case File NN3891, Records of the Judge Advocate Gen-

eral's Office (Army), RG 153, National Archives, Washington, D.C. (hereafter cited by case file alone).

3. KK159.

4. II756.

5. All soldiers presented here have the rank of private unless indicated otherwise.

6. II914.

7. II873.

8. II876.

9. II679.

10. II583.

11. II694.

12. II852.

13. II583.

14. II878.

15. II879.

16. KK244.

17. II948.

18. II961.

19. MM141.

20. MM216.

21. KK555.

22. KK432.

23. KK555.

24. II984.

25. II875.

26. NN3888.

27. KK325.

28. KK66.

29. II679.

30. II702.

31. KK553.

32. KK555.

33. II952.

34. KK463.

35. KK325, KK373.

36. KK387.

37. KK207.

38. KK207.

39. Ibid.

40. II773.

41. NN116.

42. II869.

43. Records of the Adjutant General's Office, RG 94, G737–849, Box 56, National Archives.

44. II819.

45. United States War Department, *War of the Rebellion: Official Records of the Union and Confederate Armies* (Washington, D.C.: Government Printing Office, 1880–1901), series I, vol. 51, pt. 2, 386–87.

46. II712.

47. See http://www.pohick.org/history.html.

48. II676.

49. Letter File, Fredericksburg-Spotsylvania National Military Park, Fredericksburg, Va.

50. KK765.

51. LL219.

Richmond, the Confederate Hospital City

David J. Coles

In July 1862 the Confederate capital of Richmond, Virginia, was still recovering from the Peninsula Campaign, which saw a massive Union army under Maj. Gen. George McClellan approach to within a few miles of the city before being pushed back down the peninsula to Harrison's Landing. A reporter for the *Charleston (S.C.) Mercury* had returned by train to the capital after a one-month holiday. "One feels the dread of infection as he gets nearer and nearer this war-scarred city," he related. "Soldiers crowd the cars—dirty convalescents from the country hospitals—sick trains pass him on the way; he catches the odor of suppurating wounds in Manchester, and this odor increases to a stench as he crosses the James river, where the tainted breezes from the vast wards on Chimborazo Heights have free play." Reaching town shortly after dusk, the reporter noticed "a strange stillness about the streets. . . . The doors of the great dry goods and clothing houses are open and guarded by sentinels. Looking in, he beholds multitudes of beds and ministering angels passing to and fro. Well he knows what forms lie stretched on those narrow beds. They are the heroes who have suffered in the great cause. How horrible is war!"[1]

The citizens of Richmond would know well the horrors of war. As capital of the Confederacy, the city was the object of a number of Federal military campaigns, resulting in a series of battles occurring in its proximity in 1862 and again in 1864–1865. The thousands of casualties from these engagements, along with the even greater number of soldiers felled by disease, required medical care on a scale never before seen in America. Consequently, Confederate and state authorities would establish in the city a variety of hospitals to treat Southern casualties, while a number of privately operated facilities also came into existence. By 1862 Richmond had developed into the medical as well as a political, economic, and military center of the new nation. By war's end the various hospitals in Richmond had treated between 200,000 and 300,000 sick and wounded, a number unequaled in the Confederacy.[2]

The initial hospital system established by the Confederate government worked adequately until casualties from the Peninsula Campaign overwhelmed the existing facilities. In 1862, authorities turned to a combination of larger "encampment" hospitals as well as smaller general hospitals, often established to treat soldiers from a particular state. Ultimately, in a mid-war consolidation effort, many of the smaller to medium-sized hospitals were closed, and the great majority of patients housed in the larger facilities. The result was a system barely adequate to meet the critical situation faced by the South, but one that did compare favorably to that of the better equipped and better financed Northern hospitals.[3]

During the Civil War more than 600,000 Americans died from battle wounds and disease. The magnitude of the crisis they faced caught both Union and Confederate medical officials unprepared. While the U.S. Army moved to expand its small medical department, the new Confederate government would have to create an entirely new agency. The Confederate Congress authorized the establishment of a medical bureau in February 1861, which would be led by Surgeon General Samuel Preston Moore for most of the war. A graduate of the Medical College of South Carolina, Moore had been an assistant surgeon, surgeon, and medical purveyor in the U.S Army for more than twenty-five years.[4] His priorities included the creation of an administrative hierarchy of medical directors, inspectors, and boards; the selection of medical purveyors to procure supplies; the recruitment of qualified surgeons and assistant surgeons to serve in the Confederate military; and the establishment of a variety of hospitals throughout the South. Eventually, the Confederate Medical Department opened some 154 "principal" hospitals, as well as many smaller facilities. Virginia, with thirty-nine principal hospitals, had more than any other state except Georgia, which had fifty. Although the Confederates established military hospitals throughout the Old Dominion, the largest number would reside in the Confederate and state capital of Richmond.[5]

The third-largest city in the Confederacy at the outbreak of the war, Richmond grew from a population of about 40,000 to perhaps 150,000 during the conflict. With national and state offices established throughout the city and with a huge influx of government employees, relatives of soldiers, refugees, and others flocking to the new capital, office and residential space soon became extremely expensive or entirely unavailable.[6] Finding sufficient hospital space proved a major problem, particularly early in the conflict. Richmond had five hospitals when the war began: the Richmond City Hospital, the Main Street Hospital, the Medical College of Virginia Infirmary, the St. Francis de Sales Infirmary, and Bellevue Hospital. All were small and handled more outpatients than inpatients.[7]

In June 1861, already recognizing the need for additional space for military patients, the Confederate government began renting from the city the newly constructed Alms House, designating it General Hospital and later General Hospital No. 1. The large structure had a capacity of four hundred to five hundred and it was used to house Union prisoners after the Battle of Manassas, as well as smallpox patients and Confederate sick and wounded.[8] In the period following the victory at Manassas in July, Confederate wounded flooded Richmond, overwhelming the few hospitals then established. Churches, hotels, and private homes all served as makeshift hospitals. Mayor Joseph Mayo held a meeting in Capital Square to form committees to both assist wounded soldiers in reaching Richmond and to establish additional medical facilities in the capital.[9]

Robertson Hospital, the most famous of the private hospitals established during this period, opened its doors on July 31, 1861. Miss Sally Tompkins and other women from St. James Episcopal Church operated the facility, which one historian has described as "the epitome of order, neatness, and cleanliness and the food was of high quality and prepared by ladies who considered the patients their guests." In September 1861 Tompkins received a commission as a Confederate officer in order to keep the hospital open as at least a quasi-official facility, and the surgeon of a nearby general hospital also served as Robertson's surgeon-in-charge. Despite the efforts of some in the Confederate Medical Department to close the hospital, it remained in operation until the war's end.[10]

During the late summer and fall of 1861 a number of medium-sized hospitals were established, which were later designated as general hospitals. In all, twenty-eight general hospitals, so-called because they admitted soldiers from more than one unit, were established between 1861 and 1863. Many originated as private or state sponsored facilities. The earliest included

Byrd Island Hospital, later General Hospital No. 3; the St. Charles Hotel, later General Hospital No. 8; the Globe Hospital, later General Hospital No. 11; Moore's Hospital, later General Hospital No. 24; Springfield Hall, later General Hospital No. 26; and the Company G Hall Hospital, later General Hospital No. 27. A number of these hospitals were converted from tobacco warehouses and most had patient capacities of one hundred to three hundred.[11]

In 1861–1862 individual states also established Richmond hospitals for their soldiers. The Georgia Hospital Association eventually operated four with a capacity of nearly seven hundred soldiers, and Mrs. Juliet O. Hopkins oversaw the establishment of three Alabama hospitals. The Louisiana Soldier's Relief Association operated a medical facility on the grounds of the Baptist College, assisted by a group of the Sisters of Charity, while a South Carolina hospital was established in Manchester. The state of Florida provided assistance for another hospital, as did the Ladies Cumberland Hospital Association of North Carolina. In addition to the benefit of recuperating from illness or wounds in the company of comrades from one's own state, the housing of patients by state improved morale by ensuring that supplies, visitors, and mail could more easily find patients and in general promoted a more peaceful atmosphere. The smaller size of these hospitals undoubtedly led to more personalized care as well. Consequently, even in facilities operated directly by the Confederate government, including the large encampment hospitals, efforts were made to house patients together by state.[12]

Perhaps most surprising, given the state's small population and remote location, was Florida's support for its troops in Virginia, which initially included the Second Florida Infantry Regiment, and later the Fifth and Eighth Infantry. A separate Florida hospital was established in Richmond during the late summer of 1862, with Dr. Thomas M. Palmer of Jefferson County, and Mary Martha Reid, the widow of a former territorial governor, the most prominent individuals associated with its operation. Palmer had originally been a surgeon in the Second Florida, while Reid had worked as a nurse at a military hospital in Lake City, Florida.

In the summer of 1862, Reid and several other prominent Floridians began urging the state government to create a Florida hospital in Richmond. Officials selected the former James H. Grant & Company tobacco warehouse, located on 19th Street, near its intersection with Franklin Street, as the location of the new Florida Hospital, which was officially referred to as

General Hospital No. 11. Built in 1853, the building had a capacity of 150 beds. It had formerly been known as the Globe Hospital. Floridians donated money and matériel to supply the hospital, and the state provided additional funding. Florida governor John Milton, "[a]t the request of many prominent citizens, . . . agreed to aid in the management of the Hospital." He appointed Dr. Palmer as superintendent and director, and Dr. Green Hunter as special agent to procure supplies.[13]

Francis Fleming, a soldier in the Second Florida Infantry who served a term as Florida governor after the war, noted in a letter home that the creation of a state hospital "is something that we very much need and should have been attended to long ago. Our sick & wounded are scattered all over the city, and unless you accidentally know in what hospital a man is, it is almost an impossibility to find one." Several months later Fleming visited the Florida Hospital and wrote that Mrs. Reid "has it nicely fixed up."[14] During its existence the Florida Hospital had cared for 1,076 patients with only 53 deaths, a mortality rate of less than 5 percent, perhaps the lowest of any of the Richmond hospitals. The *Richmond Enquirer* gave credit to surgeons Palmer and Babcock, as well as to Reid, the "gentle, energetic and devoted Matron . . . more familiarly known to her patients as the '*buena madre*.'"[15]

By April 1862 twenty hospitals were in operation in the capital. That number increased during the late spring and summer of 1862, as more opened in response to the fighting on the Virginia peninsula, which flooded Richmond with thousands of casualties. In addition to these smaller and medium-sized facilities, Confederate authorities also moved in late 1861 and early 1862 to establish a number of large "encampment" hospitals with a capacity of several thousand patients. Ultimately six encampment hospitals were established in Richmond during the conflict: Chimborazo, Winder, Howard's Grove, Louisiana, Jackson, and Stuart. The first three, however, were generally the largest and best known.[16] Chimborazo was organized in late 1861, while Howard's Grove and Winder came into existence the following year. Probably the most famous of any Confederate military hospital, Chimborazo, with a capacity of over 3,000, treated nearly 78,000 patients during its three and one-half years of operation and was rivaled in size only by Winder Hospital.[17]

Chimborazo was located on a prominent hill east of Richmond, and military units had initially trained there during the war's early months. In addition, Confederate authorities maintained a facility on the heights to guard Union prisoners. In the fall of 1861, preparations were made to build winter quarters at Chimborazo for Confederate soldiers. Reporting on the new facility on November 11, 1861, the *Richmond Dispatch* commented: "On the hill east of Richmond, known as Hospital Hill, or Chimborazo Heights, there has suddenly sprung up a city, which, while it does not rival the metropolis in architectural construction, makes a very formidable show in the number of its houses. These buildings have been put up for winter quarters, and will furnish accommodations for thousands of troops. It is worth any one's trouble to go and see the new city of Chimborazo."[18] Ultimately these structures would house the Confederacy's most famous military hospital.

In October 1861, Gen. Joseph E. Johnston had approached Confederate Surgeon General Samuel Moore about establishing a hospital in Richmond to alleviate overcrowding in his field hospitals. Moore met with Dr. James Brown McCaw, a respected Richmond physician and professor at the Medical College of Virginia, and asked McCaw to establish such a hospital and to accept the position as surgeon-in-chief.[19] McCaw selected the Chimborazo site, located on a bluff of about forty acres overlooking the James River and named for an Ecuadorian volcano. He supervised construction of the wards and supporting structures, which were installed over the next several months using slave labor. Quickly built using cheap "balloon" construction techniques and a "pavilion" design to improve ventilation, Chimborazo already housed several hundred sick soldiers by November 1, 1861. One month later the patient population had risen to 1,200, with plans made to house an additional thousand convalescents, and the numbers typically remained over 3,000 for most of 1862. The overcrowded conditions at Chimborazo later contributed to the decision to establish two other large encampments in Richmond, Winder and Howard's Grove, as well as several new general hospitals.[20]

Chimborazo's facilities were impressive for the period. Eventually more than 150 buildings were constructed. The nearly one hundred wards measured eighty by twenty-eight feet and could house up to thirty-two patients. In addition to the wards, the complex included a headquarters building, various kitchens, a bakery, a soap house, icehouses, a stable, guardhouses, a chapel, carpentry and blacksmith shops, apothecaries, a bathhouse, and latrines built into the hill's slope. Five wells provided sufficient water, and in the vicinity the hospital also ran a brewery, dairy, sawmill, and garden.[21]

McCaw divided the complex into five divisions, each with a separate surgeon in charge. He also hired the staff that, while never reaching the levels authorized by the Confederate government, did at one point consist of a medical staff of forty-five matrons and a support staff of several hundred.[22] Frequently McCaw placed ads in the Richmond papers, such as one in April 1862, requesting the services at Chimborazo of "fifty young NEGRO MEN, to nurse the sick."[23] The following month, with McClellan's army threatening Richmond, McCaw expressed concern that the owners of the more than 250 slaves working as cooks and nurses "are threatening to remove them to the interior of the country." He asked Surgeon General Moore that these servants, with as many others as may be needed, be "immediately impressed, as it will be utterly impossible to continue the Hospitals without them."[24]

In addition to staffing difficulties, Chimborazo also occasionally suffered from shortages of food, clothing, and supplies. In May 1862 authorities asked "the ladies, who have done much for this hospital," to supply "bandages of different kinds, poultices, &c."[25] Two months later the *Enquirer* asked citizens "engaged in the labor of love and patriotism, or relieving the wants of our sick and wounded soldiers, [to come] to the large hospital on our eastern limits, known as Chimborazo." The size of the facility "is so great as to require very liberal and frequent contribution; while its remoteness is such as to make it liable to be overlooked."[26]

Women played an important role at Chimborazo and other Confederate military hospitals. Many local women volunteered their time writing letters, reading, and generally comforting the sick and wounded, while others, both black and white, worked as laundresses and cooks. Still others served in the position of matron, formally established by the Confederate Congress in September 1862. For a monthly salary of forty dollars, matrons were to supervise "the entire domestic economy of the hospital," to include the patient's diet "and all such other duties as may be necessary."[27] Assistant and ward matrons, meanwhile, had responsibility for the hospital's laundry and bedding, for the administering of medicine, and for the supervision of nurses. Some women worked as matrons out of necessity, while others emphasized the patriotic self-sacrificing aspect of their work. Many Southerners contended that white women, particularly from the middle and upper classes, had no business working in the horrific conditions often encountered in military hospitals. Surgeons and other male officials often resented the women's presence as well, with a modern historian referring to the hospitals as "a battleground of class and gender, exacerbated by the new legislation appointing and empowering women."[28]

Arguably the most famous female hospital worker of the war would be employed at Chimborazo. Phoebe Yates Pember was born into a prominent Jewish family of Charleston in 1823. Her husband had died in 1861, and Pember went to live with her family in Georgia. In November 1862 she received an offer to work at Chimborazo and she arrived there the next month, serving as head matron of the hospital's Division No. 2. Apparently the first matron employed at the complex, Pember noticed a distinct coolness on the part of her male coworkers when one remarked, "in a tone of ill-concealed disgust, that 'one of them had come.'"[29] During her tenure, Pember grew to admire the stoic courage of the desperately wounded and ill patients, commenting that "[n]o words can do justice to the uncomplaining nature of the Southern soldier."[30] She did, however, criticize some of the hospital staff. The matron found many of the nurses, usually male convalescents, "not practiced or expert in their duties," and requiring "constant supervision and endless teaching." A complex the size of Chimborazo also housed a small army of clerks, stewards, and related positions, often held by "forgotten hangers-on, to whom the soldiers gave the name of hospital rats in common with would-be invalids who resisted being cured from a disinclination to field service."[31] Pember also endured a "long and bitterly waged contest" for control over the distribution of liquor to the patients for medicinal purposes. Previously some of the male staff, including surgeons, had appropriated the alcohol for their own use. Control over the distribution "eventually became a symbol of authority in a tussle between the male and female contingents of the hospital staff."[32]

In evaluating Chimborazo, historian Carol Green determined that the facility's "quality of organization appears to have been very high," while medical treatment "was as good or better than at any other hospital during the Civil War." Patient mortality rates were less than 11.5 percent, comparing favorably to those of better-equipped Northern hospitals. Green also praises the planners and staff for "innovations in patient care, such as separating patients by ailments, and the performance of clinical drug tests," for "creative use of the hospital fund," and for designing the "first American hospital, North or South" in the pavilion style for "maximum ventilation."[33]

Along with Chimborazo, Winder Hospital, established in 1862, was one of Richmond's "two sister mega-hospitals." It eventually expanded into the largest facility of its kind in the Confederacy, treating nearly as many patients during the war as its more famous sibling. Located on the city's western outskirts and named for John Winder, a brigadier general and provost marshal, Confederate authorities established Camp Winder in April 1862. Alexander G. Lane served as Winder's surgeon-in-chief. At 125 acres, the complex was three times the size of Chimborazo with accommodations for one thousand more patients. The hospital was organized into five divisions, later expanded to six, with an additional tent division. Once completed, the sprawling complex included 180 buildings with its own steam bath, bakery, dairy, icehouse, and library.[34] Despite these amenities, the camp had a reputation for a lack of cleanliness. John Tucker of the Fifth Alabama visited Winder in May 1862 and proclaimed it "the nastiest place I ever saw in my life."[35]

By early May 1862, Winder housed approximately 2,500 sick soldiers, but Surgeon Lane's professional staff consisted only of himself and six assistants. Thousands of soldiers wounded during the fighting on the Virginia peninsula soon inundated the complex. While noting that Lane "has done everything in his power to promote the sanitary condition of the place, and to minister to the relief of the patients," the *Richmond Whig* reported, "[I]t is obvious, however that this force is inadequate." The paper urged local "medicine men" to volunteer their services.[36] Such a large facility also required an extensive support staff, and Winder's administration turned initially to Richmond's free black population to fill this need. In late April 1862, with the camp's organization still incomplete, Surgeon Lane advertised for "One hundred male free Negroes," who "are wanted immediately, as nurses, at the Winder Hospital." He noted ominously that, "If the parties go willingly, good wages will be paid and kind treatment afforded them. If they do not volunteer they will be impressed, and run the risk of receiving such treatment and pay as is generally awarded under such circumstances."[37] A few days later Lane again placed an advertisement for "80 Nurses and Waiters for Winder Hospital, from fifteen to eighteen dollars per month will be paid for men and women, or white men over thirty-five years of age, (not subject to military duty by conscription)."[38]

During its early weeks of operation, shortages of food, medicines, and other items dogged the camp. Pleas went out for donations, to be deposited at a local chapter of the YMCA for the hospital's use. In addition, authorities asked Richmond's citizens to donate "empty vials, old pill boxes," and any "supplies of provisions, suitable for sick and convalescent soldiers," pleading that all such items were "much needed."[39] Lane also requested "the ladies of Richmond . . . to visit the Winder Hospital at all hours, and provide the sick with any food or comforts they need."[40]

Several letters from patients provide a glimpse into conditions at Winder during the hospital's difficult early months of operation. Thomas Gaither of the Fourth North Carolina wrote a letter home in May 1862 from "Camp Winder Horsepittle." While complaining that "my back and legs hurts me so that I can scarcely get about I am faring tolerable well," Gaither added that "as for eating [I] get plenty I have a straw bed to lay on but it seams to lay hard." The Southern soldier claimed that he "hope[d] to be able for duty now in a few days" while reporting "there is thousands of sick soldiers here now they are sending them off as fast as possible ever[y] day to Danville and peters burge there is a great many Dieing ever[y] day . . . I have thought that I had seen hard times but was mistakin."[41] In correspondence written several weeks later Gaither reported that he would rejoin his regiment the following day. He also commented on the high price of food and drink, and claimed that Virginians "do not treat the North Carolina Troops with much respect the Va always does all the fighting to hear them tell it[.] I am sorry that I left the state and [wish] that [I] could get back there."[42] Gaither survived his time at Winder and returned to his regiment, only to be killed the following year at Chancellorsville.

In August 1862, Georgian James M. Garrett spent time as a patient in Winder's Division No. 2, Ward No. 47. Evidently his accommodations were satisfactory, as he noted in a letter to his mother: "I have a good bed to ly [*sic*] on and a good house to stay in and plenty to eat such as it is." He did complain, however, about the quality and monotony of the rations: "we get bread and coffee for supper and the same for breakfast and a little fat bacon boiled and for dinner we have a little fat bacon and bread. That is not fitten for a sick man to eat." Garrett complained about the cost of purchasing supplemental rations, noting, "If I did not have money I would be in a bad fix here and every thing is so high it takes a heap of it to do a man." He added, "I would like very much to get a box of vituals from home if you get the chance."[43]

Winder remained crowded through the end of 1862 with the sick, and with wounded from the Seven Days' Battles and subsequent campaigns. At the end of each of the last four months of that year, reports showed patient populations of 3,402; 3,302; 2,713; and 2,316, respectively. In September 1862, for example, Winder's hospital lists showed a total of 3,161 patients remaining from the previous month, with 2,860 new patients being admitted. That same month 153 patients died, while 39 deserted, 30 received discharges, 164 were transferred, 432 were furloughed, and 1,801 returned to duty. The number of patients decreased dramatically throughout the late winter and early spring of 1863, before spiking again in May following Chancellorsville. Not until the summer of 1864, however, would the numbers remain consistently as high as they did during the hectic months of 1862.[44]

In December 1862, both patients and staff looked forward to the holiday season, marking as it would an end to the bloody first full year of the conflict. Mrs. Mason, the matron of Winder's Division No. 1, requested assistance from the women of Richmond in providing a Christmas dinner for the men under her care. "It went off famously—everybody delighted" she reported in a Richmond paper, with the convalescents receiving turkey, chicken, duck, corned beef, pies, and cider, and the sick rice custard, pudding, oysters, and eggnog. "Woman's hands collected, and woman's hands prepared and dispensed the feast," the paper reported. "Perhaps we should not be unwarranted in speaking of this as an illustration of the benefit of introducing matrons into our hospitals. The considerate kindness that provides Christmas dinners, is not restricted to Christmas; but shows itself in a thousand gentle influences and attentions such as come only from the heart and the hand of woman."[45]

Except for the months following Chancellorsville and Gettysburg, the number of patients at Winder remained relatively low for most of 1863. During this period the camp also housed a large number of convalescent soldiers who worked on the Richmond defenses. During the latter stages of the war the complex suffered damage from a storm and a fire, and it would briefly close for cleaning in early 1864. That same year a newspaper account described Winder as "most healthily located, and . . . supplied by a number of wells with clear, cold, pleasant water." The visitors noted that the facility also "[h]ad a central register for the information of enquiring friends, a library for the use of patients, a bath house, and a bakery at which the whole of the bread for the hospital is baked."[46] A minor controversy involving Winder arose in June 1864, when representatives from North Carolina in the Confederate Congress complained that patients from their state were being neglected by the hospital staff, a charge hotly denied in a Richmond newspaper editorial.[47] Louisiana soldier James Roden also criticized conditions at Winder, particularly the diet. His discontent over the rations of bread, rye coffee, corn bread, bacon, stewed beets, and potato vine leaves led to an altercation with a nurse and with Roden being threatened with the guardhouse. Roden survived his hospitalization, leaving Winder "after a stay of eight weeks, with a glad heart, feeling thankful that I had been spared."[48]

Howard's Grove was the third of the large, government-run hospitals established in the Confederate capital during 1861–1862. A prewar "picnic-recreation area," Howard's Grove was located on the Mechanicsville Turnpike northeast of the city. It served early in the war as a training facility for newly arriving troops. The Confederate Quartermaster's Department constructed buildings on the site for storage, but in June 1862 the Medical Department took control of the site for conversion into a hospital complex. The original buildings were used for a time as wards, a guardhouse, a dead house, and a laundry, but these were eventually removed and a total of sixty-two uniform, one-story wood frame structures erected.[49] Though still unfinished and with a capacity far less than that of Chimborazo or Winder Hospitals, Howard's Grove opened in time to treat the sick and wounded of the Seven Days' fighting. The number of patients there during the last four months of the year averaged fewer than four hundred.[50]

In the fall of 1862 William A. Carrington, medical director and inspector of hospitals, conducted inspections and issued reports on most of the hospitals then open in Richmond. His November 13 report on Howard's Grove provides the most details on that facility during the early months of its operations. Carrington reported that the complex was located "in a beautiful grove of towering pines & lovely oaks unsurpassed for the beauty of scenery or the elements of health." Howard Grove's wards were of higher elevation and farther apart than those at either Winder or Chimborazo and had better ventilation. In addition to wards for the sick, the complex included a kitchen, mess room, storeroom, drug store, linen room, laundry, dead house, guardhouse, and offices for surgeons. No bathhouse had as yet been constructed, though "two very fine springs have been walled in." Unfortunately, Carrington noted, "the privies are old & insufficient."[51]

The hospital's First Division, with a capacity of 544 patients, was then in operation while construction of the Second Division's wards was not yet complete. The facility's capacity would total 1,100 upon completion of the

Second Division. A surgeon-in-chief and eight assistant surgeons treated the sick and wounded, aided by four matrons, five stewards, seventy-seven nurses, twelve cooks, and eleven laundresses. Carrington recommended an increase in the number of cooks and laundresses, and noted that the matrons "are efficient & of great benefit to the service." The hospital guard needed to be increased, and Surgeon Rice "complained [of] much contrivancy [*sic*] & disobedience of orders by attendants & patients until he . . . introduced bucking & gagging as a firmer resort in addition to the guard house—with the most beneficial effects."[52]

Few accounts written by Howard's Grove patients in 1862 have been identified but John Ussery, an 1863 patient in Ward H of the First Division, was complimentary of conditions in the facility. "All is clean and nice. I can get clean shirts &c as often as [I] need them," he reported to his sister. "The M.D. was very attentive. The Ward Master I must give you his name. I hope that you all will pray for him & thank God that raised up so many kind friends in a strange place."[53] The soldier also commented, "I do not have to burn my hands cooking now—it is brought to my bed. I wish I had some fruit though I know my Dr. would not allow me to eat it." Ussery's one complaint concerned the prices of various commodities. Tomatoes cost two dollars per dozen and peaches "the size of a hickory nut and nearly as hard," sold for three dollars a dozen.[54]

Howard's Grove continued in operation until the end of the war, except for a brief period during the winter of 1863 and a longer period during the winter and spring of 1864 when it temporarily closed because of a low number of patients. Two new divisions were established and the complex received additional patients following the closing of a number of the city's smaller military hospitals in 1863–1864, and by the summer of 1864 it averaged 1,100 to 1,400 patients per month. In 1863, Howard's Grove became the location of a smallpox hospital for the city's black population, and military patients with smallpox were also evidently sent to that location.[55]

The year 1862 had proven to be most critical in the establishment of a relatively efficient hospital system in Richmond, though one that still dealt with periodic overcrowding and regular shortages of food and supplies. In April, a committee of the Confederate House of Representatives reported that the twenty military hospitals in Richmond could house between five thousand and six thousand patients. The report noted a shortage of medicines, "but otherwise found the men adequately attended."[56] The Peninsula

Campaign, however, had shown the number of beds to be insufficient, leading to an expansion in the number of hospitals during the remainder of 1862.

The Confederate Congress returned to the subject of medical facilities in September 1862 when it passed "An Act to Provide for the Sick and Wounded of the Army in Hospitals." The passage of this act followed an investigation and report by the Senate Select Committee on Hospitals, in which investigators visited all of the principal military hospitals in Richmond. The committee reported that, "though many of the complaints made by the sick, are well founded in fact, yet they are in no manner attributable to the inattention or neglect of the surgeons in charge." The complaints, they noted, "relate to a want of proper food, both in quantity and quality; a proper preparation of it, additional clothing and competent and skillful nurses." Most of these problems were not "under existing laws and regulations, in the power of surgeons in charge to remove."[57] Consequently, the committee report led to the passage of an act designed to improve the administration of and the conditions in the military hospitals. As described previously, the act established the positions of matron and assistant matron in military hospitals, as well as authorizing additional nurses, cooks, and ward masters. It also increased the amount hospitals received for the commutation of rations for hospitalized soldiers, thus allowing for the purchase of more food; authorized the increased distribution of clothing; called for the housing of patients together by state; made it easier for hospitalized soldiers to receive their pay; and established procedures to improve the transportation of the wounded and ill. The *Richmond Enquirer* noted the act "strikes at the real evils which have added to the discomforts of our sick soldiers. It has been customary to lay everything upon the Surgeons. Now that the true causes have been diligently probed and discovered, we are gratified that the Senate, by unanimous vote, has prepared for the corrective."[58]

With the passage of the Hospital Act, and the establishment and expansion of Chimborazo, Winder, and Howard's Grove hospitals, the Confederate government had moved to increase the efficiency and improve the conditions in Richmond's hospitals. To further these aims, the Medical Department moved in late 1862 to reduce the number of privately operated and state-sponsored hospitals that had been established in Richmond during 1861 and early 1862. In the fall of 1862, Medical Director and Inspector William Carrington inspected a number of these hospitals. He found conditions in some of the facilities, such as the Louisiana Hospital, outstanding, reporting:

"The Surgeon in charge has faithfully [discharged] his duties in inspiring & providing order & cleanliness in the whole establishment." Continuing, Carrington stated: "I cannot praise too highly the order and cleanliness of the wards—Stewards pantry and apothecary shop & etc and I may favorably mention this Hosl records." He recommended "that immediate steps be taken to remove to this Hosl all the sickest of the Louisianians in the Hosls in Richmond."[59] Carrington also praised conditions in General Hospital No. 19, formerly the Third Georgia Hospital, calling the wards and bedding "notably neat and cleanly and really worthy of honorable mention."[60] In fact, conditions at most of the hospitals appeared satisfactory, with a few problems noted such as poorly maintained records, insufficient guards, inadequate privies, or, as was the case with General Hospital No. 17, the lack of a bath, which caused the patients to "suffer for personal cleanliness."[61] At General Hospital No. 12, Carrington found the condition of the ward and offices "unacceptable."[62]

After the close of 1862, following his round of inspections, Carrington directed that the privately operated Robertson, Samaritan, Soldier's Home, St. Francis de Sales, and Medical College hospitals be closed, that patients be transferred "to the Hospitals of their respective states," and the facilities "hereafter receive no sick or wounded soldiers except on written authority." All property of the Confederate States government was to be turned in to the medical purveyor and all staff members reassigned.[63] Carrington subsequently explained this decision to Surgeon General Moore. He argued that the five facilities did not fall "under military control," that there was a "want of military discipline . . . necessary for the good order for soldiers," and that they "keep soldiers longer from duty and induced the belief, among others, that few had peculiar privileges and exemptions not enjoyed by the most." Carrington also claimed that the sick "did not receive the attention that they did in the large Hospitals, when one Medical officer is always on duty." He added, "Confed. Soldiers are not an object of charity, being beautifully cared for by the Confed. States Authorities, [and] that their care and subsistence are liberally provided for." Finally, Carrington argued that with more than 6,200 "empty beds in Richmond Hospitals," it was unnecessary and uneconomical for Confederate soldiers to be patients in private hospitals.[64] Despite Carrington's order, the Robertson Hospital remained open, probably due to the popularity of its director, Sally Tompkins, and the fact that it had an unusually low death rate of 5.5 percent. The Samaritan Hospital did close, but evidently not for six months, and while the Soldier's Home Hospital did close in February 1863, it reopened the next year under the auspices of the Association for the Relief of Maimed Soldiers. The Medical College Hospital ceased admitting Southern soldiers after February 1863, and, while the St. Francis Hospital remained open throughout the war, it may also have stopped serving as a military hospital.[65]

Carrington's and Moore's consolidation efforts would continue throughout 1863 and early 1864. By March of 1864 thirty-five hospitals had been closed, including both privately operated facilities and general hospitals, mainly those caring for fewer than one hundred patients. The Florida Hospital, for example, closed in late 1863, with the patients and staff transferred to Howard's Grove, where a ward was reserved for Floridians. Moore allowed some of the private hospitals to continue to operate for a time, "[a]s the ladies are very desirous of attending to sick soldiers, they should be gratified."[66] The new Jackson and Stuart "encampment" hospitals, which opened respectively in 1863 and 1864, replaced most of the beds lost with the closure of the general hospitals, and a series of "wayside" hospitals along major railroads also alleviated the need for some of the Richmond facilities. Thus by late 1863 far fewer hospitals operated in Richmond, and those that did were larger and more directly under Confederate government control.[67]

Historians have argued the relative merits of the Confederacy's decision to close the smaller hospitals in Richmond and to focus primarily on the larger encampments. To some, "there is no doubt that the patients in smaller hospitals fared better. They were easier to manage, and most were under the watchful eye of a devoted Southern lady with a penchant for good food and cleanliness."[68] They also promoted state pride and recognition and maintained death rates below those of the larger hospitals. Others contend that the success of larger hospitals like Chimborazo made it "the best-known and perhaps the most well-respected hospital in the Confederacy" and "an obvious model to follow."[69] From the perspective of Confederate authorities, maintaining such a large number of smaller facilities in Richmond proved administratively and logistically uneconomical, and the obvious answer to these problems was to establish a smaller number of larger hospitals. While probably the correct decision, it is impossible to determine whether it ultimately saved or cost lives. Students of the Confederate Medical Department might marvel at its ability to create a hospital system that rivaled that of the Federal government, but it cannot diminish the fact that Civil War hospitals

North and South remained places of suffering and death unequaled in any other American conflict.

Notes

1. *Charleston (S.C.) Mercury,* July 26, 1862.

2. While the exact number of sick and wounded admitted into Richmond hospitals during the entire war is unknown, a report in the *Richmond Enquirer* of September 29, 1862, records a total of 99,508 patients by that early war date. Transcribed at *Civil War Richmond,* http://www.mdgorman.com. This invaluable site, maintained by Michael D. Gorman, contains a remarkable amount of material concerning the capital city during the war, including a variety of written accounts, maps, and photographs, with a particularly strong collection of material relating to prisons and hospitals.

3. H. H. Cunningham, *Doctors in Gray: The Confederate Medical Service* (Baton Rouge: Louisiana State University Press, 1958), 45–53; Carol C. Green, *Chimborazo: The Confederacy's Largest Hospital* (Knoxville: University of Tennessee Press, 2004), 5–18; Rebecca Barbour Calcutt, *Richmond's Wartime Hospitals* (Gretna, La.: Pelican Publishing Company, 2005), passim.

4. Cunningham, *Doctors in Gray,* 27–28.

5. Ibid., particularly 21–98. This work, though nearly fifty years old, remains the standard source on the subject. In addition, *The Medical and Surgical History of the War of the Rebellion* (Washington, D.C.: Government Printing Office, 1870–1888) provides detailed correspondence and case studies.

6. The three best studies of wartime Richmond that detail the establishment of the Confederate governmental facilities, including some information on the city's hospitals, are Alfred Hoyt Bill, *The Beleaguered City: Richmond, 1861–1865* (New York: Knopf, 1946), 34–166; Emory M. Thomas, *The Confederate State of Richmond: A Biography of the Capital* (Austin: University of Texas Press, 1971), 32–125; and Ernest B. Furgurson, *Ashes of Glory: Richmond at War* (New York: Knopf, 1996), 49–196.

7. Calcutt, *Richmond's Wartime Hospitals,* 23. This is the most complete work on the subject, though Robert W. Waitt, *Confederate Military Hospitals in Richmond* (Richmond, Va.: Richmond Civil War Centennial Committee, 1964; reprint, Eastern National, 2002), remains a valuable source.

8. Calcutt, *Richmond's Wartime Hospitals,* 41, 110–12; Waitt, *Confederate Military Hospitals in Richmond,* 11.

9. Furgurson, *Ashes of Glory,* 72–73; Bill, *Beleaguered City,* 70–71; Thomas, *Confederate State of Richmond,* 54–59.

10. Calcutt, *Richmond's Wartime Hospitals,* 42, 172–74.

11. Cunningham, *Doctors in Gray,* 45; Calcutt, *Richmond's Wartime Hospitals,* 110–83.

12. Carol Cranmer Green, "Chimborazo Hospital: A Description and Evaluation of the Confederacy's Largest Hospital," (Ph.D. diss., Texas Tech University, 1999), 168–70.

13. Waitt, *Confederate Military Hospitals in Richmond,* 7, 13–14. An 1862 list shows the Florida Hospital as being located at Fifteenth Street and Cary. Such a facility may have been briefly located there, but no records of it exist. *Journal of the Proceedings of the Senate of the General Assembly of the State of Florida, at the Twelfth Session, Begun and Held at the Capitol, in the City of Tallahassee, on Monday, November 17th, 1862* (Tallahassee: Office of the Florida Sentinel, 1862), 52–53.

14. John P. Ingle Jr., "Soldiering with the Second Florida Infantry Regiment," *Florida Historical Quarterly* 59 (January 1981), 338; Edward C. Williamson, ed., "Francis P. Fleming in the War of Southern Independence: Letters from the Front," *Florida Historical Quarterly* 28 (July 1949), 44–45; Samuel Penezet [?], private secretary to John Milton, to Mary Martha Reid, March 2, 1865, John Milton Letterbook, Florida Historical Society, St. Augustine.

15. Thomas M. Palmer to John Milton, November 2, 1863, in *Documents Accompanying the Governor's Message* (Tallahassee, Fla., 1863 [?]), 70–72; *Richmond (Va.) Enquirer,* October 19, 1863.

16. Waitt, *Confederate Military Hospitals in Richmond,* 19–22. Jackson Hospital eventually grew to become the third largest in the Confederacy, but it was not established until mid-1863.

17. Green, *Chimborazo,* viii–ix.

18. *Richmond (Va.) Dispatch,* November 11, 1861.

19. Green, *Chimborazo,* 7.

20. Ibid., 9–15. For the number of patients in Chimborazo for the period from September 1862 through August 1864, see Statistical Reports of the Hospitals of Virginia, 1862–1864, RG 109, chap. 6, vol. 151, pp. 43–44, National Archives, transcribed at *Civil War Richmond,* http://www.mdgorman.com. General information on McCaw and Chimborazo can be found in "Chimborazo Hospital and J. B. McCaw, Surgeon-in-Chief," *Virginia Magazine of History and Biography* 62 (April 1954): 190–200.

21. Green, *Chimborazo,* 8–18.

22. Ibid., 19.

23. *Richmond (Va.) Dispatch,* April 11, 1862.

24. J. B. McCaw to S. P. Moore, May 17, 1862, Letters Received and Sent,

Chimborazo Hospital, 1861–1864, RG 109, chap. 6, vol. 707, p. 101, National Archives, transcribed at *Civil War Richmond*, http://www.mdgorman.com.

25. Ibid., May 13, 1862.

26. *Richmond (Va.) Enquirer,* July 11, 1862.

27. Quoted in Drew Gilpin Faust, *Mothers of Invention: Women of the Slaveholding South in the American Civil War* (Chapel Hill: University of North Carolina Press, 1996), 97.

28. Ibid., 100. For an earlier discussion on the subject of matrons, see also Francis Butler Simkins and James Welch Patton, *The Women of the Confederacy* (Richmond: Garrett and Massie, 1936), 87–94. For the memoir of the most well-known Richmond hospital matron, see Phoebe Yates Pember, *A Southern Woman's Story: Life in Confederate Richmond,* ed. Bell Irvin Wiley (Jackson, Tenn.: McCowat-Mercer Press, 1959). The most recent study of women in Civil War hospitals is Jane E. Schultz, *Women at the Front: Hospital Workers in Civil War America* (Chapel Hill: University of North Carolina Press, 2004).

29. Pember, *Southern Woman's Story,* 26.

30. Ibid., 68.

31. Ibid., 27–28.

32. Bell Irvin Wiley, introduction to ibid., 6.

33. Green, *Chimborazo,* 153–55.

34. Calcutt, *Richmond's Wartime Hospitals,* 58, 181–83; Waitt, *Confederate Military Hospitals in Richmond,* 21–22.

35. Gary Wilson, ed., "The Diary of John S. Tucker: Confederate Soldier from Alabama," *Alabama Historical Quarterly* 43 (Spring 1981): 12.

36. *Richmond (Va.) Whig,* May 7, 1862.

37. *Richmond (Va.) Dispatch,* April 28, 1862.

38. *Richmond (Va.) Enquirer,* May 5, 1862. In early May, notices in Richmond newspapers still noted a shortage of physicians and attendants at Winder. See *Richmond (Va.) Dispatch,* May 6, 1862.

39. *Richmond (Va.) Whig,* May 24, 1862.

40. *Richmond (Va.) Dispatch,* May 18, 1862; *Richmond (Va.) Dispatch,* May 6, 1862; *Richmond (Va.) Whig,* May 7, 1862.

41. Thomas W. Gaither to Dear friends at home, May 10, 1862, Gaither Family Papers, Southern Historical Collection, University of North Carolina, Chapel Hill.

42. Thomas W. Gaither to Mr. Gaither, May 30, 1862, ibid.

43. *Confederate Reminiscences and Letters, 1861–1865* (Atlanta: Georgia Division, United Daughters of the Confederacy, 2000), vol. 14.

44. Statistical Reports of the Hospitals of Virginia, 1862–1864, RG 109, chap.

6, vol. 151, pp. 37–38, National Archives, transcribed at *Civil War Richmond,* http://www.mdgorman.com. By mid-March 1863 the number of patients at Winder had dropped so low that William Carrington recommended temporarily closing several of the hospital's divisions and consolidating the men into two or three divisions. William A. Carrington to A. S. Mason, March 12, [1863], William Carrington Compiled Service Record, National Archives Microfilm Publication M331, Confederate General and Staff Officers and Non-Regimental Enlisted Men.

45. *Richmond (Va.) Enquirer,* December 31, 1862.

46. *Richmond (Va.) Whig,* June 15, 1864.

47. *Richmond (Va.) Whig,* June 8, 1864.

48. James E. Roden, "Experience in the War Hospitals," *Richmond (Va.) Times-Dispatch,* June 30, 1907, transcribed at *Civil War Richmond,* http://www.mdgorman.com.

49. Calcutt, *Richmond's Wartime Hospitals,* 159–61; Waitt, *Confederate Military Hospitals in Richmond,* 19–20.

50. Statistical Reports of Hospitals in Virginia, 1862–1864, RG 109, chap. 6, vol. 151, pp. 39–40, National Archives, transcribed at *Civil War Richmond,* http://www.mdgorman.com. Another document transcribed on this Web site, from the September 29, 1862, issue of the *Richmond (Va.) Enquirer,* indicates that as of late September 1862, Howard's Grove had only admitted a total of 531 patients.

51. William A. Carrington to E. S. Gallard, November 13, 1862, Carrington Compiled Service Record, M331, National Archives.

52. Ibid.

53. John C. Ussery to Dear Sister, July 28, 1863, Mary Livinia Ussery Papers, Virginia Historical Society, Richmond.

54. John C. Ussery to Mary Livinia Robertson Ussery, August 2, 1863, ibid.

55. Calcutt, *Richmond's Wartime Hospitals,* 160; Green, *Chimborazo,* 16; United States War Department, *War of the Rebellion: Official Records of the Union and Confederate Armies* (Washington, D.C: Government Printing Office, 1880–1901), series I, vol. 33, 1197–1198; William Carrington to Surgeon McCaw, January 28, 1864, Letters Received and Sent, Chimborazo Hospital, 1861–1864, RG 109, chap. 6, vol. 709, pt. 1, p. 18, National Archives, transcribed at *Civil War Richmond,* http://www.mdgorman.com. On temporary closings, see *Richmond (Va.) Dispatch,* January 12, 1863; *Richmond (Va.) Enquirer,* January 13, 1864; and C. D. Rice to J. B. McCaw, March 31, 1863, Letters Received and Sent, Chimborazo Hospital for smallpox hospital, transcribed at *Civil War Richmond,* http://www.mdgorman.com.

56. Cunningham, *Doctors in Gray,* 45–46.

57. *Richmond (Va.) Enquirer,* September 29, 1862.

58. *Richmond (Va.) Enquirer,* September 26, 1862; Cunningham, *Doctors in Gray,* 73.

59. William Carrington to E. S. Gaillard, November 15, 1862, Carrington CSR, typescript at Richmond National Battlefield Park Library, Richmond, Va.

60. William Carrington to E. S. Gaillard, December 6, 1862, ibid.

61. William Carrington to E. S. Gaillard, November 16, 1862, ibid.

62. William Carrington to E. S. Gaillard, November 8, 1862, ibid.

63. William Carrington to Chief Surgeon Mason, January 21, 28, 1863, ibid.

64. William Carrington to Dr. S. P. Moore, [ca. January 1863], RG 109, chap. 6, vol. 416, 67–68, National Archives, typescript at Richmond National Battlefield Park Library.

65. Calcutt, *Richmond's Wartime Hospitals,* 172–74, 176–78. See the *Wadesboro (N.C.) Argus,* June 19, 1862, for an account praising Tompkins and the Robertson Hospital.

66. Quoted in Green, *Chimborazo,* 16.

67. Calcutt, *Richmond's Wartime Hospitals,* 73–74; Green, *Chimborazo,* 16; *Richmond (Va.) Dispatch,* February 23, 1863.

68. Calcutt, *Richmond's Wartime Hospitals,* 67.

69. Green, *Chimborazo,* 18.

Virginians See Their War

Harold Holzer

On September 13, 1862, more than a year after the Confederate government established itself in Richmond, Virginia, the capital city finally welcomed its first illustrated newspaper, the *Southern Illustrated News*. At last, after nearly fourteen months of war, civilian readers would finally enjoy access to something Northern audiences had long taken for granted: regularly published pictures of the battles and leaders of their cause.

Until the war began, Virginians, too, had surely subscribed to non-Southern pictorial sheets like *Harper's Weekly, Frank Leslie's Illustrated Newspaper,* and even the *London Illustrated News*. But these picture-rich periodicals became unavailable to readers in the Confederacy once the war and the blockade cut the region off from most commerce.

Understandably, the widely anticipated new Richmond weekly promised from the first to live up to the high standards set by its famous and popular predecessors. "By the aid of pen and pencil," its first editorial vowed, the *Southern Illustrated News* would "present more vividly to the reader the grand and imposing events that are happening before us." The most "competent and experienced artists" would furnish only "handsomely embellished" pictures.[1]

Furthermore, the editors promised that, unlike Union-made prints, its illustrations would be unfailingly realistic: "We cannot engage to give pictures of victories that were never won, or to sketch the taking of capitals that never have surrendered, as have the illustrated weeklies of Yankeedom," that first editorial asserted, in a slap at the Northern weeklies. Clearly, the war of propaganda was taken seriously—not only by publishers, but also by audiences. Even Confederate soldiers in the field worried that their Union foes had the advantage not only in "good wagons, fat horses, and . . . pontoon trains, of splendid material and construction," but also in "illustrated papers, to cheer the 'Boys in Blue' with sketches of the glorious deeds they did not do." The *Southern Illustrated News* boasted it would never reproduce "fancy sketches originating only in the brain of our artists."[2]

But the maiden issue of the Confederacy's answer to *Harper's* and *Leslie's* also cautioned against overexpectation: "While we expect each week to increase the number of engravings, yet our aim shall be, not *number* but *quality.*" In fact, the woodcuts published in the *Southern Illustrated News* never approached the success of those published by its Northern counterparts—in either quantity or quality. It managed instead to sputter along for only a few years, publishing coarse-looking portraits of military celebrities with decreasing frequency, forced from time to time to advertise desperately on its own pages for artists and supplies. It even earned criticism from other Southern journals appalled by its amateurism, with one newspaper in Georgia assailing its artists, during that first year of publication in 1861, for producing what it called "miserable daubs." These included early attempts to portray military heroes "Stonewall" Jackson, Turner Ashby, and Joseph E. Johnston (figures 1, 2, 3), all of whose crudely engraved and uninspiring likenesses appeared on its pages in 1862.[3]

Fig. 1. John W. Torsch, *General "Stonewall" Jackson.* Woodcut engraving, published in the *Southern Illustrated News,* Richmond, Virginia, September 13, 1862.

Fig. 2. Probably John W. Torsch, after William H. Caskie, *General Turner Ashby*. Woodcut engraving, published in the *Southern Illustrated News,* Richmond, Virginia, October 18, 1862.

Fig. 3. John W. Torsch after a photograph by Julian Vannerson, *General Joseph E. Johnston*. Woodcut engraving, cover of the *Southern Illustrated News,* Richmond, Virginia, November 1, 1862.

Fig. 4. William B. Campbell after "Rees" (Mathew B. Brady), *Robert Edmund* [sic] *Lee / Commander-in-Chief of the Confederate Forces.* Woodcut engraving, published in the *Southern Illustrated News,* Richmond, Virginia, December 13, 1862. (Author's collection)

Not until the year was nearly over, in December 1862, did the Confederacy's sole illustrated newsweekly acknowledge, in an extraordinarily candid editorial, that "Numerous enquiries" had been pouring in from readers "in regard to the publication" of a picture of the most celebrated hero of the Army of Northern Virginia: Robert E. Lee. These "enquiries," the paper was forced to admit, it had yet to answer. Only now could the newspaper report that its artists were at last "engaged on a magnificent full-page picture of the great Captain, which will be published in a short time. The engraving will be executed with the greatest care, and we feel warranted in saying, will be one of the most artistic pieces of work of its kind ever gotten up in the South."[4]

But when the long-awaited woodcut by staff artist William B. Campbell (figure 4) appeared two weeks later, it proved nothing more than a mundane adaptation of a hopelessly outdated Mexican War–era photograph of the general, wearing a dark moustache, but with no evidence of the white beard for which he had already become famous. The newspaper confessed that "the General now looks somewhat different from the picture herewith represented, his face at present being covered with a heavy, snowy beard."

Yet it promoted its picture as a representation of the newspaper's "best style." Sadly, this was probably true. The editors apparently did not even know the general's name: they identified him as Robert *Edmund* Lee.[5]

Such "mediocre pictures" in the *Southern Illustrated News,* as the *Southern Literary Messenger* later mocked them, might not have been mediocre enough to seal the weekly's premature doom, not in a region whose readers were so starved for any pictures of its early wartime heroes.[6] But the demise of the weekly that, as it proved, simply could not manage to successfully illustrate current events in the Confederacy in a timely manner, served at least to illustrate something larger: the insurmountable problems faced by the entire Confederate picture-making industry by 1862. The ever-worsening lack of supplies, for example, crippled the picture business. "Thousands upon thousands of dollars invested in printing materials are now lying idle . . . for want of paper," the *Richmond Enquirer* lamented that year, after the Federal army captured Nashville, one of the last remaining sources of the precious material. The problem only became more acute as the war dragged on.[7]

Engravers and lithographers dwindled, too. Subject like all other Confederate citizens to military conscription, civilian artists quickly became a scarce commodity in war-torn Virginia. Those who remained, like the employees of Richmond's principal printmaking firm of J. C. Hoyer & Charles Ludwig, were typically assigned to "official" art like the design of Confederate currency (figure 5). Earlier, the firm had been able to create a fine display print of *Jefferson Davis/First President of the Confederacy,* along with an equestrian portrait of a uniformed Davis at Bull Run in early 1861 (figure 6), one that, judging by the abundance of surviving copies in major collections, remained a popular best seller in Virginia well into the war. By 1862, however, Hoyer & Ludwig was compelled to focus on "a want that which has heretofore seriously taxed the public endurance"—postage stamps.[8]

Such government-ordered printing obligations restricted printmaking firms' ability to create icons for home display, the kind of portraits and scenes that, since the dawn of the nineteenth century, had earned honored places in America's family parlors. There, they testified to their owners' political loyalties and patriotism, and earned handsome profits for the publishers who produced them. Instead, Hoyer & Ludwig directed its dwindling workforce to projects such as *An ordinance to repeal the ratification of the Constitution of the United States of America by the State of Virginia;* a *Map Showing the Battle Grounds of the Chickahominy* drawn by the artist Edwin Sheppard

Fig. 5. Examples of Confederate currency produced circa 1862, the fifty dollar note depicting President Jefferson Davis. These notes were published in Columbia, South Carolina. (Author's collection)

Fig. 6. Hoyer & Ludwig, *President Jefferson Davis / Arriving in the Field of Battle at Bull Run*. Hand-colored lithograph, Richmond, Virginia, circa 1861. (Author's collection)

in 1862; and illustrated plates for a Virginia Military Institute *Manual of Infantry and Rifle Tactics* authored by William H. Richardson.[9] To say the least, none was designed to inspire home-front audiences.

Judging from the eroding quality of the sketch-work produced in Virginia at this time, it is easy to believe that the best artists had been drafted into service in the army topographical departments, or the treasury or post office departments. Virginians could not have been much inspired by William Baumgarten's *True Plan of the Battle near Leesburg, Va., fought 21st Oct. 1861,* nor taken much solace from the boast that the picture had been modeled "from a drawing furnished by an eye witness after the battle." Not until 1863 would the Richmond lithography firm of Ayres & Wade publish a decent Ernest Crehen portrait print of "Stonewall" Jackson—not for home display, but merely as the frontispiece of a small biography. Not long thereafter, Ayres & Wade, like its competitor, Hoyer & Ludwig, was back to work on a more typical "official" project: a manual of military surgery, with gruesome if simplistic illustrations, issued "by order of the Surgeon-General."[10] Theirs were now hardly the sort of pictures the general public would purchase, much less display, to invigorate patriotic resolve.

Notwithstanding all these formidable impediments to commercial success, Virginians might have been reliably supplied with display prints for their parlor walls for the remainder of the war had other Southern cities maintained the ability to supply and ship the pictures they had routinely generated before secession. But two of the leading publishing centers in the South, New Orleans and Baltimore, proved unable to do so. The "Crescent City" fell to the Union in 1862, and thereafter pictures sympathetic to the Confederacy were confiscated there. Local printmaker A. Blackmar, a lithographer who had published an early portrait of President Davis, could never produce another. One of the South's leading publishers of illustrated patriotic sheet music, his output dwindled and died.[11]

Baltimore, of course, remained in Union hands throughout the war. Judging from their early 1861 efforts, its most famous lithographers, August and Ernest Hoen, were entirely sympathetic to the Confederate cause. But Union authorities did not permit them to publish such pictures after they took control of the city. A. Hoen & Co.'s temporarily idle factory, though it later resumed production and continued to churn out pictures into the 1930s, became—and remains today—a ghostly reminder of the once-vibrant picture publishing industry in the South.[12]

The searing, prolific output of a Baltimore-based, Bavarian-born etcher named Adalbert Volck might have filled the void brilliantly. Volck's anti-Lincoln cartoons (figure 7) were no less powerful than his sympathy-inducing pro-Confederate sentimentals, like *Offering of Church Bells to be Cast into Cannon* (figure 8) and *Scene in Stonewall Jackson's Camp* (figure 9),

Fig. 7. Adalbert Johann Volck, *Passage through Baltimore*. Etching from *Sketches from the Civil War in North America*, Baltimore, circa 1863. (Author's collection)

(*Above*) Fig. 8. Adalbert Johann Volck, *Offering of Church Bells to be Cast into Cannon.* Etching, Baltimore, circa 1863–1864. (The Lincoln Museum, Fort Wayne, Indiana, #3685) (*Below*) Fig. 9. Adalbert Johann Volck, *Scene in Stonewall Jackson's Camp.* Etching, Baltimore, circa 1863–1864. (Library of Congress)

both published mid-war. But working from an "occupied city," Volck could only publish his work secretly in limited editions. Today these etchings convincingly demonstrate his acute artistic vision, and keen eye for iconic scenes, and are often seen in modern book and magazine illustrations. But it is important to remember that they had little impact while the war continued; they were virtually underground publications. Volck, a professional dentist, later boasted that he smuggled medicine into the Confederacy, and it is possible he may have carried his portfolios of pictures there, too, though they were far more likely to attract unwelcome notice than a cache of small bottles. But even if he did so, it strains credulity to imagine that he brought enough pictures South during the war to make the mark he deserved.[13]

Early in the war, surprisingly, the largest city in the North, though firmly in Union hands, proved an unlikely but reliable source for Confederate pictures. By way of explanation, printmakers there had long enjoyed, and taken full commercial advantage of, a nonpartisan, or more accurately stated, a multi-partisan, publishing tradition. (Surely it helped as well that so many New York entrepreneurs, long engaged in trade with the South, were at first sympathetic with Southern objections to Northern interference on the slavery issue.) As proof of their commercial independence during the 1860 presidential election, local firms with national distribution outreach like industry leaders Currier & Ives, routinely published both pro-Republican and pro-Democratic portraits, as well as lampoons designed to criticize the candidates of each. They were inspired by profits, not politics, and they aimed for the widest audiences possible, as long as the audience remained available.

But when the Southern audience evaporated, Northern publishers turned exclusively to the topical work from which it could profit—pro-Union imagery.[14] One angry Southern critic complained that "with a cunning, [Yankees] fostered the intellect of their section" through their "established publishing houses." It was an accurate observation. As *DeBow's Review* worried shortly before the new year of 1862 began: "[H]ow are we to relieve ourselves from our degrading dependence upon our enemies for . . . our chief sources of information and pleasure?" The answer came soon enough: "we" would not.[15]

Thus it comes as a surprise that the American Bank Note Company of New York provided some of the Confederacy's earliest currency, and might have continued to do so for a while longer had not Richmond's Hoyer &

Fig. 10. E[rnest] Crehen, *Jeff. Davis.* Lithograph, published by Jones & Clark, New York, 1861. (Library of Congress)

Fig. 11. E[rnest] Crehen, *Gen. Lee C.S.A.* Lithograph, published by Jones & Clark, New York, 1861. (Library of Congress)

Ludwig petitioned Jefferson Davis's government to "give us preference to Northern Houses."[16] And yet another New York printmaking outfit, Jones & Clark, rushed out commercially motivated portraits of Jefferson Davis (figure 10) and Robert E. Lee (figure 11) created by Richmond-based lithographer Ernest Crehen—perhaps manufactured to appeal to a curious North (although the prints were based on prewar photographs) as well as a hero-worshipping South. It is entirely possible that examples of both found their way into Virginia homes before 1862. Historians have been unable to unearth evidence that might indicate that the firm was officially urged by Union authorities to cease and desist the production of such morale-building pictures. But even in the absence of formal censure, Jones & Clark doubtless found it increasingly, even unprofitably, difficult after 1861 to produce pictures for an audience it could no longer reach via antebellum shipping arrangements. Once the New York firm was cut off from its Southern audiences, it no longer produced pictures specifically designed to appeal to them.

Similarly, Boston lithographer Louis Prang, who would earn fame and fortune for a series of pro-Union Civil War battle chromos published a generation after the guns fell silent, issued a group portrait of Davis and his generals in 1862 (figure 12). But by entitling the image *Enemies of Our Union*, no doubt to appeal to prospective customers in the North, Prang also guaranteed that, even if his pictures could be shipped into the Confederacy, audiences there would have little interest.

The fact that Confederate printmaking died aborning from want of supplies, artists, and independence from Federal censorship, and that Union publishers stopped or were forced to stop providing pictures that might otherwise have filled the gap, helps explain the dearth of surviving Confederate imprints after 1861. The Confederacy boasted only fifteen paper mills at the start of the war, and they could not keep up with demand alone.[17] That is perhaps why, astonishing as it may seem, as long as the Confederacy lived, its engravers and lithographers never succeeded in providing a single separate sheet display image of its greatest hero, Robert E. Lee. Not until the war had ended, and Northern printmakers were able to resume the mass production of pictures aimed at the long-denied Southern print buyer, did manufacturers help illustrate the Lost Cause with the emblematic icons that, in the century-and-a-half since, have come to illustrate the Confederate struggle for independence. In truth, most of these pictures were published retrospectively. They were manufactured a safe distance from former enemy

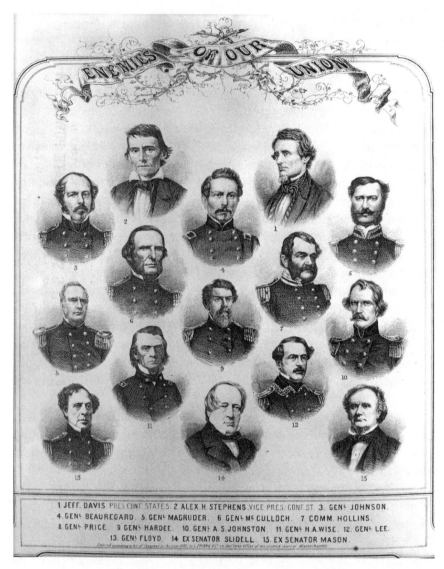

Fig. 12. L[ouis] Prang & Co., *Enemies of Our Union*. Lithograph, Boston, 1862. (Library of Congress)

soil once peace was restored, and commerce between North and South re-opened. It is important to remember that, by and large, pictures remained painfully scarce to Southern audiences while the fighting raged.

To be sure, there were exceptions to this rule of iconographical depriva-tion. Portraits of Jefferson Davis, some optimistically identified as "Our First President," no doubt to invite comparisons to George Washington while also implying that a second, and third, president would inevitably follow, were doubtless still on display in Virginia in 1862. Richmond's Hoyer & Ludwig designed one such print portrait (figure 13), which was published in Augusta, Georgia, another indication that Richmond's presses were by then otherwise engaged in official business.

Davis himself proved stubbornly unwilling at first to provide new pho-

Fig. 13. Hoyer & Ludwig after J. Wissler, *Jefferson Davis / First President of the Confederate States of America*. Lithograph, published by Tucker & Perkins & Co., Augusta, Georgia, copyrighted by James T. Paterson, Virginia, 1861. (Museum of the Confederacy, Richmond, Virginia)

tographs for the printmakers. Hoyer & Ludwig desperately needed such a model to create twenty-cent stamps "with President Davis' portrait," warning Postmaster General John H. Reagan that it was up to Davis himself "to furnish us with a good likeness." Ultimately Davis cooperated, and the appearance of the bust-portrait stamps, however crude, supplied the need. The *Richmond Daily Dispatch* applauded, crediting "Messrs. Hoyer & Ludwig, of this city" for "supplying the Government with these needed articles."

Yet if Virginia's "public" also needed larger-sized images with which to express their belief in their struggle for independence, the hardships of that struggle ironically made production of such keepsakes nearly impossible. Meanwhile, publishers in Northern cities like New York, Boston, Philadelphia, Chicago, and Cincinnati continued to illustrate, and stoke, Union patriotism with a seemingly unending flood of portraits and battle scenes. No print more dramatically exposed this disparity than New York lithographer William M. Davis's *carte de visite* photograph, *The Neglected Picture* (figure 14), showing a mutilated Southern-made print of Jefferson

Fig. 14. William M. Davis, "*The Neglected Picture.*" *Carte de visite* photograph of a *trompe l'oeil*-style print, New York, 1862. (Author's collection)

(*Above*) Fig. 15. Artist unknown, *Schoolmaster Lincoln and His Boys / Lincoln: Waal, boys, what's the matter with yer, you haint been hurt, hav yer?* Woodcut engraving, published in the *Southern Illustrated News,* Richmond, Virginia, January 31, 1863. (Author's collection) (*Below*) Fig. 16. Artist unknown, *Master Abraham Lincoln Gets a New Toy.* Woodcut engraving, published in the *Southern Illustrated News,* Richmond, Virginia, February 28, 1863. (Author's collection)

Davis, its glass rudely smashed. Whether the printmaker knew it or not, he was pictorially summarizing the decline of the Confederate image—if only for lack of supplies, not will.[18]

Northern audiences of the day were also being exposed to a robust outpouring of political cartoons, which proliferated, perhaps, to provoke laughter that might ease the pain of casualty and carnage. They were published both as separate sheets and in the weekly press. But the Confederate response was at best feeble. Most of the Lincoln caricatures in the *Southern Illustrated News* (figures 15, 16), for example, proved so uninspired and uninformed they barely resembled the man they were lampooning. If laughter ebbed, so did music. Richmond publisher J. W. Randolph managed to publish an Ernest Crehen equestrian portrait of "Jeb" Stuart around 1862, for a sheet music cover entitled *Riding a Raid* (figure 17). But it was a rarity. Confederate publishers issued a surprising 870 recorded sheet music titles during the Civil War, but most lacked illustrated covers, and with presses stilled in New Orleans and Baltimore, the number was actually smaller than it might have been had not Union forces occupied those cities. In the North, meanwhile, patriotic sheet music proliferated.[19]

Deprivations notwithstanding, the South, Virginia in particular, could boast a rich reserve of native talent in the fine arts. But skilled local painters like Conrad Wise Chapman were assigned to army service, though in Chapman's case a mysterious wartime injury—combined with family connections to the governor of Virginia—ultimately earned him a reassignment to Gen. P. G. T. Beauregard's staff in Charleston. There the artist spent much of 1864 creating a vivid artistic record of deteriorating conditions in that besieged port city. But little of it was seen outside Charleston during the war.[20]

In Richmond, painter Benjamin Franklin Reinhardt produced canvases of both Robert E. Lee (figure 18) and "Stonewall" Jackson (figure 19) for a Southern patron in 1862, though his portraits were, like those of the generals published in the *Southern Illustrated News,* all too obviously based on prewar photographs. Lacking access to more recent models, Reinhardt let his imagination run wild, dressing Lee in a gaudy uniform with fur lapels. In truth, Lee had by this time lost much hair, and what remained had turned grey. Moreover, as Confederate war clerk John B. Jones noted in November 1862, General Lee was by then "hardly recognizable, for his beard, now quite white, has been suffered to grow all over his face."[21]

Another Virginia artist, W. B. Cox, was inspired by the Confederacy's first

Fig. 17. E[rnest] Crehen, *Riding a Raid*. Lithographed sheet music cover, depicting General J. E. B. Stuart, published by J. W. Randolph, Richmond, Virginia, circa 1862. (Library of Congress)

Fig. 18. Benjamin Franklin Reinhardt, *Robert E. Lee.* Oil on canvas, 12–3/4 x 9–1/2 inches. Signed right: *Reinhardt '62.* (R. W. Norton Art Gallery, Shreveport, Louisiana)

Fig. 19. Benjamin Franklin Reinhardt, *Thomas Jonathan "Stonewall" Jackson.* Oil on canvas, 14–1/2 x 11–1/2 inches. Signed lower left: *B. Reinhardt.* (R. W. Norton Art Gallery, Shreveport, Louisiana)

Fig. 20. W. B. Cox, *The Heroes of Manassas,* circa 1862–1865. Oil on canvas, 20 x 26-1/2 inches, showing, left to right: P. G. T. Beauregard, "Stonewall" Jackson, Jefferson Davis, J. E. B. Stuart, and Joseph E. Johnston. (West Point Museum Collections, United States Military Academy, West Point, New York)

military triumph to paint a group equestrian portrait of Beauregard, Jackson, Davis, Stuart, and Johnston as *The Heroes of Manassas* (figure 20), a small undated canvas from 1862 or 1863 that might have received public display in the Confederate capital. So, too, undoubtedly, did a bravura series of six heroic-sized equestrians of Confederate leaders by the French-born Louis Mathieu Didier Guillaume (Figures 21, 22), painted in Richmond around the same time. The flamboyant Guillaume, a local favorite, might have gone on to even greater success in the city had not the shortages that crippled print publishers afflicted him as well. At one point he stopped selling paintings and started selling his artist's supplies.[22] By the time another Virginia painter, William De Hartburn Washington, displayed his genre classic *The Burial of Latane* in Richmond a year or so later, wartime shortages were so

Fig. 21. L. M. D. Guillaume, *Jefferson Davis Reviewing a Louisiana Regiment at Richmond, Va.,* circa 1862–1865. Oil on canvas, 36 x 29 inches. (R. W. Norton Art Gallery, Shreveport, Louisiana)

acute that viewers at its first exhibition tossed valuables into a pail set up beneath the canvas, in order to show support to the Cause. This triumph of Confederate iconography remained little known even in the South until, typically, a New York printmaker engraved it in 1868.[23]

Perhaps no episode of the war speaks more eloquently to this disparity in Union and Confederate image making than the 1862 Peninsula Campaign in Virginia. Northern publishers responded with an abundance of romanticized print portraits of the commander of the Army of the Potomac, George B. McClellan, whether the vain and self-promoting general deserved them or not.[24] But their Southern counterparts, as noted, lacked the photographic models, the artists, the ink, and the paper to counter with even one display portrait of the defender of the peninsula, Robert E. Lee.

But the successful defense of Richmond did inspire one final burst of artistic creativity from Richmond: a strange but remarkable quartet of large, 11.5 by 16.5-inch cartoon prints entitled *Dissolving Views of Richmond,* created by a lithographer named Blanton Duncan in, of all places, Columbia, South Carolina. The prints in the series were designed to lampoon the "great noble and victorious" Union invader, in the words of one of the cartoons, who by then, of course, had been driven from Virginia. It is interesting to note that the artist clearly had access to current photographs of the general, for the McClellan he portrayed in three of the four sheets certainly bears a strong resemblance to the commander as he looked in 1862. The South, on the other hand, still had no idea what Lee looked like.

In the first *Dissolving Views* sheet, *The youthful Napoleon quietly sitteth down upon his base before Richmond intending to take it when he gets ready* (figure 23), a complacent McClellan (evidently wearing a mask to look like the French general for whom he was nicknamed) wears a comically huge Napoleonic hat and carries an oversized sword, looking ridiculously immature and unconcerned as the American eagle whispers encouragement. The print also takes a swipe at what was clearly a Confederate obsession: the resentment, as expressed in the premier edition of the *Southern Illustrated News,* over the belief that Union prints routinely overstated Federal military successes and masked military failures. In the Duncan print, telegraph poles are literally abuzz with exaggerated messages testifying to McClellan's "victories" in the Seven Days' Battles.

In the second print, *He concludeth to change ye base of his operations, and is ably seconded therein by ye gallant Stonewall . . .* (figure 24), McClellan was

Fig. 22. L. M. D. Guillaume, *Col. John Singleton Mosby,* circa 1862–1865. Oil on canvas, 42 x 34 inches. (R. W. Norton Art Gallery, Shreveport, Louisiana)

(Above) Fig. 23. Artist unknown (W. J. or J. W.), *Dissolving Views of Richmond / Scene 1st. The youthful Napoleon quietly sitteth down 'upon his base' before Richmond intending to take it when he gets ready.* Lithograph, published by Blanton Duncan, Columbia, South Carolina, circa 1862. (The Boston Athenaeum) *(Below)* Fig. 24. Artist unknown (W. J. or J. W.), *Dissolving Views of Richmond / Scene 2nd. He concludeth to change ye base of his operations, and is ably seconded therein by ye gallant Stonewall. He giveth way to pressure coming from the rear.* Lithograph, published by Blanton Duncan, Columbia, South Carolina, circa 1862. (The Boston Athenaeum)

accurately portrayed, albeit upside down, his Napoleonic mask falling to the ground to reveal the real Federal commander. Yet the printmaker evidently had no clue about the appearance of the Confederacy's own "Stonewall" Jackson. He portrayed him as a generic, dandified cavalier with a cockaded hat. Once again, the absence of updated models in the picture-bereft South had made an accurate depiction impossible. Realistically drawn or not, Jackson is shown majestically driving McClellan off the peninsula at the point of a bayonet. The hapless Union commander is happy to see his gunboats nearby, "for although I'm not running or retreating," he explains unconvincingly, "I'me [*sic*] getting devilish tired of this 'Strategic movement[']."

The fourth and final *Dissolving Views* print, *The "small" Napoleon after the fatigues of the week* (figure 25), showed the ridiculous McClellan as he

Fig. 25. Artist unknown (W. J. or J. W.), *Dissolving Views of Richmond / Scene 4th. The "small" Napoleon after the fatigues of the week, congratulates his victorious companions on the 4th July for their gallant deeds.* Lithograph, published by Blanton Duncan, Columbia, South Carolina, circa 1862. (The Boston Athenaeum)

"congratulates" his soldiers "for their gallant deeds," while his bedraggled, wounded, and unflatteringly drawn Irish soldiers (speaking with brogues) reply that "hell's full of just such victories as this."

The Blanton Duncan set of *Dissolving Views* succeeded not only at taunting the hapless McClellan, and celebrating his defeat, but in so doing—in background scenes showing safe cities dominated by church steeples—assured audiences that Richmond, and other Virginia towns, were now safe from the foreign-born invaders. Had Duncan boasted the distribution power of his Northern counterparts, larger Southern audiences, and indeed, Northern ones as well, might have been exposed to these clever pictures. But their rarity today suggests they were originally printed in small quantities, and reached scant numbers of buyers.

All this said, it is remarkable that accomplished pictures like these, not to mention an ambitious newspaper like the *Southern Illustrated News,* ever managed to appear at all during the chronic shortages of 1862. The *News* in fact managed to limp along, albeit with increasingly irregular editions, for two more years. A powerful rejoinder to recent historiography attributing Southern defeat to a lack of will or patriotism, its modest success was clearly attributable to the Southern yearning for easily available, affordable, and emblematic images of its battles and leaders. The gutted Southern printmaking industry simply proved incapable of supplying them.

Virginians probably never saw the series of comic envelopes, produced by J. H. Tingley in New York in 1861, showing Abraham Lincoln engaging Jefferson Davis in a five-round prize fight (figure 26). But the amusing pictures might have served well as a metaphor for the North versus South battle for pictorial dominance in 1862. In the struggle to supply its citizens with inspiring images to gird home-front morale, the Confederacy's printmakers had the will, the talent, and the customers—but not the means—to succeed.

In the end, Virginians enjoyed access to fewer prints in 1862 than they had in 1861, and would see progressively fewer still in 1863, 1864, and early 1865. Not until peace was restored that April, and Northern printmakers resumed supplying the Southern marketplace with popular prints, beginning with Appomattox surrender scenes that acknowledged the nobility of Robert E. Lee, did icons of the Lost Cause finally appear in abundance.

It was probably no surprise that within two years, none other than the neglected subject of Confederate printmaking, Robert E. Lee, would find

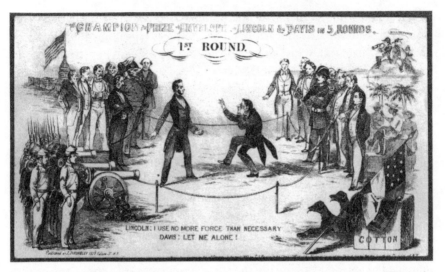

Fig. 26. J. H. Tingley, *Champion Prize Envelope—Lincoln & Davis in 5 Rounds.* Woodcut engraving, New York, 1861. (Author's collection)

himself seeking shelter one day in a remote Virginia cabin whose walls featured his portrait.[25] Surely a Northern printmaker had supplied it. But as one Richmond citizen observed not long thereafter, picture-starved Southerners by then were giving "of their poverty gladly" to own such icons, no matter where they originated.[26]

Notes

1. *Southern Illustrated News,* September 13, 1862. The author consulted original copies in the collections of the New York Public Library and the New-York Historical Society for the preparation of Mark E. Neely Jr., Harold Holzer, and Gabor S. Boritt, *The Confederate Image: Prints of the Lost Cause* (Chapel Hill: University of North Carolina Press, 1987).

2. Carlton McCarthy, *Detailed Minutiae of Soldier Life in the Army of Northern Virginia, 1861–1865* (Richmond, Va.: Carlton McCarthy, 1884), 6.

3. *Savannah (Ga.) Republican,* December 1862, reprinted in *Southern Illustrated News,* December 27, 1862. In turn, the *News* viciously attacked the critic for "hepatic derangement" requiring "a course of blue pills."

4. *Southern Illustrated News,* December 13, 1862.

5. *Southern Illustrated News,* December 27, 1862.

6. *Southern Literary Messenger* 37 (April 1863): 1, 4.

7. Bell Irvin Wiley, *Embattled Confederates: An Illustrated History of Southerners at War* (New York: Harper & Row, 1964), 201–2.

8. *Richmond (Va.) Dispatch,* October 17, 1861.

9. T. Michael Parrish and Robert M. Willingham, *Confederate Imprints: A Bibliography of Southern Publications from Secession to Surrender* (Austin, Tex.: Jenkins Publishing, n.d.), 386, 533, 443; Neely, Holzer, and Boritt, *Confederate Image,* 13. This extraordinary compilation is the best source of data about printing in the wartime Confederacy.

10. *The Life of Stonewall Jackson by a Virginian* (Richmond, Va.: Ayres & Wade, 1863); *Manual of Military Surgery for Use by the Confederate States Army with Illustration* (Richmond, Va.: Ayres & Wade, 1863).

11. See, for example, *Confederates' Grand March* by William H. Hartwell from early 1862, featuring a portrait of a Confederate flag bearer, in Parrish and Willingham, *Confederate Imprints,* 582.

12. Harry Twyford Peters, *America on Stone: The Other Printmakers to the American People* (New York: Doubleday, 1931), 218–20. Passengers on Amtrak trains approaching Baltimore still pass by the long-empty red brick building as they approach the city's terminal. One can still read the fading whitewashed sign, A. Hoen, looming close to the busy southbound tracks.

13. Neely, Holzer, and Boritt, *Confederate Image,* 47.

14. In truth, Civil War portraits and scenes occupied only a small portion of the catalogues of wartime publishers like Currier & Ives, who enjoyed their largest trade in prints of little girls, animals, and genre scenes. See *Currier & Ives: A Catalogue Raisonné* (Detroit: Gale Research, 1984).

15. Richard Harwell, *More Confederate Imprints* (Richmond: Virginia State Library, 1957), 1: xiii–xiv; *DeBow's Review,* October–November 1861, quoted in Parrish and Willingham, *Confederate Imprints,* 11.

16. Brian M. Green, *The Confederate States Five-Cent Green Lithograph* (New York: Philatelic Foundation, 1977), 1, 3.

17. Joel Munsell, *A Chronology of Paper and Papermaking,* an 1864 report, quoted in Parrish and Willingham, *Confederate Imprints,* 12. These mills, the authors show, fell into disrepair or were burned in 1862 and 1863 (12–13).

18. Ibid., 1, 3; *Richmond (Va.) Dispatch,* October 17, 1861.

19. Parrish and Willingham, *Confederate Imprints,* 573–630.

20. See, for example, *Flag of Fort Sumter, October 20, 1863,* and *Submarine Torpedo Boat H. L. Hunley, December 6, 1863,* both of which are in the collection of the Museum of the Confederacy, Richmond, Va. For reproductions see

Harold Holzer and Mark E. Neely Jr., *Mine Eyes Have Seen the Glory: The Civil War in Art* (New York: Orion Books, 1993), 108–9.

21. John B. Jones, *A Rebel War Clerk's Diary at the Confederate States Capital* (Philadelphia: J. B. Lippincott, 1866), 1:179.

22. Annabel Shanklin Perlik, "Signed L. M. D. Guillaume: Louis Mathieu Didier Guillaume, 1816–1892" (master's thesis, George Washington University, Washington, D.C., 1979), 71.

23. Emily J. Salmon, "The Burial of Latane: Symbol of the Lost Cause," *Virginia Cavalcade* 29 (Winter 1979): 124–27. For reproductions, see Holzer and Neely, *Mine Eyes Have Seen the Glory,* 219 (painting), and Neely, Holzer, and Boritt, *Confederate Image,* xii (engraving).

24. See Mark E. Neely Jr. and Harold Holzer, *The Union Image: Popular Prints of the Civil War North* (Chapel Hill: University of North Carolina Press, 2000), 36–43.

25. Robert E. Lee, *Recollections and Letters of General Robert E. Lee* (New York: Doubleday, 1907), 273.

26. *New York Times,* May 30, 1890.

Virginia's Troubled Interior

Brian Steel Wills

The year 1862 opened inauspiciously for Union and Confederate forces facing each other in the far reaches of southwestern Virginia. During the previous year of conflict, little of a military nature had occurred in the region compared to the action that took place in the northwestern and central portions of the state. Area citizens had little direct exposure to the war that raged around them, although the existence of gaps through the mountainous terrain, the proximity of the Virginia & Tennessee Railroad, and the ambitions of commanders in the region portended an alteration in that state of affairs.

There were few exclusive advantages for either side in southwest Virginia. Neither North nor South had an absolute claim on the loyalties of the people of the area. Voters in the eight southwest Virginia counties had expressed their preferences in the volatile 1860 presidential election for either the Southern Democrat John C. Breckinridge or the moderate Constitutional Union candidate John Bell, with only modest support for Northern Democrat Stephen Douglas and none for Republican Abraham Lincoln.[1]

Despite the region's physical location within the boundaries of the Confederate States of America, historian William Marvel noted that "Southwest Virginia greeted secession with the least enthusiasm in the state" outside of the counties that would ultimately constitute West Virginia.[2] A major reason for this ambivalence lay in the fact that the area contained few slaves.[3]

Enthusiasm for the Confederacy existed, as evidenced by the number of enlistees to Southern service that historian Jeffrey Weaver explained occurred "in proportions matching their eastern cousins," although most of these ultimately served outside of the region.[4] Southern sympathy vied with Unionism for supremacy in the hearts and minds of many southwest Virginians. These communal divisions ensured a form of internecine warfare that would exacerbate prewar quarrels and feuds and pit families against each other as the relative constraints of peace gave way to war.

Geographical isolation mitigated the large-scale concentration of troops or the movement of great armies. Nevertheless, important targets such as the saltworks and lead mines of Saltville and Wytheville, and the depots, rolling stock, rails and bridges of the Virginia & Tennessee Railroad could be threatened easily by Union forces penetrating the region. Weaver concluded that once Kentucky ended its neutrality, this "left Pound Gap and Wise County the main potential avenue of invasion and commerce."[5]

Such an avenue lay open for each side to exploit. In early 1862 Confederate Brig. Gen. Humphrey Marshall sought to do so at the head of his grandiosely titled Army of Eastern Kentucky. His counterpart, Ohio native and schoolteacher James A. Garfield, preferred to seize the initiative for himself. As a result, the fate of southwest Virginia would be decided in the opening months of 1862 by military actions taking place across the border in Kentucky.

From the beginning, Marshall seemed destined for disappointment. He anticipated potential throngs of sympathizing citizens embracing him as a liberator. Instead, he found at best only a lukewarm reception that he complained to a superior emanated from individuals who were either "perfectly terrified or apparently apathetic" to the Confederate cause. "These people should learn that they belong to the Southern Confederacy," the Southern commander observed caustically to Albert Sidney Johnston.[6]

The result of Marshall's foray into Kentucky was an inconclusive fight at Middle Creek, on January 10, 1862.[7] Yet, neither side was in a better position to capitalize on the situation. Conditions deteriorated badly under heavy, cold rain that swelled the rivers and turned the already primitive road system into quagmires.[8] A Confederate staff officer who had an uncomfortably close look at these conditions labeled the roads eastward from Pound Gap "the most desperate roads—I had ever yet beheld." Edward Guerrant, who had recently joined Marshall's staff, assessed the situation glumly, noting, "I cannot imagine worse roads than the 8 or 10 miles beyond the Gap toward Wise C.[ourt] H.[ouse] or Gladesville." The Kentucky native concluded simply, "The mud is almost 'swimming' except where brush has been thrown in & [even] there [the road] is almost impassable."[9]

Since Marshall and his intrepid band of Southerners depended on these roads for their sustenance, he should hardly have been surprised to receive an order in late January to pull back across the mountains to Pound Gap in Virginia.[10] It would take a few days for the instructions to reach Marshall and even then he was reluctant to comply. Poor supply conditions as well as sickness and exposure threatened his men. Troops had stripped the area in the borderland region of supplies over the previous months. Marshall noted to Adj. and Insp. Gen. Samuel Cooper on February 2 that "the subsistence of the country about Pound Gap for 20 miles is literally exhausted." Bemoaning the difficulty of procuring sufficient resources, he added dejectedly, "You can have no conception of the state of affairs, here, general; starvation stares these people in the face." Under such circumstances the local residents were uncooperative at the very least. "They are most averse to parting with a peck of corn or a pound of meat and daily the women beg for the retention of the means of sustaining themselves and their children."[11] To further the subsistence of his command, Humphrey Marshall dispatched the Twenty-ninth and Fifty-fourth Virginia Infantry regiments to Gladeville. The little town was closer to Abingdon and the Virginia & Tennessee Railroad. These troops had permission to proceed in that direction should sufficient supplies prove difficult to obtain where they were initially supposed to establish camp.[12]

Marshall could hardly be comforted by what he found at Pound Gap, the gateway through which forces could pass to and from Virginia and Kentucky in the region. A few log cabins and rough earthworks guarded the summit, which one Southern staff officer deemed "the most practicable route into Virginia." Buffeted by winds, the 300 to 400 Confederates there under Maj. John B. Thompson endured the elements and awaited the enemy behind such defenses as they could muster. "I counted 8 cannon & accompanying caissons on the mountain," Guerrant recalled as he and Marshall proceeded to Gladeville for more comfortable accommodations.[13] When he arrived there, the Confederate aide noted that the little hamlet boasted only "9 resident families" and a handful of homes and small businesses, in addition to a large courthouse. The population of the community, he observed, could be set at "about 1000 minus 965."[14]

A surgeon with the Confederates offered his own assessment of the situation to Gen. Joseph E. Johnston on February 11. He noted that the Southern commander at Pound Gap remained composed in the face of impending danger and was "as cheerful in the presence of these difficulties as if no great events were passing around." Indeed, he had intimated that his "ragamuffins are ready and willing to dispute every inch of ground from Pound Gap to Abingdon."[15] Such bravado was bound to be tested in the weeks to come.

Indeed, the Federal threat to southwest Virginia continued to develop. Although Colonel Garfield did not have the numbers attributed to him by jittery Confederate rumors, he was organizing troops in eastern Kentucky to test the Confederate grip on Pound Gap. He was also well-informed about the conditions and dispositions of his adversaries across the Virginia-Kentucky border.[16]

Marshall's position was precarious. He rightfully worried that measures to subsist his command at the expense of the locals "cannot advance our cause or make converts to it to starve the best friends we have in this population." In early February he had felt confident that "in this country we have . . . a considerable majority of the people."[17] However, a month later, Marshall was less sure of the loyalties of the people with whom he had now lived for a time. "In Wise County I found whole districts of the country as false as could be," he lamented to President Jefferson Davis. "I have the names of at least twenty-five leading men in Wise County who are false to us," he added, with the additional information that Unionists were supplying the names of secessionists for future punishment. As far as General Marshall was concerned, only the imposition of martial law on the region would end the unruliness that festered in it.[18]

In his exasperation, the politician-general exhibited a pattern of exaggeration that was common for him. In this case he suggested a heavy Unionist presence in Wise County that did not appear to be indicative of sentiment there. Weaver exposed the level of hyperbole in Marshall's alarmist communication. "In proportion to their population," he explained in a study of Buchanan and Wise counties in the Civil War, "these counties furnished a greater percentage of their sons to the Confederacy than any other part of the Old Dominion."[19]

Southwest Virginia was entering into a state of flux that would only worsen the military situation for its defenders. Uncertainties and upheavals were beginning to unravel a delicate social and racial balance. In February, one resident recorded in her diary that "15 Negroes ran off from the neighborhood last night," including one of her own.[20] Although the slaves would be quickly recaptured and returned, their actions signaled more than a desire to gain a measure of control over their lives; they also revealed the vulnerabilities of the slave system under the stresses and strains of war.

Poor weather and scarce resources continued to affect the region. On February 15, 1862, General Marshall noted that some six inches of snow blanketed the area and more was "falling rapidly."[21] Despite these circumstances, he tried to remain vigilant. Marshall undertook short reconnaissance missions to keep an eye on Federal dispositions and scattered his units to accommodate their supply needs.[22] Finally, he felt the necessity to shift his headquarters to Lebanon, Virginia, in nearby Russell County. The change in base put the Southerners closer to Abingdon, but farther from what the Confederate general deemed the critical position at Pound Gap. He also took such steps as he could to augment his authority to provide greater security to his area of responsibility.[23]

Security for the region would increasingly become a necessity as Union attentions turned to the ways in which actions in southwest Virginia could contribute to a grander strategy for winning the war. From Washington, D.C., Maj. Gen. George B. McClellan inquired of Maj. Gen. Don Carlos Buell: "Cannot Garfield reach the Virginia and Tennessee Railway near Abingdon?"[24] The disruption of that line would have obvious negative implications for Confederate supply and communication. But apparently Buell preferred a more immediate impact, reporting that he was going to employ Garfield to "chase Marshall entirely out of Kentucky."[25]

Thus, as the worst of the winter weather began to subside, Union Col. James Garfield intended to probe toward Pound Gap with the notion of advancing against it in force. "I particularly desire you to gather all of the information in your power of the whereabouts of General Marshall or any force in the vicinity of Pound Gap," he instructed a subordinate in early March.[26] Initial efforts proved frustrating, but Garfield continued to gather accurate intelligence on his opponents and indicated that he also saw a shift in the loyalties of local residents that had concerned Marshall. "There has been a marked change in favor of the Union among the citizens of Buchanan, Wise, Scott and other counties," he explained to a subordinate.[27]

On March 14, Garfield set out with a small force of 600 men consisting of contingents of the Fortieth Ohio, the Forty-second Ohio, and the Twenty-second Kentucky, supplemented by 100 cavalry. Weather remained a determining factor, affecting the roads and morale of the men on both sides.[28] Even so, the Union commander had his men in position on the morning of March 16 to launch their attack against Pound Gap. A combined assault carried out by forces approaching from different directions overwhelmed Confederate resistance. After a short, but sharp fight, the Southern "raga-muffins" fell back in disorder, ultimately retreating to Gladeville to await further developments.[29]

Despite the pyrotechnics, only a handful of men fell on either side in the Battle of Pound Gap. The victorious Federals captured two Confederate camps that they subsequently consigned to the flames. Having taken such plunder as could be removed before destroying the remainder, the Union troops withdrew to Kentucky, the mission of defeating and dispersing the Confederate defenders of Pound Gap having been accomplished.[30]

Marshall was left to explain the loss of what he had once considered a vital position. Now, having given the point up to the enemy, he was not so certain of its value. He continued to advocate the implementation of mar-tial law as a remedy for the various evils he had identified in the behavior of local residents whose loyalty he questioned. It was classic Humphrey Marshall, detailing the reasons why he was not responsible for the disaster that had befallen the troops he had left in isolation to guard a position he now deemed untenable.[31]

From his headquarters at Lebanon, Marshall summoned local militia to fill the ranks until reinforcements could arrive. Now that Union forces had "taken Pound Gap and have invaded the State of Virginia in force," he used his authority as the regional commander to activate the citizen soldiers of the counties to the defense of southwest Virginia. When the dragnet for recruits was complete, Marshall boasted a command that had been increased by 1,614 troops.[32] Of course, the order had the adverse effect of convincing Unionists in the region who had not already done so to seek the safety of Union lines.

Humphrey Marshall was not the only Southern commander to face Federal challenges. Buell had his sights set on taking the position at Con-federate-held Cumberland Gap as well. In mid-March, he informed his superior, Henry W. Halleck, of his intention to send a mixed column of infantry, cavalry, and artillery against the Confederates there.[33] Various early efforts failed to secure the target, but they gained the attention of Maj. Gen. Edmund Kirby Smith, the newly arrived commander headquartered in east Tennessee. In response, he sent word that the post must be held to the "last extremity."[34] Kirby Smith also called upon Humphrey Marshall across the border in Virginia for assistance in that sector, but the subordinate commander felt too consumed by the responsibilities he faced on his immediate front.[35] Termed most harshly by one historian as "utterly incompetent,"[36] Marshall certainly earned his reputation from another as "a hard commander from whom to get even the semblance of co-operation."[37]

The defense of the southwestern portion of the commonwealth received what looked to be a boost in May with the creation of the Virginia State Line. Expected to be composed only of citizens who were not subject to the newly passed Confederate conscription act, the unit would help to defend the border region. Southwest Virginia native John B. Floyd, a former secretary of war and Confederate general with a reputation sullied by his actions at Fort Donelson, Tennessee, earlier in February held the command.[38]

Southwest Virginians did not rush into the ranks of the Virginia State Line with equal enthusiasm. Russell County supplied the most men with 133 out of a free population of 9,030. Wise provided 97 from its 4,416 and Buchanan 73 of 2,762. Of the more populous counties, only Washington offered comparable recruits with 70 of its 14,098 free citizens enrolling.[39]

In the meantime, Humphrey Marshall seemed to have a running feud with anyone with whom he was supposed to work. Always jealous of his prerogatives, the Kentuckian clashed with Floyd, just he had done and would do in 1862 with Department of Western Virginia commanders William W. Loring and Samuel Jones.[40] When not engaged in such lengthy contentious correspondence with his superiors or rousting recruits for his command, Marshall kept his command busy with scouts and drills.[41] His fears had at least some basis in fact, for the Federals remained interested in using the route from Pound Gap as an avenue for threatening the saltworks in Saltville, Virginia.

In early June, the Union commander of the Fortieth Ohio pushed a probe toward Gladeville. Only a small force of Virginia militia barred the way, and these men presented no obstacle to the Federals. The Union troops captured local officials, confiscated the county's treasury, and burned several structures before departing.[42] One of these officials, Morgan T. Lipps, served as a preacher as well as a county clerk. When his captors learned of his religious avocation, they insisted that he offer a sermon on their behalf. Lipps defiantly replied that he would not "cast pearls before swine." Fortunately for the Southern loyalist, such a declaration did not prevent him from being released a short time later.[43]

Individuals with Unionist leanings were also targets for harassment or retaliation. Bushwhacking, physical or psychological intimidation, and murder were not uncommon activities in the region as a whole. Union Gen. George Morgan dispatched a force into Lee County, Virginia, to capture one such "band," whose leader had allegedly executed a person "who was said to entertain Union feelings."[44] In a separate incident, a group of disguised pro-Confederate raiders whipped and threatened the life of an individual thought to be supplying the Federals with intelligence.[45] Similar actions could be attributed to Union soldiers or sympathizers against pro-Southern or Confederate civilians.

These experiences represented the scale of warfare in the region. The conflict in southwest Virginia occurred on the most personal level, where life and death existed not in the maelstrom of large-scale battles, but in the isolated mountain passes and hollows. One Confederate noted that the nature of warfare seemed to bring out the "worst passions" in people, some of whom followed "a course of life termed 'laying out,'" or "watching for opportunities to slay some solitary political or personal opponent."[46] How often these private grudges were settled in this manner is not known, but the conflict in southwest Virginia created an environment that was certainly conducive to such activities.

At the end of July, an editorial in a local newspaper lamented the fates of several regional counties now that the war had more directly reached their thresholds. "The gallant little county of Wise has already been overrun," the writer explained, "her town burnt down, her citizens captured and driven from their homes and despoiled of their property." For neighboring Russell, "true to our cause as the needle to the pole," and Scott counties, the situation was just as dire. The writer was convinced that "never was southwestern Virginia and east Tennessee since the beginning of the present struggle in more danger of invasion and dissolution than at this very time."[47]

Edward Guerrant returned to the town later in the year and recorded the effects of the Union raid on the village. "We arrived at Gladesville—the 'burnt city,'" he explained. "*Few houses* ever stood in Gladesville—now much fewer are left save in their smoldering ruins & charred & blackened skeletons."[48]

In the meantime, Federal pressure continued to mount on Cumberland Gap. By June, the effort was underway in earnest. General Morgan was set to advance on the morning of June 18. Already diminished in numbers through the reassignment of men to other posts, the remaining Confederate defenders proved no match for the bluecoats. Morgan reported subsequently that he took "the American Gibraltar without the loss of a single man."[49] Yet the success was not nearly as rewarding as it might have seemed. By mid-September, it was the Federals who had to consider the viability of holding Cumberland Gap as they faced the same set of obstacles for maintaining the position as the Confederates. Their answer was to destroy everything that could not be removed and evacuate the position; a task the Union troops completed early on September 17. The Confederates had insufficient numbers to prevent the withdrawal and the Northerners made their way back into Kentucky with only minimal harassment, but Cumberland Gap was once more in Southern hands.[50]

Humphrey Marshall also began to embrace visions of returning to Kentucky. He still brimmed with confidence in his ability to rally Bluegrass recruits to his side. "The news I have is that the people of the mountains in Kentucky, where I was last fall and winter, are excited and can be induced now to come into the contest, but we must have arms" he observed in a communication with the secretary of war.[51] Marshall confided optimistically to President Davis that, "I cannot refrain from expressing in the very strongest terms my conviction that this is the golden moment."[52]

Edmund Kirby Smith had earlier briefed Marshall on plans for a Confederate invasion of Kentucky and the subordinate was clearly anxious to secure a large command for himself if he were going to cooperate in the venture. Smith planned to advance toward Richmond, Kentucky, in conjunction with the invasion of Gen. Braxton Bragg's Army of Tennessee into the Bluegrass State, and he expected Marshall to join him. But Marshall's vanity and his tendency to engage in internal leadership squabbles hindered the efficiency of the Confederate efforts in this regard.

On August 20 Smith informed the temperamental Kentuckian that he would leave Barbourville for Lexington. "Please move forward rapidly into Morgan County, Kentucky," he requested, "and co-operate with me."[53] This was the first of many such calls.[54] However, Marshall remained in Virginia, sending an additional request to Secretary of War Randolph for arms and reinforcements.[55] Finally, Kirby Smith had to plead with President Davis directly to compel Marshall to "advance at once through Pound Gap," and coordinate with his command.[56]

Marshall did not set out from his base at Lebanon until September 7.

By then, a contingent of Smith's troops had already defeated the Federals decisively at Richmond, as they moved into the heart of central Kentucky. Even with the command on the march, Marshall's ardor apparently began to wane. Smith tried to encourage him with repeated admonitions, but the effort seemed to be of no avail. Finally, Jefferson Davis intervened with the brooding subordinate. "No one can have an independent command," the president explained rather mildly, reminding the general of the value of cooperating with other forces. Then, with a gentle dig designed to prod Marshall along, he added: "It was expected that you would have moved with General Smith into Kentucky."[57]

Throughout the Kentucky Campaign, Marshall remained a less than ideal partner. He simply would not be hurried in forming any conjunction that might diminish his independence and authority, whatever the consequences to the war effort. Finally, an exasperated Smith observed almost fatalistically to Braxton Bragg, with whom he was supposed to be cooperating while in Kentucky, that his "fear" was that Marshall simply "will not come."[58] Such an exchange revealed much about the Confederate war effort and ultimate Southern fortunes in far southwestern Virginia and neighboring Kentucky in 1862 and beyond. Private fiefdoms and territorial disputes clearly predominated over wartime realities, limiting the effectiveness of military operations.

The overall campaign ended with a bloody fight at Perryville on October 9, although Marshall's Southerners remained in Kentucky until late in the month before winding their way through the mountainous terrain to Virginia.[59] John B. Jones, the Confederate war clerk whose diary captured his assessments through the conflict, reflected the disappointment. "Gen. Humphrey Marshall met with no success in Kentucky," he explained. Attributing the failure of the campaign to the Kentuckians themselves, Jones concluded that "the brave hunters of former days have disappeared from the scene."[60]

The Confederates returned to harsh circumstances in the Old Dominion. Marshall's men continued to gather such supplies as they could, usually through the military expedient of impressment. These measures added to the scarcity that wracked local citizens, made worse by inflation and hoarding. To meet the needs of their destitute constituents some county officials had to range into neighboring North Carolina to secure adequate resources.[61]

Nor would the end of the year bring relief from the threat of Union raids.

In December, Union Brig. Gen. Samuel P. Carter pushed a Federal force into the region with the object of damaging the vital Virginia & East Tennessee Railroad.[62] Near the little community of Stickleyville, Carter gathered his command early on December 29, where it captured a handful of prisoners. The column reached Estillville (now Gate City) in neighboring Scott County later in the day and pushed ahead to Blountville, Tennessee, which they took easily in the early morning hours of December 30.

The Union commander had to satisfy himself with damaging or destroying the transportation network in the region. Having consigned as much to the flames as he could, and facing the imminent threat of Confederate columns being gathered against him, Carter deemed his mission complete. A force of Confederates managed to induce a brief firefight at Jonesville with the Union rearguard, but they could not halt the withdrawal to Kentucky.[63]

As 1862 closed, Confederate fortunes in southwestern Virginia paled in comparison to the promise of a year earlier. Far from moving into and holding eastern Kentucky for the Confederacy, Southern commanders remained consumed with defending southwestern Virginia from Union incursions. Even the grand invasion of Kentucky by the combined forces of Bragg, Smith, and Marshall failed to resurrect Confederate hopes there. Instead, infighting and recrimination were the order of the day for the Southerners.

While major engagements such as the Seven Days' Campaign, Second Manassas, or Fredericksburg marked the conflict in other areas of Virginia, the people of the southwest experienced the war on a smaller scale. Soldiers and sympathizers on both sides conducted raids, endured bushwhacking, and suffered from shortages and disease. Harassment of women, children, and other noncombatants occurred with daunting frequency. Some individuals fled from their homes to avoid these threats or as refuge from the conscript or recruiting agents that frequently roamed the area. In every case, they became acutely aware of the presence of the war they were now experiencing firsthand.

Throughout 1862, southwest Virginia continued to serve as little more than a military backwater, although the existence of vital facilities like those at Saltville and Wytheville would ensure that such operations would encroach upon the region with greater intensity. If the region that included far southwest Virginia was a "contested borderland," as historian Brian McKnight has asserted, the contest was weighing heavily in the favor of the soldiers in blue by the end of 1862.[64]

Notes

The author wishes to thank Brian D. McKnight for providing access to his excellent study *Contested Borderland: The Civil War in Appalachian Kentucky and Virginia* (Lexington: University Press of Kentucky, 2006), which was not published at the time of writing this essay.

1. Jeffrey Weaver, *The Civil War in Buchanan and Wise Counties: Bushwhackers' Paradise* (Lynchburg, Va.: H. E. Howard, 1994), 35–36.

2. William Marvel, *The Battles for Saltville: Southwest Virginia in the Civil War* (Lynchburg, Va.: H. E. Howard, 1992), 1.

3. Washington County accounted for the largest number of slaves, but as Marvel pointed out, some of their owners were Unionist or moderate. Ibid., 1–2. Jeffrey Weaver noted that Southwest Virginia had a free population of just under 70,000 in 1860 and 7,296 slaves, or 9.4 percent of the total population, in the nine counties he considered. *Civil War in Buchanan and Wise Counties,* 20. Randall Osborne and Jeffrey Weaver substituted Wythe County for McDowell, elevating the number of slaves by 2,162 (McDowell had none listed). *The Virginia State Rangers and State Line* (Lynchburg, Va.: H. E. Howard, 1994), 31.

4. Weaver, *Civil War in Buchanan and Wise Counties,* 91 and 99.

5. Ibid., 67.

6. H. Marshall to A. S. Johnston, January 3, 1862, United States War Department, *War of the Rebellion: Official Records of the Union and Confederate Armies* (Washington, D.C.: Government Printing Office, 1880–1901), series II, vol. 2, 1410–11 (hereafter cited as *OR*).

7. H. Marshall Report, *OR,* series I, vol. 7, 46–50; J. A. Garfield Report, January 14, 1862, *OR,* series I, vol. 7, 30–31.

8. Garfield Report, 31. See also R. H. Chilton to H. Marshall, January 24, 1862, *OR,* series I, vol. 7, 58.

9. William C. Davis and Meredith L. Swentor, eds., *Bluegrass Confederate: The Headquarters Diary of Edward O. Guerrant* (Baton Rouge: Louisiana State University Press, 1999), February 7, 1862, 24–25.

10. S. Cooper to H. Marshall, 1862, January 24, 1862, *OR,* series I, vol. 7, 59–60.

11. Marshall Report, February 2, 1862, *OR,* series I, vol. 7, 57.

12. H. Marshall to S. Cooper, February 2, 1862, *OR,* series I, vol. 7, 59–60.

13. Davis and Swentor, *Bluegrass Confederate,* February 7, 1862, 25.

14. Ibid., February 14, 1862, 32.

15. B. C. Duke [to J. E. Johnston], February 11, 1862, *OR,* series I, vol. 52, pt.

2, 270–71. Gladeville, which Duke, Marshall, and others spelled "Gladesville," is the current town of Wise, Va.

16. J. A. Garfield to Capt. J. B. Fry, March 7, 1862, *OR*, series I, vol. 10, pt. 2, 17–18; J. A. Garfield to W. S. Rosecrans, March 10, 1862, *OR*, series I, vol. 10, pt. 2, 28.

17. H. Marshall to S. Cooper, February 2, 1862, *OR*, series I, vol. 7, 52.

18. H. Marshall to Jefferson Davis, March 8, 1862, *OR*, series I, vol. 52, pt. 2, 283–84.

19. Weaver, *Civil War in Buchanan and Wise Counties*, 117.

20. Bonnie Ball, "The Involvement of Russell County in the Civil War," *Historical Sketches of Southwest Virginia* 16 (1983): 18–19.

21. H. Marshall to S. Cooper, February 15, 1862, *OR*, series I, vol. 7, 885.

22. H. Marshall to S. Cooper, February 19, 1862, *OR*, series I, vol. 7, 892.

23. General Orders, No. 6, March 14, 1862, *OR*, series I, vol. 10, pt. 1, 37; H. Marshall, Circular, March 14, 1862, *OR*, series I, vol. 10, pt. 1, 38–40. President Davis issued such a proclamation in May 1862. See Jefferson Davis, General Order No. 35, May 3, 1862, *OR*, series I, vol. 10, pt. 1, 484–85.

24. Geo. B. McClellan to D. C. Buell, February 24, 1862, *OR*, series I, vol. 7, 660.

25. D. C. Buell to McClellan, March 3, 1862, *OR*, series I, vol. 7, 679.

26. J. A. Garfield to Capt. David Garrard, March 5, 1862, *OR*, series I, vol. 10, pt. 2, 9.

27. J. A. Garfield to Capt. J. B. Fry, March 7, 1862, *OR*, series I, vol. 10, pt. 2, 17–18.

28. James A. Garfield Report, March 17, 1862, *OR*, series I, vol. 10, pt. 1, 33–34.

29. James A. Garfield Report, March 18, 1862, *OR*, series I, vol. 10, pt. 1, 33–34; John B. Thompson Report, March 21, 1862, *OR*, series I, vol. 10, pt. 1, 41–42.

30. Garfield Report, March 18, 1862, *OR*, series I, vol. 10, pt. 1, 34.

31. Humphrey Marshall Report, March 20, 1862, *OR*, series I, vol. 10, pt. 1, 35–36.

32. J. Milton Stansifer, Special Order No. 38, March 19, 1862, *OR*, series I, vol. 10, pt. 1, 40.

33. Don Carlos Buell to Henry W. Halleck, March 14, 1862, *OR*, series I, vol. 10, pt. 2, 37.

34. H. L. Clay to J. E. Rains, March 23, 1862, *OR*, series I, vol. 10, pt. 2, 356–57.

35. E. Kirby Smith to Humphrey Marshall, April 27, 1862, *OR*, series I, vol. 10, pt. 2, 457.

36. Earl J. Hess, *Banners to the Breeze: The Kentucky Campaign, Corinth, and Stones River* (Lincoln: University of Nebraska Press, 2000), 51.

37. Joseph Howard Parks, *General Edmund Kirby Smith, C.S.A.* (Baton Rouge: Louisiana State University Press, 1954), 222.

38. Osborne and Weaver, *Virginia State Rangers,* 25–26.

39. Ibid., 31.

40. Weaver, *Civil War in Buchanan and Wise Counties,* 135, 154–55. See, for example, Marshall to Randolph, *OR,* series I, vol. 16, pt. 2, 764–66.

41. H. Marshall to R. E. Lee, April 25, 1862, *OR,* series I, vol. 16, pt. 2, 444–49.

42. Weaver, *Civil War in Buchanan and Wise Counties,* 136–37.

43. Charles A. Johnson, *A Narrative History of Wise County, Virginia* (Norton, Va.: Norton Press, 1938; reprint, Johnson City, Tenn.: Overmountain Press, 1988), 325–26; Luther F. Addington, *The Story of Wise County (Virginia)* (Wise County, Va.: Centennial Committee and School Board of Wise County, 1956), 102.

44. George W. Morgan to Capt. J. B. Fry, July 18, 1862, *OR,* series I, vol. 16, pt. 2, 182.

45. McKnight, *Contested Borderland,* 117–19.

46. Micajah Woods to My Dear Father, December 16, 1862, quoted in ibid., 122.

47. Editor of the *Goodson* [or Bristol, Va.] *Southern Advocate,* July 31, 1862, quoted in Osborne and Weaver, *Virginia State Rangers,* 26.

48. Davis and Swentor, *Bluegrass Confederate,* September 7, 1862, 142.

49. George W. Morgan to E. M. Stanton and D. C. Buell, June 18, 1862, *OR,* series I, vol. 16, pt. 2, 38. See also George W. Morgan Report, June 22, 1862, *OR,* series I, vol. 16, pt. 2, 57. References to Cumberland Gap as a "Gibraltar" or a "Thermopylae" appear in various forms, particularly in soldiers' accounts as quoted in McKnight, *Contested Borderland,* 72–73, 75.

50. McKnight, *Contested Borderland,* 87–88.

51. H. Marshall to George W. Randolph, August 19, 1862, *OR,* series I, vol. 16, pt. 2, 765.

52. Quoted in Hess, *Banners to the Breeze,* 26.

53. E. Kirby Smith to Humphrey Marshall, August 20, 1862, *OR,* series I, vol. 16, pt. 2, 767.

54. See E. Kirby Smith to Humphrey Marshall, September 10, 1862, *OR,* series I, vol. 16, pt. 2, 807, and Smith to Marshall, September 12, 1862, *OR,* series I, vol. 16, pt. 2, 814–15.

55. H. Marshall to George W. Randolph, August 21, 1862, *OR,* series I, vol. 16, pt. 2, 767.

56. E. Kirby Smith to Jefferson Davis, August 21, 1862, *OR,* series I, vol. 16, pt. 2, 769.

57. Jefferson Davis to Humphrey Marshall, September 19, 1862, *OR,* series I, vol. 16, pt. 2, 851.

58. E. Kirby Smith to Braxton Bragg, September 18, 1862, *OR,* series I, vol. 16, pt. 2, 846.

59. Davis and Swentor, *Bluegrass Confederate,* October 13, 1862, 159.

60. John B. Jones, *A Rebel War Clerk's Diary at the Confederate States Capital* (Philadelphia: J. B. Lippincott, 1866), 1:195.

61. Addington, *Story of Wise County,* 99.

62. For an examination of this raid, see William Garrett Piston, *Carter's Raid: An Episode of the Civil War in East Tennessee* (Johnson City, Tenn.: Overmountain Press, 1989).

63. Samuel P. Carter Report, January 9, 1863, *OR,* series I, vol. 20, pt. 1, 88–92; Humphrey Marshall Report, January 7, 1863, *OR,* series I, vol. 20, pt. 1, 95–103; Marshall Report, January 31, 1863, *OR,* series I, vol. 20, pt. 1, 103–18.

64. McKnight, *Contested Borderland,* 137.

Lee Rebuilds His Army

Dennis E. Frye

No battle had stressed Robert E. Lee more than Antietam. Sixteen of Lee's brigades had not arrived when Gen. George B. McClellan attacked astride the Hagerstown Pike at dawn on September 17. Three of the Confederate commander's nine divisions were still en route from nearby Harpers Ferry. Lee faced a foe more than double his strength when the fighting commenced north of Sharpsburg. Quickly the disparate numbers exacted their toll.

Lee's left buckled as farmer Miller's cornfield converted into a Confederate killing field. Lee's center collapsed after a three-hour defense at the Bloody Lane. Lee's right recoiled following a stubborn stand at the bridge bullied by Gen. Ambrose E. Burnside. Everywhere Lee's line was precarious. A breach anywhere promised disaster.

Twelve hours of close-order combat mercifully ceased at dusk on September 17, but Lee's stress continued. Could the Confederate chieftain hold his position on the morrow? More than one-quarter of the Army of Northern Virginia was dead or wounded. Yet Lee had no reserves. His Harpers Ferry contingent had arrived—barely in time, and inserted immediately into the melee at breaking points throughout the day—but now the reserves were bruised and battered. Retreat loomed as a rational response, but Lee refused. His army would continue to stand on the blood-soaked slopes of Sharpsburg. Indeed, Lee intended more than a stand on September 18. He determined to attack. His target was the Union right flank, straddling the Hagerstown Turnpike about two miles north of Sharpsburg. Summoning Maj. Gen. Thomas J. "Stonewall" Jackson, directing the left wing of the army, and cavalry commander J. E. B. Stuart, Lee instructed them to find a weakness in the Federal position. The offensive on Maryland soil must continue. If the Confederates could wrestle the Hagerstown Turnpike from McClellan, the avenue toward Pennsylvania (only twenty miles distant) would be reopened. After intense scouting, both generals, however, reported unfavorable news. "I found that the [Potomac] River made such an abrupt bend that the enemy's batteries were within 800 yards of the brink of the stream," reported Stuart, making "it impossible to have succeeded in the movement proposed." Jackson concurred, declaring it "inexpedient to hazard the attempt."[1]

Faced with this frustration, Lee remained intent on turning the Federal army. If it could not occur at Sharpsburg, perhaps a broader flanking maneuver could work elsewhere. With this option in mind, reinforced by a retreat recommendation from Maj. Gen. James Longstreet, Lee determined to withdraw from his stubborn defense of the Antietam's ridges, even though McClellan did not attack on September 18. Subsequently, throughout the night of September 18–19, the Army of Northern Virginia silently slipped away, crossing the Potomac at Boteler's Ford, three miles west of Sharpsburg.

Lee had retreated, but he did not regard himself as defeated. He deemed the move from Antietam as a redeployment, not a conclusion to the Maryland Campaign. "The morning of the 19th found us satisfactorily over on the south bank of the Potomac, near Shepherdstown," Lee wrote President Jefferson Davis the day after. "The army was immediately put in motion toward Williamsport."[2]

Williamsport was a Maryland river town about twelve miles northwest of Sharpsburg. It had captured Lee's strategic attention long before the collision along the Antietam Creek. Now he intended to recross the river to continue the invasion by a different avenue. Throughout the first invasion of the North, Lee intended to utilize the good ford at Williamsport to shuttle supplies northward from Winchester (the forward base of operations in the Shenandoah Valley) to Hagerstown, Lee's destination in Maryland. By withdrawing back into Virginia, and then racing upstream to recross the Potomac at Williamsport, Lee hoped to outflank McClellan's army, which he expected to remain concentrated at Sharpsburg, and renew the offensive near Hagerstown.

Executing this bold maneuver would be difficult. Lee understood that it required crossing of the Potomac twice—first with the withdrawal at Boteler's Ford, and second with an advance at Williamsport. Lee appreciated also that the enemy had the advantage of interior lines—direct roads leading to Williamsport and Hagerstown, without the necessity of crossing any river. Lee realized that his proposed march would require speed, stealth, and screening; but if he succeeded it would redeploy his army in western Maryland and continue the fall offensive in Union territory.

Convinced he could overcome any difficulties, Lee instructed Stuart to inaugurate this new initiative. "In order to threaten the enemy on his right and rear and make him apprehensive for his communications, I sent the cavalry forward to Williamsport," he reported to Davis. Stuart wasted no time. As the main army withdrew near Shepherdstown on the night of September 18, Stuart and Wade Hampton's brigade splashed north and west, crossing into Virginia at a "very obscure and rough ford . . . [where] many got over their depth and had to swim the river." By daylight of September 19 Hampton's horsemen had recrossed the Potomac near Williamsport. There they discovered the undefended town had already been seized by the Twelfth Virginia Cavalry and a battalion of the Second Virginia Infantry. Lee's new bridgehead into Maryland was secure—but only temporarily.[3]

Three subsequent events thwarted Lee's rapid return to Maryland. All occurred on September 20, and all were initiated by McClellan. First, McClellan's pursuit toward Boteler's Ford, although neither aggressive nor strong, produced exaggerations at Lee's headquarters during the night of September 19–20 that the entire reserve artillery of his army had been captured. This created consternation and chaos in the Confederate rear. "I am now obliged to return to Shepherdstown, with the intention of driving the enemy back," Lee bemoaned to President Davis early on September 20. As a result, "the march of the army toward Williamsport was arrested."[4]

McClellan's second move, provoked by the sudden appearance of Stuart's cavalry at Williamsport, was swift and decisive. When Union scouts reported 4,000 enemy cavalry and six pieces of artillery at Williamsport on September 19, as well as 10,000 infantry marching upon the same point from the direction of Virginia, McClellan rushed two brigades of his own cavalry and a Federal division toward the town. The following day, he ordered the entire Union VI Corps toward Williamsport. This impressive force, numbering nearly 18,000 men, compelled Stuart to abandon his beachhead at Williamsport on the night of September 20. McClellan effectively had blocked Lee's intentions to return to Maryland.[5]

The third action by McClellan that forced Lee to reconsider his reintroduction into Maryland involved Harpers Ferry. By September 20, a division of the Union XII Corps had been transferred from the Antietam battlefield with orders to reoccupy the town. Two full Yankee corps soon followed, and within one week of the Battle of Antietam, McClellan had nearly 20,000 men concentrated at Harpers Ferry. This massive force, located on the same side of the river as Lee's army, threatened Confederate communications and Lee's right flank. With the Federals holding Harpers Ferry in strength, Lee's options to move north were erased.[6]

Despite McClellan's deterrents, General Lee remained fixated with returning the army to Maryland. "When I withdrew from Sharpsburg into Virginia, it was my intention to recross the Potomac at Williamsport, and move upon Hagerstown," Lee reiterated to President Davis in a message dated eight days after Antietam. "In a military point of view," Lee confided, "the best move, in my opinion, the army could make would be to advance upon Hagerstown and endeavor to defeat the enemy at that point." Lee painfully admitted, however, that "the condition of the army" and its diminished numbers prevented a new strike north. He regretfully informed the president, "I am, therefore, led to pause."[7]

Robert E. Lee's definition of "pause" did not mean taking a rest. Though hesitantly acknowledging that the condition of his army precluded offensive operations in Maryland or Pennsylvania in the autumn of 1862, Lee could still fight—especially if the fight was in Virginia. Thus he responded to the changing situation before him and developed a new strategy. "If we cannot advance into Maryland, I hope to draw him into the [Shenandoah] Valley," declared Lee on September 24 in a letter to Maj. Gen. Gustavus W. Smith, in command of Confederate forces around Richmond. The next day, Lee shared a similar thought with Maj. Gen. William W. Loring, the theater commander in western Virginia. "McClellan's army is on the north bank of the Potomac, stretching from Hagerstown to Harpers Ferry." After describing the situation, Lee offered his strategy. "I hope to be able to retain them on the Potomac, or, if they cross, to draw them up the valley." President Davis acquiesced in Lee's desire to "occupy the enemy on this frontier . . . [or] to draw them into the Valley, where I can attack them to advantage." Davis, in fact, calmed Lee's distress about his failure to drive into Union territory. "The feverish anxiety to invade the North has been relieved by the counter-irritant of apprehension for the safety of the capital in the absence of the army."[8]

Unbeknownst to Lee, on the north side of the Potomac George McClellan was devising a Union strategy that cooperated perfectly with Confederate plans. "After a full consultation with the corps commanders in my vicinity,"

McClellan informed General-in-Chief Henry W. Halleck, "I have determined to adopt the line of the Shenandoah for immediate operations against the enemy." McClellan preferred this alternative for two reasons. First, his army easily could be supplied at Harpers Ferry by the Baltimore & Ohio Railroad; and second, he could best protect Maryland and Pennsylvania from invasion by driving into the Valley and, at the same time, holding the Potomac River line. McClellan confidently claimed that his objects were "to fight the enemy if they remain near Winchester, or . . . to force them to abandon the Valley of the Shenandoah." The twin strategies of the two commanders, although devised in camps on opposite sides of the Potomac, appeared to ensure an inevitable clash in the Valley.[9]

Yet no battle occurred. Weeks passed, but McClellan did not advance. Even when delivered a preemptory order from President Lincoln on October 6 to "cross the Potomac and give battle to the enemy or drive him south," McClellan delayed. General Lee noticed this odd lack of initiative. "General McClellan's army is apparently quiescent," he informed President Davis on October 2. "I have been in hopes that he would cross the river and move up [south into] the Valley, where I wish to get him, but he does not seem so disposed."[10]

Although perplexed by McClellan's posture, Lee perceived the Union intentions. Based upon the obvious buildup of Federal forces, fortifications, and supplies at Harpers Ferry, the Confederate commander repositioned his army on September 27, shifting it south and west from the vicinity of Martinsburg further into the Valley's interior north of Winchester. This new position along Mill Creek, Lick River, and the Opequon Creek better prepared the army for any Federal threat from Harpers Ferry against Lee's right or rear.[11] Thus, with McClellan inclined toward defense—"to hold the army about as it is now, rendering Harpers Ferry secure and watching the river closely"—and Lee conditionally content with defense, "not deeming it prudent to . . . reenter Maryland," the two armies avoided collision.[12]

This frustrated Lee greatly, but the Confederate commander regretfully acknowledged that the dreadful condition of his own army prevented renewed campaigning. "Its present efficiency is greatly paralyzed by the loss to its ranks of the numerous stragglers," Lee confided to President Davis on September 21. "I have taken every means in my power to correct this evil, which has increased rather than diminished." Lee then concluded that his army could not return to Maryland and continue the offensive because of this "desertion of their comrades." "This is a woeful condition of affairs," judged Lee, "and I am pained to state it."[13]

Lee first identified straggling as a problem on September 7, only three days after commencing the Maryland Campaign. "One of the greatest evils . . . is the habit of straggling from the ranks," Lee notified President Davis from his headquarters near Frederick, Maryland. "It has become a habit difficult to correct," fumed a frustrated Lee. With his anger increasing, Lee condemned these men as "cowards of the army [who] desert their comrades in times of danger." Six days later, from his new headquarters at Hagerstown, Lee continued his harsh complaint. "One great embarrassment is the reduction of our ranks by straggling," the offended commander wrote to Davis. "Our ranks are very much diminished—I fear from a third to one-half the original numbers."[14]

Wherever that absent fraction of the army went before the battle, apparently it was not to Antietam. Lee reported "this great battle was fought with less than 40,000 men on our side." Five days later, following the withdrawal to Virginia, 41,520 Confederates answered roll call near Martinsburg. Then something extraordinary occurred. On September 30, only eight days after the initial muster, 62,713 Rebels answered "here" at roll call, an increase of over 20,000 (or one-third of the army). By October 8, the Confederate ranks ballooned to 78,204, nearly double the size of Lee's force at Antietam. Thus, since returning to Virginia, the Confederate army had multiplied and replicated to almost twice its Maryland size in only eighteen days.[15]

Although pleased to see his graycoats returning, Lee knew he could not predicate his future on unpredictable turnout. "It [straggling] occasions me the greatest concern in the future operations of the army," reflected a despondent Lee to President Davis. "It is true that the army has had hard work to perform, long and laborious marches, and large odds to encounter . . . but not greater than were endured by our revolutionary fathers." Lee offered no patience for the stragglers. "It ought to be construed into desertion in face of the enemy," he groaned, "and thus brought under the Rules and Articles of War." While puzzling over the causes of the straggling, Lee concluded: "I hope by a few days rest . . . to restore the efficiency of the army."[16] Yet Lee realized that rest, alone, would not resolve his problems. The Confederate commander understood that straggling was a symptom, and not the cause, of the bad conduct of his troops. On September 21, only one day after the army's return to Virginia, Lee commenced an aggressive addressing of his army's degradation and its causes—discipline, depravation, and destitution.

General Lee directed his attention first to discipline—for those still within the army, and for those who had dropped out. First he had to establish order. On September 21, Lee directed Brig. Gen. George H. Steuart (just returning to the army after recovering from a wound suffered at Cross Keys three months earlier) to proceed to Winchester to "systematize operations at that point." Lee's instructions were deliberate and his tone beyond debate. In priority order, the commanding general required Steuart to: 1) establish a provost guard to keep "perfect order and quiet"; 2) organize the commissary and quartermaster's department so that all supplies may be issued; 3) forward stragglers, convalescents, and new recruits "to this army immediately"; and 4) establish hospitals for the sick and wounded in barns or buildings. Lee demanded immediate response, and offered no patience for mishap. "The foregoing requirements will be rigidly enforced."[17]

For those stalwarts still within the ranks, Lee described his program in a lengthy, detailed letter to wing commanders Jackson and Longstreet. Roll calls would occur daily at reveille. Morning reports would be tabulated and forwarded daily to regimental, brigade, and division commanders. Arms and equipments would be inspected weekly. A brigade guard would march in rear of each brigade and drive up all stragglers. Officers would ensure that marching ranks were closed up at all times. Sentinels would protect private property. A permanent provost guard, under an "efficient, energetic, and firm officer," would be established in each wing to correct and punish violations of orders.

Routine apparently had been ignored. To reinstate routine, Lee pleaded with his two principal lieutenants to meet with generals and officers and offer "personal explanations and calls upon their sense of duty." Lee instructed Longstreet and Jackson to "infuse a different spirit among our officers, and to inspire them . . . to bring about a better state of discipline." Lee's final paragraph personalized his plea to every officer, appealing to the inner soul of the Confederate soldier. If we exhibit strengths like "better discipline, greater mobility, and higher inspirations," Lee reasoned, we can "counterbalance the many advantages over us, both in numbers and material, which the enemy possesses."[18]

If eloquence did not inspire, removal and replacement of officers was Lee's remedy. "There is great dereliction of duty among the regimental and company officers," Lee confided to Secretary of War George Randolph on September 23, "and unless something is done the army will melt away." Many of the derelicts had been elected by the ranks in the spring of 1862, and this failed experiment in military democracy required rectification. Lee thus recommended that the Confederate Congress authorize the president to degrade officers upon "clear proof of bad conduct." Secretary Randolph readily agreed, and in an endorsement to the chairman of the Confederate Senate's Military Committee, he declared: "The vast amount of stragglers which now paralyze our Army and defeat all attempts to re-enforce it is mainly due to the inefficiency of the regimental and company officers." Randolph added that "it is useless to increase the Army unless it can be properly officered. Numbers are only a source of weakness in a badly-organized, ill-disciplined army, and it is impossible to discipline an army without efficient regimental and company officers." Randolph then bluntly warned: "Unless we apply a speedy remedy great disasters to our arms may be expected." The Confederate Congress heeded these warnings, and on October 13, passed an ordinance that relieved the army of "disqualified, disabled, and incompetent officers."[19]

Vanished officers began to reemerge in the army during a stragglers sweep of the lower Shenandoah Valley during the first week after Antietam. "The number of officers back here was most astonishing," reported a stunned Gen. J. R. Jones, commander of the Stonewall Division. "After due notice, I ordered the cavalry to arrest and bring to the rendezvous all officers, as well as men, found in the rear without proper leave. It created quite a stampede in the direction of the army." By September 27, Jones had rounded up between 5,000 and 6,000 stragglers.[20]

Even with the stragglers and errant officers returning, Lee recognized he had limited authority to punish the offenders. That purview belonged to the court-martial—a laborious process that occurred in Richmond or some other convenient city, but never accompanied a field army. Lee required a system of justice that moved where he moved, a system that would correct "daily evils" with "promptness and certainty of punishment." To accomplish this, Lee requested that President Davis ask the Confederate Congress to adopt legislation that would permit a military commission to accompany the army. "I know of no better way of correcting this great evil," Lee concluded. With a military commission present, offering the ill-disciplined penance or penalty, Lee believed he could defeat those showing "backwardness in duty, tardiness of movement, and neglect of orders" who brought discredit to his army. The Confederate Congress concurred, adopting a law on October 9 that placed military courts in the field with the armies.[21]

Not all of Lee's frontline officers were absent due to dereliction. Many were dead. The incessant campaigning of the past three months had killed or maimed many of the best leaders in the Confederate army. The Second Virginia Infantry of the famed Stonewall Brigade had its colonel killed, its lieutenant colonel mortally wounded, its major dead, and half of its company commanders deceased or out of action, all without having fought at Antietam. At Sharpsburg Lee lost three brigadier generals, had ten colonels killed and twenty-three wounded, six lieutenant colonels killed and eleven wounded, and four majors killed and eleven wounded. In Richard Ewell's proud division, eleven of the fifteen commanders were gunned down near the Cornfield. In the Third North Carolina Infantry, twenty-three of twenty-seven line officers were casualties on September 17.[22]

Lee understood he could not replace his line officers quickly, but his discipline program, designed to restore rigor, routine, and righteousness in the ranks, showed initial success. "The returns of September 30 will show an increase of our strength," Lee reported to President Davis. "But our ranks are still thin," he cautioned, "and our sick are very numerous." This sickness problem was the result of dual depravations: rest and food. Incessant marching, maneuvering, and fighting since the last week of June had debilitated the Confederate physique. Virtually every foot soldier in the Rebel army suffered from extreme fatigue. Simply stated, Lee's army was tired. Although difficult for Lee to admit, the thousands of stragglers he complained of were thousands of weary warriors—warriors who could no longer maintain Lee's persistent pace. Even with a year's perspective, Lee failed to acknowledge fatigue as a principal problem with his army. "Although not properly equipped for invasion, lacking much of the material of war, and feeble in transportation," Lee wrote in his August 1863 report of the Maryland Campaign, the army was "yet believed to be strong enough" to conduct offensive operations in the North. Lee defined strength by numbers and materials, but he overlooked the shrinking stamina of each soldier. Nowhere did General Lee accept the physical breakdown of his men as a primary source of his ranks' reductions. Even two weeks after Antietam, he seemed perplexed by his army's extended exhaustion. "Strange to say," he wrote President Davis, "our sick are very numerous."[23]

Union commander George McClellan ultimately provided the Confederate soldier with the best remedy. As the Army of the Potomac reorganized, reequipped, and reconnoitered, it did not move forward. Despite emphatic demands for action from President Lincoln, McClellan offered repeated excuses and remained glued to the Potomac. As a result of McClellan's hesitance, Lee's army remained stationary for nearly six weeks. Hence, through the inactivity of the enemy, the Shenandoah Valley became a haven of rest.

During this welcome respite, Lee addressed the diet depravation that had hampered his army in September. Throughout the Maryland Campaign, Confederate food was so deficient that thousands of soldiers subsisted on green corn and green apples. This nonnutritious combination further decayed weakened Confederate constitutions, producing an epidemic of diarrhea and dysentery. It was not so much the shortage of food, but its delivery, that produced problems for the army while in Maryland. The shift of supply lines to Winchester, west of the Blue Ridge, had outraced the army's concurrent move across the mountains, resulting in a temporary severance of supplies that was compounded by Lee's stringent orders against foraging. The Confederate soldier nearly starved while in Maryland.

When Lee returned to Virginia on September 20, his supplies at Winchester were now within reach. Stockpiles of food began to flow to the famished army. Every day more than seven thousand pounds of fresh-baked bread came out of the ovens at Winchester. Cattle herds were butchered, and the army began consuming one thousand head of beef per week. "We have plenty of beef and flour for our troops," Lee informed President Davis on September 23, but he judiciously requested that "it is also important that such stores as may be needed for future use should be collected by the Commissary Department." Unbeknownst to General Lee, shortages in beef, hogs, and grain were looming. Due to the severe drought in Virginia in the summer of 1862, the wheat crop was one-fourth its average yield, and cattle and hogs were thin and not in great numbers. "The chances of procuring sufficient supplies are becoming every hour more and more doubtful," warned Col. L. B. Northrop, commissary-general of subsistence, in a letter to the secretary of war on November 3. "I think it would be imprudent to estimate full supplies in January, and a fatal error to rely on full supplies after that time." Despite these dire predictions, General Lee's army fattened up during the fall of 1862 during the largest eating orgy in the army's history.[24]

With food flowing into the company messes, the destitution of the army became Lee's next challenge. On September 21, while still deciding whether to return to Maryland, Lee fired off a blunt assessment to Col. A. C. Myers, the Confederate quartermaster general. "I desire to call your attention to the great deficiency of clothing in this army," Lee opened, "the want of which there is much suffering." Lee then elaborated some details. More than 900 men at Winchester did not participate in the recent campaign because they had no shoes. Between four thousand and five thousand pairs of shoes were purchased while in Maryland, but "this was by no means sufficient to supply the men without them." Lee's demand reflected his urgency: "The near approach of cold weather renders it all the more necessary that clothes, and especially underclothing, be supplied."

Lee commenced the Maryland Campaign fully aware of the destitution of his soldiers. "The army is not properly equipped for an invasion," Lee informed President Davis on September 3, "and the men are poorly provided with clothes, and in thousands of instances are destitute of shoes." Despite these shortcomings, the military offensive prevailed. "[W]e cannot afford to be idle," he reminded Davis, "and though weaker than our opponents . . . [we] must endeavor to harass if we cannot destroy them."

Nearly one month later, Lee offered no apologies for the Maryland Campaign, but his army still suffered destitution. "The number of barefooted men is daily increasing," he reported to President Davis on September 28, "and it pains me to see them limping over the rocky roads." Lee fully appreciated the debilitating effects of the destitution, and he reminded Davis that if arrangements could be made to "furnish [the troops] with clothes, shoes, and blankets, we could yet accomplish a great deal this fall."[25]

Arrangements, indeed, were underway. On the first of October, 4,400 pair of shoes arrived at Winchester, followed the next day by an additional 2,000 pairs. Lee was pleased. "I hope [this] will cover the bare feet in the army," he scribed to Davis. Then the Confederate Congress worked to address a long-term remedy. On October 8, the congressmen adopted legislation to "encourage the manufacture of clothing and shoes for the Army," including the authorization of duty-free importation of cloth, leather, and machinery. On the same day, the Congress repealed the onerous law requiring commutation for soldiers' clothing, instead ordering the secretary of war to provide "in kind to the soldiers the uniform clothing prescribed by the Regulations of the Army." Finally, on the following day, the Congress permitted the president to detail up to 2,000 men from the army who are "skilled in the manufacture of shoes" to commence a program of mass shoe production. As an incentive, the Congress offered these skilled soldiers thirty-five cents per pair of shoes in addition to their regular pay and rations.[26]

With discipline decreed and enforced, rest retained, food in abundance, and the arrival of clothing and shoes, the condition of Lee's army improved dramatically. "I wish we could fight with McClellan's army about Sharpsburg again," wrote Sandie Pendleton, one of Jackson's staff officers. "The result would be very different from that of the battle of September 17. Our army is twenty-five thousand stronger [now, on October 8] . . . and in far better condition in every respect." Pendleton deemed the army anxious for action. "We have been idle now for more than three weeks, and our generals are not given to inaction. Activity and motion have gotten to be a necessity for us, as giving some food to the mind."[27]

Activity and motion depend upon transportation, and here Lee faced another problem. "[O]ur horses have been so reduced by labor and scant food," he informed President Davis on September 28, "that, unless their condition can be improved before winter, I fear many of them will die." The condition of the army's motive power was so deplorable that General Lee issued orders dealing only with this matter. "The commanding general desires to impress upon all officers in charge of horses of the army the urgent necessity of energetic and unwearied care of their animals." Specifically, Lee instructed wagon train officers not to permit their teams to be "overdriven, misused, or neglected." Turning to artillery horses, Lee was even more adamant about diligence and responsibilities. Battery horses should in no instance be ridden. During the march, any halting place must be selected where water and food were available. During battle, horses must receive every possible opportunity for "resting, watering, and feeding." For those animals "worn down" or "past recovery," Lee ordered them turned over to the chief quartermaster to send them off to "good pasturage." Lee acknowledged that rest was the best remedy for his animals, "yet I see no way of affording it." Even though the fall of 1862 provided a respite from the battlefield, the army transportation continued to toil as Lee daily supplied his army from his base at Staunton to his forward position at Winchester, a trek of nearly ninety miles.[28]

Only the cavalry's horses remained in good condition, but Lee grasped this as an opportunity to conduct an offensive. On October 8, Lee summoned Stuart to his headquarters and informed him that "an expedition into Maryland . . . is at this time desirable." Lee likely chose this moment because Federal newspapers reported that President Lincoln had just completed a conference with McClellan at the Union commander's headquarters near Sharpsburg. Correctly anticipating Lincoln's desire to renew the Union offensive, Lee determined to strike first.

Mindful of the omnipresent threat of another invasion posed by the Confederate army, Lee conceived a demonstration. He could terrorize the North with his swift-footed cavalry. Subsequently, Lee ordered Stuart to cross the Potomac above Williamsport with 1,200 to 1,500 men and to proceed beyond Maryland. The target became Chambersburg, Pennsylvania, about twenty miles north of the Mason-Dixon Line. Lee had practical goals, such as destruction of the railroad bridge at Chambersburg (thus disrupting one of McClellan's supply lines), and the opportunity to gain information on "the position, force, and probable intention of the enemy." Lee's real purpose, however, was to "impede and embarrass the military operations" of McClellan and to keep the Union army frozen as a border patrol and to ensure that theater operations remained on "this frontier."[29]

At 3:00 A.M. on October 10, Stuart attacked McCoy's Ferry and commenced his mission northward. During the next sixty hours, his force galloped 180 miles in a circuitous arc north to Chambersburg, east toward Gettysburg, south toward Frederick, and back across the Potomac at White's Ford near Poolesville by noon on October 12. Along the way, Stuart's men captured 1,200 horses. Despite orders to McClellan that not a Rebel "should be permitted to return to Virginia," Stuart suffered no killed and only one wounded. At Chambersburg, the Confederates fired the Cumberland Valley Railroad depot and machine shops, but failed to destroy the iron bridge spanning the Conococheague Creek. Despite this setback, Stuart was pleased. "The results of this expedition, from a moral and political point of view, can hardly be estimated," he informed General Lee two days after his return. "[T]he consternation among property holders in Pennsylvania beggars description."[30]

Union response was swift—over the telegraph lines. During the two weeks following Stuart's successful scurry, and General McClellan's failure to stop him or catch him, McClellan complained incessantly about his own broken-down horses. "I have just read your dispatch about sore-tongued and fatigued horses," President Lincoln snapped at McClellan. "Will you pardon me for asking what the horses of your army have done since the battle of Antietam that fatigues anything?"

Lee's strategy with Stuart's Pennsylvania raid certainly embarrassed Lincoln and McClellan, and it revealed the vulnerability of the Federal army's defense of the Potomac and Pennsylvania borders. Unfortunately for Confederate strategy, the Pennsylvania romp backfired. General Lee did not achieve his ultimate outcome of maintaining McClellan's masses on the Shenandoah Valley frontier. Exasperated with McClellan's defensive obstinacy, Lincoln exhausted his patience. "[I]f the enemy had more occupation south of the river," Lincoln chastised McClellan on October 14, "his cavalry would not be so likely to make raids north of it."[31]

Subsequently, the administration ordered McClellan to commence an offensive in Virginia, but not into the Shenandoah Valley. Considering Washington the army's "proper base of operations," and not Harpers Ferry, as McClellan had argued, General-in-Chief Halleck looked at the map and reasoned two simple perspectives: 1) the most direct route to Richmond or the railroad center at Lynchburg was east of the Blue Ridge; and 2) a Federal move east of the mountains would compel Lee to abandon the Shenandoah Valley in order to protect the Confederate capital and its communications. To comply with this new line of operations, McClellan began shifting the army toward Berlin (modern-day Brunswick), Maryland, about five miles downstream from Harpers Ferry, on October 23. Three days later, an infantry division of the IX Corps commenced the latest invasion of Virginia. By November 2, virtually all of the Army of the Potomac had returned to Confederate soil.[32]

Lee's scouts immediately detected McClellan's move. In fact, Lee anticipated it after witnessing no indications that McClellan would advance in the Valley. On October 22, four days prior to the renewal of the Union offensive, Lee directed John G. Walker's division to cross the Blue Ridge at Ashby's Gap "with a view of checking the incursions of the enemy in that region and watching more closely his movements east of the mountains." When it became evident that the Army of the Potomac was beginning a new offensive, Lee moved his headquarters to Culpeper. First, however, he continued his penchant for unconventional strategy by promptly splitting his army. He ordered Longstreet's corps to cross the Blue Ridge at Chester's Gap and to concentrate at Culpeper. Lee instructed Jackson's corps to remain in the Valley at Berryville, near its eastern edge. From this position, Jackson could either swing across the mountain to reinforce Longstreet or threaten the Union rear and flank east of the Blue Ridge. Jackson's presence in the Valley also presented a continued menace to Maryland and Pennsylvania, a strategy Lee hoped would keep Federal troops penned along the Potomac.[33]

Unbeknownst to the Confederate commander, the Rappahannock, and not the Potomac, was the Federals' next target. The two armies nervously eyed each other from the new Union headquarters at Warrenton and from Lee's post at Culpeper until mid-November, while Union authorities were hatching plans to dash south. The race to Fredericksburg and their next great clash thence commenced.

Notes

1. United States War Department, *War of the Rebellion: Official Records of the Union and Confederate Armies* (Washington, D.C.: Government Printing Office, 1880–1901), series I, vol. 19, pt. 1, 820, 957 (hereafter cited as *OR*).

2. Ibid., 142.

3. Ibid., 142, 820–21.

4. Ibid., 142. Brig. Gen. William Nelson Pendleton, Lee's chief of artillery who was commanding the Confederate rear at Boteler's Ford, was the source of this erroneous report that all forty-four cannon in the artillery reserve had been captured. In actuality, the Federals had seized only four or five cannon. Ibid., 830–32, 339–40.

5. Ibid., 68, 821; ibid., pt. 2, 334.

6. Ibid., vol. 51, pt. 1, 855–56.

7. Ibid., vol. 19, pt. 2, 626–27.

8. Ibid., pt. 1, 143; ibid., pt. 2, 625–27, 634.

9. Ibid., pt. 1, 11.

10. Ibid., 10; ibid., pt. 2, 644.

11. Ibid., pt. 2, 628–29.

12. Ibid., pt. 1, 70–71; ibid., pt. 2, 633.

13. Ibid., pt. 1, 143.

14. Ibid., 597, 606.

15. Ibid., pt. 2, 621, 639, 660.

16. Ibid., pt. 1, 143.

17. Ibid., pt. 2, 614–15.

18. Ibid., 618–19.

19. Ibid., 622–23; ibid., series IV, vol. 2, 97–98, 205.

20. Ibid., series I, vol. 19, pt. 2, 629.

21. Ibid., 597; ibid., series IV, vol. 2, 202–3.

22. Dennis E. Frye, *2nd Virginia Infantry* (Lynchburg, Va.: Harold Howard, 1984), 32, 39; James V. Murfin, *The Gleam of Bayonets: The Battle of Antietam and Robert E. Lee's Maryland Campaign* (New York: Thomas Yoseloff, 1964), 359–73.

23. *OR,* series I, vol. 19, pt. 2, 643; *OR,* series I, vol. 19, pt. 1, 144.

24. Ibid., pt. 2, 623, 625; ibid., series IV, vol. 2, 158–59, 192–93.

25. Ibid., series I, vol. 19, pt. 2, 614, 590–91, 633.

26. Ibid., series IV, vol. 2, 111, 202, 204.

27. William G. Bean, *Stonewall's Man: Sandie Pendleton* (Chapel Hill: University of North Carolina Press, 1959), 81.

28. *OR,* series I, vol. 19, pt. 2, 633, 642–43.

29. Ibid., 55; ibid., pt. 1, 143–44, 152.

30. Ibid., pt. 2, 52–54, 59.

31. Ibid., 485, 421.

32. Ibid., 442–43, 485–86, 531–32.

33. Ibid., 675–76, 685–86.

Diary of a Southern Refugee during the War, January– July 1862

Judith Brockenbrough McGuire
Edited by James I. Robertson Jr.

Refugee life in the second year of the Civil War was laborious for Judith Brockenbrough McGuire, her feeble minister-husband, and her two step-daughters. For eight months after abandoning their Alexandria home, the McGuires had made temporary residences with friends and neighbors in the Clarke County and Winchester areas. They departed Winchester on Christmas Eve, 1861. By stage and rail the husband, wife, and two daughters made their way to the Brockenbrough estate, "Westwood," just north of Richmond in Hanover County.

That stay lasted two weeks before the family moved to Richmond, the crowded center of the Confederate government. Judith McGuire had grown up amid Richmond aristocracy. Now the forty-nine-year-old homeless wife found herself in an environment of want. Reverend McGuire had been a minister and schoolteacher for thirty-seven years. His health at the age of sixty-two kept him from seeking a chaplaincy in the army, and no teaching positions were available amid the chaos of war. So the minister began searching for any kind of employment.

Meanwhile, Judith McGuire had to endure the embarrassment of going from door to door in search of living quarters. Her husband soon obtained a clerkship in the Post Office Department. The job was drudgery and the salary was small, but it was a job.

A two-week search by Mrs. McGuire ended with the family's securing a single room on Grace Street. The building once housed schoolboys but now was filling with refugees. Mrs. McGuire volunteered as a nurse in hospitals for sick and wounded soldiers comprising a large percentage of Richmond's wartime population. Federal threats from without added to the anxieties from within as the McGuires struggled to exist. An occasional visit to the home place, "Westwood," brought but temporary relief.

In the summer, Reverend McGuire became ill. The couple made a six-week visit to Lynchburg and Charlottesville. While in Lynchburg, Mrs. McGuire and a friend went for a carriage ride. "I almost fancy that we are taking one of our usual summer trips," she wrote, "and then I am aroused as from a sweet dream, to find myself a homeless wanderer, surrounded by horrors of which my wildest fancy had never conceived a possibility, in this Christian land and enlightened day."

By autumn, Reverend McGuire's health had improved sufficiently for the family to return to Richmond. No suitable quarters could be obtained in the capital, so the McGuires and four other couples moved into "a cottage with eight small rooms" in Ashland, twelve miles north of Richmond. Reverend and Mrs. McGuire commuted by train to their government and nursing duties.

Judith McGuire's highly quotable diary entries for 1862 are a revealing mixture of military reports and rumors, the activities of family members and friends in the army, and her personal observations of life, faith, and the future. Occasionally she would recite in depth the travails of the innocent abused by war—such as a Kentucky widow trying desperately to reach her wounded soldier-son in Virginia, but encountering obstacle after obstacle in what proved to be an empty pilgrimage.

When reporting a battle, especially in the eastern theater, Mrs. McGuire was always more concerned about the human casualties than of the consequences of the engagement. Certain that God was with the South, she continued to be optimistic about the eventual triumph of the Southern Confederacy. Her daily jottings are alternately filled with moments of concern for loved ones in service, expressions of thanksgiving over positive news, and unbending resolution when setbacks occurred. One such expression came in late winter, 1862: "Our people continue to make every effort to repel the foe, who, like the locusts of Egypt, overrun our land, carrying the bitterest enmity and desolation wherever they go."

A bonus in Mrs. McGuire's 1862 journal was the inclusion of a long excerpt from the diary of an in-law and close friend, Hanover County resident

Mary Newton. Those daily observations not only contain insights into the initial stage of Gen. J. E. B. Stuart's "Ride around McClellan" but also provide the first personal account written of the burial of Capt. William Latane.

Diary of a Southern Refugee

Westwood,[1] *Hanover County, January 20, 1862*—I pass over the sad leave-taking of our kind friends in Clarke [County] and Winchester. It was very sad, because we knew not when and under what circumstances we might meet again. We left Winchester, in the stage, for Strasburg at ten o'clock at night, on the 24th of December. The weather was bitter cold, and we congratulated ourselves that the stage was not crowded. Mr. [McGuire] and the girls were on the back seat, a Methodist clergyman, a soldier, and myself on the middle, and two soldiers and our maid Betsey on the front seat. We went off by starlight, with every prospect of a pleasant drive of eighteen miles. As we were leaving the suburbs of the town, the driver drew up before a small house, from which issued two women with a baby, two baskets, several bundles, and a box. The passengers began to shout out, "Go on, driver; what do you mean? There's no room for another; go on!" The driver made no answer, but the women came to the stage-door, and began to put in their bundles; the gentlemen protested that they could not get in—there was no room. The woman with the baby said she *would* get in; she was "agwine to Strasburg to spend Christmas with her relations, whar she was born and raised, and whar she had not been for ten year, and nobody had a better right to the stage than she had, and she was agwine, and Kitty Grim[2] was agwine too—she's my sister-in-law; and so is baby, 'cause baby never did see her relations in Strasburg in her life. So, Uncle Ben!" she exclaimed to the driver, "take my bag, basket, and box by you, and me and Kitty and baby, and the bundles and the little basket, will go inside." All this was said amidst violent protestations from the men within: "You can't get in; driver, go on." But suiting the action to the word, she opened the door, calling, "Come, Kitty," got on the step, and thrust her head in, saying: "If these gentlemen is gentlemen, and has got any politeness, they will git out and sit with Uncle Ben, and let ladies come inside." A pause ensued. At last a subdued tone from the soldier in the middle seat was heard to say: "Madam, if you will get off the step, I will get out." "Very well, sir; and why didn't you do that at first?

And now," said she, looking at the man on the front seat, "there's another seat by Uncle Ben; sposen you git out and let Kitty Grim have your seat; she's bound to go." The poor man quietly got out, without saying a word, but the very expression of his back, as he got out of the stage, was subdued. "Now, Kitty, git in, and bring the little basket and them two bundles; they won't pester the lady much." The door was closed, and then, the scene being over, the passengers shouted with laughter.

Our heroine remained perfectly passive until we got to the picket-post, a mile from town. The driver stopped; a soldier came up for passports. She was thunder-struck. "Passes! Passes for white folks! I never heard of such a thing. *I* ain't got no pass; nuther is Kitty Grim." I suggested to her to keep quiet, as the best policy. Just at that time a Tennessee soldier had to confess that he had forgotten to get a passport. "You can't go on," said the official; and the soldier got out. Presently the woman's turn came. "Madam, your passport, if you please." "I ain't got none; nuther is Kitty Grim (that's my sister-in-law); we ain't agwine to git out nuther, 'cause we's agwine to Strasburg to spend Christmas with my relations, and I ain't been thar for ten year, and I never heard of white folks having passes." "But, madam," began the official——"You needn't to 'but, madam,' me, 'cause I ain't agwine to git out, and I'd like to see the man what would put me out. This is a free country, and I'se agwine to Strasburg this night; so you might as well take your lantern out of my face." "But, madam, my orders," began the picket. "Don't tell me nothing 'bout orders; I don't care nothing 'bout orders; and you needn't think, 'cause the Tennessee man got out, that I'se agwine to git out—'cause I ain't. Ain't I got three sons in the army, great sight bigger than you is? And they fit at Manassas, and they ain't no cowards, nuther is their mother; and I ain't agwin to git out of this stage this night, but I'm agwine to Strasburg, whar I was born and raised."

The poor man looked non-plussed, but yet another effort; he began, "My dear madam." "I ain't none of your dear madam; I'se just a free white woman, and so is Kitty Grim, and we ain't no niggers to git passes, and I'se gwine 'long this pike to Strasburg. Now I'se done talking." With this she settled herself on the seat, and leant back with a most determined air; and the discomfited man shut the door amid peals of laughter from within and from without. In a few minutes we were quiet again, and all began to settle themselves for sleep, when the silence was broken by our heroine; "Kitty, is you sick?" "No," said Kitty. "Well, it is a wonder. Gentlemen, can't one of you take Kitty's seat, and give her yourn? She gits monstrous sick when she is riding with her back to the horses." There was a death-like silence, and my curiosity was aroused to know how she would manage that point. After a few moments she began again. "Kitty, is you sick?" "No," says Kitty, "not yit." "Well, I do wish one of you gentlemen would give Kitty his seat." Still no reply. All was becoming quiet again, when she raised her voice: "Kitty Grim, *is* you sick?" "Yes," said Kitty, "just a little." "I knowed it: I knowed she was sick; and when Kitty Grim gets sick, she most *in general flings up!*" The effect was electric. "My dear madam," exclaimed both gentlemen at once, "take my seat; by all means take my seat." The Methodist clergyman being nearest, gave up his seat and took hers. The change was soon effected amidst the most uproarious laughter, all feeling that they were fairly outgeneraled the third time. From that time until we reached Strasburg, at two o'clock, she kept up a stream of talk, addressed to the baby, never interrupted except once, when the quiet-looking soldier on the front seat ventured to say, "Madam, do you never sleep?" "Never when I'm a-traveling," was the curt reply; and she talked on to the baby: "Look at all them mules—what a sight of fodder they must eat! The Yankees come down to fight us, 'cause we'se got niggers and they ain't got none. I wish there warn't no niggers. I hate the Yankees, and I hate niggers too," etc., until we got to Strasburg. She then called out to "Uncle Ben" not to carry her to the depot—she was "agwine to her uncle's." "Whar's that?" cried Uncle Ben. "I don't know, but monstrous nigh a tailor's." One of the passengers suggested that we might be left by the cars, and had better go on to the depot. But she objected, and we had become a singularly non-resisting company, and allowed her to take—what we knew she would have—her own way.

In the mean time the cars arrived, crowded with soldiers. It was very dark and cold; the confusion and noise were excessive—shouting, hallooing, hurrahing. We passed through the dense crowd, and into the cars, with some difficulty. Mr. [McGuire] returned to look for the baggage. At last all seemed ready, and off we went; but what was our horror to find that Mr. [McGuire] was not in the cars! All the stories that we had ever heard of persons being thrown from the train as they attempted to get on, arose to our imagination. The darkness and crowd were great. Might he not have been thrown from the platform? We became more and more uneasy. The conductor came by; I questioned him, thinking he might be in another car. He replied, "No, madam, there is no such gentleman on the train." At this moment the Methodist minister, who had been in the stage, introduced himself as the Rev. Mr. Jones[3]; he knew Mr. [McGuire]; he offered me his purse and his protection. I can never forget his kindness. He thought Mr. [McGuire] had not attempted to get on the train; there was so much baggage from the stage that there was some difficulty in arranging it; he would telegraph from Manassas when we stopped to change cars, and the answer would meet us at Culpeper Court-House. All this was a great relief to us. At Manassas he attended to our baggage; one piece was wanting—a box, which Mr. J[ones] had seen in Mr. [McGuire]'s hands, just before the train set off; he seemed convinced that Mr. [McGuire] was detained by an ineffectual effort to get that box on the car. At Culpeper Court-House we found J[ames McGuire] waiting for us at the depot. Our kind and Rev. friend did not give up his supervision of us until he saw us under J[ames]'s care. We immediately applied at the office for our expected telegram; but it was not there. As it was Christmas-day, the office was closed at a very early hour, which seemed to me a strange arrangement, considering the state of the country. J[ames] felt no uneasiness about his father, but was greatly disappointed as he had expected to pass the day with him. I had heard in Winchester that my nephew, W. B. Phelps,[4] had been wounded in the unfortunate fight at Dranesville, and felt great uneasiness about him; but J[ames] had seen persons directly from Centreville, who reported him slightly wounded. This relieved my mind, but it was most unfortunate; for, had I known the truth, I should have gone on the return train to Manassas, and thence to Centreville, for the purpose of nursing him. We spent Christmas-day at the hotel, and dined with a number of soldiers. In the afternoon we were very much gratified to meet with the family of our neighbour, Capt. J.[5] The Captain is stationed here, and the ladies have made themselves very comfortable. We took tea with them, and talked over our national troubles: our lost homes—our scattered families and friends.

The next morning the train came at the usual hour, bringing Mr. [McGuire]. Some difficulty in putting a small box of books on the car had caused a slight detention, and as he was almost in the act of stepping on board, the train moved off, and there he was, left in the dead of a winter's night, without shelter (for, strange to say, there is no station-house at Strasburg) without light, and with no one to whom he could apply for assistance. He walked back to the village, and there, to use his own expression, he "verily thought he should have to spend the freezing night in the street." At a number of houses he knocked loud and long, but not a door was opened to him. At last a young man in an office, after giving scrutinizing glances through the window, opened his door and gave him a chair by his fire, assigning as a reason for the difficulty in getting accommodations, that the number of disorderly soldiers passing through the village made it dangerous to open the houses during the night. At daybreak he got on a freight train, hoping to find at Manassas the means of getting to Culpeper Court-House that night. In this he was disappointed, and had a most unpleasant trip on the train, which did not reach Manassas until sunset. There he found no place to sleep, and nothing to eat, until a colonel, whose name he unfortunately has forgotten, invited him to his quarters in the country. He accepted the invitation most gladly, and as it was very dark, he took a servant as a guide, who proved to know no more about the way than he did; so that both blundered and stumbled along a muddy lane, over fences, through a corn-field, over the stalks and corn-beds, until, by what seemed a mere accident, they came upon the longed-for house and found rest for the night. Next morning we joined him on the train, delighted to see him safe and sound, feeling that "all's well that ends well;"[6] we proceeded pleasantly on our journey. J[ames] accompanied us as far as Gordonsville, that he might have two hours with his father. That evening we reached this place after dark, and found a house full of friends and relatives—the house at S[ummer] H[ill] also full—so that it was a real family gathering, as in days of yore; and to add to our pleasure, our dear W. B. N.[7] was at home on furlough. Here we see nothing of war, except the uniform of the furloughed soldiers and the retrenchment in the style of living. Desserts and wine are abolished; all superfluities must go to the soldiers. In some respects we are beginning to feel the blockade; groceries are becoming scarce and high in price, but the ladies are becoming wonderfully ingenuous—coffee is so judiciously blended with parched corn, wheat or rye, that you scarcely detect the adulteration. The dressy Southern girls are giving up their handsome bonnets, wrappings, and silk dresses; they are perfectly willing to give up what once they considered absolutely necessary to their wardrobes. They say they do not enjoy such things now; they are, however, bright and cheerful; they sing patriotic songs to their furloughed friends, and listen with undying interest to anecdotes of the battle-field, with tears for the fallen, sympathy for the wounded, and the most enthusiastic admiration for deeds of daring, or for the patient endurance of the soldier. It is delightful to see the unanimity of feeling, the oneness of heart, which pervades Virginia at this time; and we believe it is so throughout the South.

We were, however, soon saddened by a letter from Centreville, from a comrade of our dear Willie Phelps to my brother,[8] saying that the wound was more severe than it was at first supposed. He immediately set out for Centreville, but none of us dreamed of real danger. The reports came from him less and less favourable; I wanted to go to him, but the letters were discouraging to me—"There was no room for me; ladies would be in the way in so small a hospital;" and some strange hallucination and blindness to danger led us to abandon the idea of going to him. We know that he had lost his arm, but did not dream of danger to his life. His mother, at her home in Covington, Kentucky, saw his name among the wounded, and notwithstanding the cold and ice, set off alone—came through Pittsburg and to Baltimore without difficulty, thence to Washington; but there no passport could be obtained to come to Virginia. Her son was but twenty miles off, certainly wounded; she knew no more. She applied in person to the proper authorities: "Is your son in the rebel camp?" was asked. "Then no passport can be given you to visit him." She remembered that General [George B.] McClellan (who had been a friend in the old army of her son-in-law, General McIntosh)[9] was in the city. She drove to his house. Mrs. [Ellen Marcy] McClellan expressed great sympathy for her, and for "your son, the interesting young man I met in Cincinnati," but regretted that General McClellan was too ill to be spoken to on any subject; he was under the influence of anodynes, etc, etc.[10] She then drove to the house of Mr. Chase,[11] who had been for many years at the bar with her husband, and on most friendly terms. The servant replied pompously that Mr. Chase never saw company at that hour. She then sent for Miss [Catherine] C[hase]. The daughter very politely regretted that her father could not be seen until the next day at ten. She could do nothing but return to the hotel for another night of suspense. Next morning, in passing through the parlours, she encountered a lady from her own State, who greeted her pleasantly; she was preparing to entertain her friends—it was New Year's day. "Won't you be with us, Mrs. P[helps]? You may meet some old friends." An apology for declining the invitation was given, by a simple statement of her object in coming to Washington. "Where is your son?" "In the Southern army." "Oh," she exclaimed, "not in the rebel camp! Not a rebel!" and she curled her lip in scorn. "Yes," was the quiet reply, "he is what you call a rebel; but it is the honoured name which Washington bore;"

and with a spirit not soothed by her countrywoman, she passed on to the street, got into a carriage, and proceeded to the house of Mr. Chase. It was ten o'clock—surely there would be no obstacle now. He soon entered—she introduced herself and her subject. Mr. C[hase] was polite, but professed to be able to do nothing for her: "I am not the proper person to whom such an application should be made." "I know that; but to whom shall I apply?" He said, "He did not know how to advise her; the case was a difficult one; your son is in the rebel camp; I think that you cannot get a passport." She then, in a state of despair, exclaimed, "Oh, Mr. Chase, he is the son of your old acquaintance, Mr. [Phelps]!" He was at once touched. "Are you his widow?" "Yes." "But how came your son to join the rebels?" "Because his father and myself were both Virginians; he was educated in Virginia, and his whole heart is in the Southern cause." He immediately wrote a note to Mr. Seward,[12] which he advised her to deliver in person; it would probably produce the desired result. To Mr. Seward's she drove. The servant invited her in, but supposed that the Secretary could not attend to business, as it was New Year's day. The note was sent up; an *attaché* soon came down to say that the Secretary could not be seen, but that a passport would be given her, to go at least as far as Fortress Monroe—no passport could be given to go immediately to Centreville. She was thankful for this permission; but it seemed too hard that she should be obliged to go around hundreds of miles, when the object could be accomplished by going twenty.

She took the evening train to Baltimore, thence, next morning, to Fortress Monroe; she reached it in safety that evening. The boat was visited by a provost-marshal as soon as it touched the wharf, who, after examining passports, took hers, and some others, to General Wool.[13] An answer from this high officer was long delayed, but at last it was brought. She could not land, but must return in the boat to Baltimore; it would leave for Baltimore next morning. She poured out her griefs to the officer, who, sympathizing with her story, said he would again apply to General Wool. He soon returned to say that she might land, and her case would be examined into next morning. Next day she was requested to walk into General Wool's office. He asked why she wanted to go into Virginia. The story was soon told. Then the stereotyped question: "Is your son in the rebel army?" with the usual answer. "Then," he replied, "you cannot go." Despair took possession of her soul. She forgot her own situation, and, with the eloquence of a mother, almost frantic with anxiety, she pleaded her cause. Even the obdurate heart of General Wool was moved. He asked her what she knew of the army at Washington. She replied, that she knew nothing; she had only seen the soldiers who passed her on the street. "What have you seen of our army here?" "Nothing, for I have been too unhappy to think of it, and only left my room when summoned by you." "Then," said he, "you may take the first boat to Norfolk." The hour for the departure of the boat came, her trunk was duly searched, and she came off to the dearly-loved Confederacy. She reached Norfolk too late for the [railroad] cars, and had to wait until the next day. On reaching Richmond, she heard that her son had been brought to this place, and was doing well. The next evening she arrived here in a carriage, and was shocked and disappointed to find that she had been misinformed. Heavy tidings reached us that night: he was not improving, as we had hoped, but decidedly worse. At two o'clock in the morning I accompanied her to the depot, eight miles off, and we went on to Manassas; reached the junction after night, and were met by our brother [W. S. R. Brockenbrough] and W. B. N[ewton]. They knew that we would be in the cars, and came to meet us. As they approached us, I saw, by the dim light of the car-lamp, that their countenances were sad. My heart sunk within me. What could it be? Why had they both left him? She had not seen them, and said to me, "Come, we must get an ambulance and go to Centreville to-night." But in another moment the whole was told. Her child had died that morning, just ten hours before. Who can describe that night of horrors? We spent it in a small house near the depot. Friends and near kindred were full of sympathy, and the people in whose house we were, were kind and considerate. The captain of his company, a noble young friend from her own home, Covington, came to see her, and to condole with her; but her first-born was not—the darling of her heart had passed away! At daylight we were in the cars again, on our melancholy return. On the third day his dear remains were brought to us, and the mother saw her heroic son, in his plain soldier's coffin, but beautiful in death, committed to God's own earth, having fallen in a glorious cause, in the faith of the Gospel, and with a bright hope of a blessed immortality. The young Kentucky friend who accompanied his remains told her his last words, which were a wonderful consolation to her: "Tell my mother that I die in the faith of Christ; her early instructions have been greatly blessed to me; and my last word is, Mother." This was said in extreme weakness. He soon slept, and never awoke in this world. One young soldier said to me that night, at Manassas: "He was one of the bravest men I ever saw, and met death like a soldier." Another said: "He died like a Christian." Scarcely had we buried him, when news was brought us that her younger, now her only son, was desperately ill on the steamer "Jamestown,"[14] on James River—he belongs to our navy. She hurried to Richmond, and thence down the river to the steamer, but found him better. He was soon well enough to accompany her to this place. She had left her home suddenly, and must return to it; so after a few days with her boy, who is now decidedly convalescent, she has left him in our care, and has set off on her weary way home. She will probably meet with no difficulties on her return from officials, as she has passports through our lines; but she has a lonely, dreary way before her, and a sorrowful story for her young daughter at home. God be with her!

Richmond, February 5—For two weeks my diary has been a closed book. After another week at W[estwood], we went to the Presbyterian Parsonage,[15] to join the refugee family who had gathered within its walls. They had made themselves comfortable, and it had quite a *home-like* appearance. After remaining there a day or two, Mr. [McGuire] received a letter announcing his appointment to a clerkship in the Post-Office Department. The pleasure and gratitude with which it is received is only commensurate with the necessity which made him apply for it. It seems a strange state of things which induces a man, who is ministered and served the altar for thirty-six years, to accept joyfully a situation purely secular, for the sole purpose of making his living; but no chaplaincy could be obtained except on the field, which would neither suit his health, his age, nor his circumstances. His salary will pay his board and mine in Richmond, and the girls will stay in the country until they or I can obtain writing from Government—note-signing from Mr. Memminger,[16] or something else. We are spending a few days with our niece, Mrs. H. A. C.,[17] until we can find board. Mr. [McGuire] has entered upon the duties of his office, which he finds confining, but not very arduous. To-morrow I shall go in pursuit of quarters.

The city is overrun with members of Congress, Government officers, office-seekers, and strangers generally. Main Street is as crowded as Broadway, New York; it said that every boarding-house is full.

February 6—Spent this day in walking from one boarding-house to another, and have returned fatigued and hopeless. I do not believe there is a vacant spot in the city.[18] A friend, who considers herself *nicely* fixed, is in an uncarpeted room, and so poorly furnished that, besides her trunk, she has only her wash-stand drawer in which to deposit her goods and chattels; and yet she amuses herself at it, and seems never to regret her handsomely furnished chamber in Alexandria.

7th—Walking all day, with no better success. "No vacant room" is the universal answer. I returned at dinner-time, wearied in mind and body. I have been cheered by suggestions that perhaps Mrs.——, with a large family and small income, may take boarders; or Mrs.——, with a large house and small family, may do the same.

8th—I have called on the two ladies mentioned above. The lady with the small income has filled her rooms, and wishes she had more to fill. She of the large house and small family had "never dreamed of taking boarders," was "surprised that such a thing had been suggested," looked cold and lofty, and meant me to *feel* that she was far too rich for that. I bowed myself out, feeling not a little scornful of such airs, particularly as I remembered the time when she was not quite so grand. I went on my way speculating on the turning of the wheel of fortune,[19] until I reached the house of an old acquaintance, and rang her bell, hoping that she might take in wanderers. This I did not venture to suggest, but told her my story in pitiful tones. She was all sympathy, and would be glad to take us in, but for the reserve of a bachelor brother to whom the house belonged. She appreciated the situation, and advised me to call on Mrs. —— on —— Street. Nothing daunted by past experience, I bent my steps to —— Street, and soon explained my object to Mrs. ——. She had had vacant rooms until two days ago, but a relative had taken both. Though she spoke positively, she looked doubtful, and I thought I saw indecision in the expression of her mouth. I ventured to expostulate: "Perhaps the lady might be induced to give up one room." She hesitated, and gave me an inquiring look. I told her my history. "An Episcopal minister," she exclaimed; "I'm an Episcopalian, and would be delighted to have a minister in the house. Do you think he would have prayers for us sometimes?" "Oh, certainly, it would gratify him very much." "Well, the lady is not at home to-day, but when she comes I will try to persuade her to do it. Call on Monday." I thanked her and was walking out, when she called me back, saying, "You will not expect a constant fire in the parlour, will you?" "Oh, no; I can take my visitors to my own room." "Well, I may be out on Monday morning; come in the evening." I returned very much pleased, and received the congratulations of my friends, who are taking much interest in our welfare.

We are suffering great uneasiness about the country. The enemy is attacking Roanoke Island furiously.[20] General Wise is there, and will do all that can be done; but fears are entertained that it has not been properly fortified.

Sunday Night—Painful rumours have been afloat all day. Fort Henry, on [the] Tennessee River, has been attacked.[21]

We went to St. James's this morning, and St. Paul's tonight. When we returned we found Mr. N. and Brother J. awaiting us.[22] They are very anxious and apprehensive about Roanoke Island.

Monday Night—Still greater uneasiness about Roanoke Island. It is important to us—is said to be the key to Norfolk; indeed, to all Eastern North Carolina, and Southeastern Virginia. We dread to-morrow's papers.

The lady on —— Street has disappointed me. She met me with a radiant smile when I went to see her this evening, saying, "She agrees; she must, however, remove the wardrobe and bureau, as she wants them herself; but there's a closet in the room, which will answer for a wardrobe. And I reckon that a table with a glass on it will do for a bureau." "Oh, yes, only give me a good bed, some chairs and a washstand, and I can get along very well. Can I see the room?" "Yes, it is a back-room in the third story, but I reckon you won't mind that." My heart did sink a little at that communication, when I remembered Mr. [McGuire's] long walks from Bank Street; but there was no alternative, and I followed her up the steps. Great was my relief to find a large airy room, neatly carpeted, and pleasant in all respects. "This will do," said I; "take the wardrobe and bureau out, and put a table in, and I shall be very well satisfied." "I have a very small table," she replied, "but no glass; you will have to buy that." "Very well, I will do that. But you have not yet told me your terms." "Will you keep a fire?" "Oh, certainly, in my room." "Then my charge is ——." I stood aghast. "My dear madam," said I, "that is twenty dollars more than the usual price, and three dollars less than our whole salary per month." "Well, I can't take a cent less; other people take less because they want to fill their rooms, but I am only going to take you for accommodation; and I can fill my rooms at any time." Now the lines of her face were not undecided. I turned, and as I walked up the already lighted streets of my native city, feeling forlorn and houseless,

> "In happy homes I saw the light
> Of household fires gleam warm and bright;"[23]

and hope that I was not envious. My friends were very sympathetic when I returned, not, however, without a certain twinkle of the eye denoting merriment, as it exactly coincided with a most provoking prophecy made by Mr. C[laiborne] as I set out; and I joined in a hearty laugh at my own expense, which was a real relief to my feelings.

No good news from Roanoke Island. Fort Henry has fallen; the loss is treated lightly, but the enemy have turned their attention to Fort Donelson, on Cumberland River, which, if taken, would give them free access into the heart of Tennessee.

Tuesday—Roanoke Island has fallen—no particulars heard.

12th—The loss of Roanoke Island is a terrible blow. The loss of life not very great. The "Richmond Blues"[24] were captured, and their Captain, the gifted and brave O. Jennings Wise, is among the fallen. My whole heart overflows towards his family; for, though impetuous in public, he was gentle and affectionate at home, and they always seemed to look upon him with peculiar tenderness. He is a severe loss to the country. Captain Coles,[25] of Albemarle [County], has also fallen. He was said to be an interesting young man, and a gallant soldier. The Lord have mercy upon our stricken country!

13th—Donelson is holding out bravely. I shudder to think of the loss of life.

Notwithstanding the rain this morning, I renewed my pursuit after lodgings. With over-shoes, cloak and umbrella, I defied the storm, and went over to Grace Street, to an old friend who sometimes takes boarders. Her house was full, but with much interest she entered into my feelings, and advised me to go to Mr. L.,[26] who, his large school having declined, was filling his rooms with boarders. His wife was the daughter of a friend, and might find a nook for us. I thought of the "Hare and many friends," and bent my steps through the storm to the desired haven. To my surprise,

Mrs. L[efebvre] said we could get a room; it is small, but comfortable, the terms suit our limited means, and we will go as soon as they let us know that they are ready for us.

We have just been drawn to the window by sad strains of martial music. The bodies of Captains Wise and Coles were brought by the cars, under special escort. The military met them, and in the dark, cold night, it was melancholy to see the procession by lamplight, as it passed slowly down the street.[27] Captain Wise has been carried to the Capitol, and Captain Coles to the Central Depot, thence to be carried to-morrow to the family burying-ground at Enniscorthy, in Albemarle County. Thus are the bright, glorious young men of the Confederacy passing away. Can their places be supplied in the army? In the hearts and homes of families there must ever be a bleeding blank.

Sunday, 16th—This morning we left home early, to be present at the funeral of Captain Wise, but we could not even approach the door of St. James's Church, where it took place. The church was filled at an early hour, and the street around the door was densely crowded. The procession approached as I stood there, presenting a most melancholy *cortege*. The military, together with civil officers of every grade, were there, and every countenance was marked with sorrow. As they bore his coffin into the church, with sword, cap, and cloak resting upon it, I turned away in sickness of heart, and thought of his father and family, and of his bleeding country, which could not spare him. We went to St. Paul's, and heard an excellent sermon from the Rev. Mr. Quintard,[28] a chaplain in the army. He wore the gown over the Confederate gray—it was strange to see the bright military buttons gleam beneath the canonicals. Every thing is strange now!

Tuesday Morning—The wires are cut somewhere between this and Tennessee. We hear nothing farther West than Lynchburg; rumours are afloat that Donelson has fallen. We are too unhappy about it to think of any thing else.

Evening—It is all true. Our brave men have yielded to overpowering numbers. The struggle for three days was fearful. The dread particulars are not known.[29] Wild stories are told of the numbers captured. God in his mercy help us!

Wednesday, 19th—We are now in our own comfortable little room on Grace Street, and have quite a home-like feeling. Our children in the city are delighted to have us so near them, and the girls have come on a visit to their cousin, Mrs. C[laiborne] and will be present at the inauguration on the 22d.

February 22—To-day I had hoped to see our President inaugurated, but the rain falls in torrents, and I cannot go. So many persons are disappointed, but we are comforted by knowing that the inauguration will take place, and that the reins of our government will continue to be in strong hands. His term of six years must be eventful, and to him, and all others, so full of anxiety! What may we not experience during those six years! Oh, that all hearts may this day be raised to Almighty God for his guidance! Has there been a day since the Fourth of July, 1776, so full of interest, so fraught with danger, so encompassed by anxiety, so sorrowful, and yet so hopeful, as this 22d of February, 1862? Our wrongs then were great, and our enemy powerful, but neither can the one nor the other compare with all that we have endured from the oppression, and must meet in the gigantic efforts of the Federal Government. Our people are depressed by our recent disasters, but our soldiers are encouraged by the bravery and endurance of the troops at Donelson. It fell, but not until human nature yielded from exhaustion. The Greeks were overcome at Thermopylae, but were the Persians encouraged by their success? Did they still cherish contempt for their weak foe? And will the conquerors of Donelson meet our little army again with the same self-confidence? Has not our Spartan band inspired them with great *respect* for their valour, to say nothing of awe?

Our neighbour in the next room had two sons in that dreadful fight. Do they survive? Poor old lady! She can hear nothing from them; the telegraph wires in Tennessee are cut, and mail communication very uncertain. It is so sad to see the mother and sister quietly pursuing their avocations, not knowing, the former says, whether she is not the second time widowed; for on those sons depend not only her comfort, but her means of subsistence, and that fair young girl, always accustomed to perfect ease, is now, with her old mother, boarding—confined to one room, using her taste and ingenuity, making and altering bonnets for her many acquaintances, that her mother may be supplied with the little luxuries to which she has always been accustomed, and which, her child says, "mother must have." "Our property," she says, "is not available, and, of course, 'the boys' had to give up their business to go into the army."

23d—Notwithstanding the violence of the rain yesterday, the Capitol Square, the streets around it, and the adjacent houses, were crowded. The President stood at the base of that noble equestrian statue of Washington, and took the oath which was taken by the "Father of his Country" more than seventy years ago—just after the "great rebellion," in the success of which we all, from Massachusetts to Georgia, so heartily gloried.[30] No wonder that he spoke as if he were inspired. Was it not enough to inspire him to have the drawn sword of Washington, unsheathed in defence of his invaded country, immediately over his head, while the other hand of his great prototype points encouraging to the South? Had he not the life-like representations of Jefferson, George Mason, and, above all, of Patrick Henry, by his side? The latter with his scroll in his outstretched hand, his countenance beaming, his lips almost parted, and seeming on the point of bursting into one blaze of eloquence in defence of his native South. How could Southern tongues remain quiet, or Southern hearts but burn within us, when we beheld our heroes, living and dead, surrounding and holding up the hands of our great chief? By him stood his cabinet, composed of the talent and the patriotism of the land; then was heard the voice of our beloved Assistant Bishop, in tones of fervid eloquence, beseeching the blessings of Heaven on our great undertaking.[31] I would that every young man, from the Potomac to the Rio Grande, could have witnessed the scene.

Last night was the first levee. The rooms were crowded. The President looked weary and grave, but was all suavity and cordiality, and Mrs. [Varina Howell] Davis won all hearts by her usual unpretending kindness. I feel proud to have those dear old rooms, arousing as they do so many associations of my childhood and youth, filled with the great, the noble, the *fair* of our land, every heart beating in unison, with one great object in view, and no wish beyond its accomplishment, as far as this world is concerned.[32] But to-day is Saturday, and I must go to the hospital to take care of our sick—particularly to nurse our little soldier-boy. Poor child, he is very ill!

27th—Nothing new or important in our army. We were relieved to hear that the number who surrendered at Donelson was not so great as at first reported; the true number is 7,000, which is *too* many for us to lose! I trust they may be kindly treated. I know that we have friends at the North, but will they dare to be friendly openly? Oh, I hope they may have mercy on our prisoners! We have had some hope of recognition by France and England, but they still look on with folded arms.

March 3—Last Friday was the third day appointed by our President as a day of fasting and prayer within nine months. The churches were filled to overflowing, with, I trust, heart-worshippers, and I believe that God, in his great mercy, will direct our Government and our army.

4th—In *status quo* as far as our armies are concerned. The *Nashville*, a Confederate steamer, that has been watched by eight Federal war vessels, came into port the other day, at Beaufort, North Carolina, after many hair-breadth escapes, bringing a rich burden.[33]

Ash-Wednesday, March 5—This morning Dr. [Richard Hooker] Wilmer gave us a delightful sermon at St. Paul's. He will be consecrated to-morrow Bishop of Alabama. To-night Bishop [Stephen] Elliott of Georgia preached for us, on the power of thought for good or evil. I do admire him so much in every respect.

6th—To-day we saw Bishop Wilmer consecrated—Bishop Meade presiding, Bishops Johns and Elliott assisting. The services were very imposing, but the congregation was grieved by the appearance of Bishop Meade; he is so feeble![34] As he came down the aisle, when the consecration services were about to commence, every eye was fixed on him; it seemed almost impossible for him to reach the chancel, and while performing the services he had to be supported by the other Bishops. Oh, how it made my heart ache! And the immense crowd was deeply saddened by it.

7th—Just returned from the hospital. Several severe cases of typhoid fever require constant attention. Our little Alabamian seems better, but so weak! I left them for a few minutes to go to see Bishop Meade; he sent for me to his room. I was glad to see him looking better, and quite cheerful. Bishops Wilmer and Elliott came in, and my visit was very pleasant. I returned to my post by the bedside of the soldiers. Some of them are very fond of hearing the Bible read; and I am yet to see the first soldier who has not received with apparent interest any proposition of being read to from the Bible. To-day, while reading, an elderly man of strong, intelligent face sat on the side of the bed, listening with interest. I read the wars of the Israelites and Philistines. He presently said, "I know why you read that chapter; it is to encourage us, because the Yankee armies are so much bigger than ours; do you believe that God will help us because we are weak?" "No," I said, "but I believe that if we pray in faith, as the Israelites did, that God will hear us." "Yes," he replied, "but the Philistines didn't pray, and the Yankees do; and though I can't bear the Yankees, I believe some of them are Christians, and pray as hard as we do; ["Monstrous few of 'em," grunted out a man lying near him;] and if we pray for one thing, and they pray for another, I don't know what to think of our prayers *clashing.*" "Well, but what do you think of the justice of our cause? Don't you believe that God will hear us for the justice of our cause?" "Our cause," he exclaimed, "yes, it is just; God knows it is just. I never thought of looking at it that way before, and I was *mighty* uneasy about the Yankee prayers. I am *mightily obleeged* to you for telling me." "Where are you from?" I asked. "From Georgia." "Are you not over forty-five?" "Oh, yes, I am turned of fifty, but you see I am monstrous strong and well; nobody can beat me with a rifle, and my four boys were a-coming. My wife is dead, and my girls are married; and so I rented out my land, and came too; the country hasn't got men enough, and we mustn't stand back on account of age, if we are hearty." And truly he has the determined countenance, and bone and sinew, which makes a dangerous foe on the battle-field. I wish we had 50,000 such men. He reminds me of having met with a very plain-looking woman in a store the other day. She was buying Confederate gray cloth, at what seemed a high price. I asked her why she did not apply to the quartermaster and get it cheaper. "Well," she replied, "I *knows* all about that, for my three sons is in the army; they gets their clothes *thar;* but you see this is for my old man, and I don' think it would be fair to get his clothes from *thar,* because he ain't never done nothing for the country as yet—he's just *gwine* in the army." "Is he not very old to go into the army?" "Well, he's fifty-four years old, but he's well and hearty like, and ought to do something for his country. So he says to me, says he, 'The country wants men; I wonder if I could stand marching; I've a great mind to try.' Says I, 'Old man, I don't think you could, you would break down; but I tell you what you can do—you can drive a wagon in the place of a young man that's driving, and the young man can fight.' Says he, 'So I will'—and he's agwine just as soon as I gits these clothes ready, and that won't be long." "But won't you be very uneasy about him?" said I. "Yes, indeed; but you know he ought to go—them wretches must be driven away." "Did you want your sons to go?" "Want 'em to go!" she exclaimed; "yes, if they hadn't agone, they shouldn't a-staid whar I was. But they wanted to go, *my* sons did." Two days ago, I met her again in a baker's shop; she was filling her basket with cakes and pies. "Well," said I, "has your husband gone?" "No, but he's agwine to-morrow, and I'm getting something for him now." "Don't you feel sorry as the time approaches for him to go?" "Oh, yes, I shall miss him mightily; but I ain't never cried about it; I never shed a tear for the old man, nor for the boys neither, and I ain't agwine to. Them Yankees must not come a-nigh to Richmond; if they does, I will fight them myself. The women must fight, for they *shan't* cross Mayo's Bridge; they *shan't* git to Richmond." I said to her, "You are a patriot." "Yes, honey—ain't you? Ain't everybody?" I was sorry to leave this heroine in homespun, but she was too busy buying cakes, etc., for the "old man" to be interested any longer.

8th—The family of Captain ——,[35] of the navy, just arrived. They have been *refugeeing* in Warrenton; but now that there is danger of our army falling back from the Potomac to the Rappahannock, they must leave Warrenton, and are on their way to Danville. Their sweet home is utterly destroyed; the house burned, etc. Like ourselves, they feel as though their future was very dark.

March 11th—Yesterday we heard good news from the mouth of James River. The ship "Virginia," formerly the Merrimac, having been completely incased with iron, steamed out into Hampton Roads, ran into the Federal vessel Cumberland, and then destroyed the Congress, and ran the Minnesota ashore.[36] Others were damaged. We have heard nothing further; but this is glory enough for one day, for which we will thank God and take courage.

13th—Our hearts are overwhelmed to-day with our private grief. Our connection, Gen. James McIntosh, has fallen in battle.[37] It was at Pea Ridge, Arkansas, on the 7th, while making a dashing cavalry charge. He had made one in which he was entirely successful, but seeing the enemy reforming, he exclaimed, "We must charge again. My men, who will follow me?" He then dashed off, followed by his whole brigade. The charge succeeded, but the leader fell, shot through the heart. The soldiers returned, bearing his body! My dear J. and her little Bessie are in Louisiana.[38] I groan in heart when I think of her. Oh that I was near her, or that she could come to us! These are the things which are so unbearable in this war. That noble young man, educated at West Point, was Captain in the army, and resigned when his native Georgia seceded. He soon rose to the rank of Brigadier, but has fallen amid the flush of victory, honoured, admired and beloved by men and officers. He has been buried at Fort Smith.[39] The Lord have mercy upon his wife and child! I am thankful that he had no mother to add to the heart-broken mothers of this land. The gallant Texas Ranger, General Ben McCulloch, fell on the same day;[40] he will be sadly missed by the country. In my selfishness I had almost forgotten him, though he doubtless has many to weep in heart-sickness for their loved and lost.

Bishop Meade is desperately ill to-day—his life despaired of.

March 14th—Our beloved Bishop Meade is dead![41] His spirit returned to the God who gave, redeemed, and sanctified it, this morning about seven o'clock. The [Episcopal] Church in Virginia mourns in sackcloth for her great earthly head. We knew that he must die, but this morning, when we had assembled for early prayers, it was announced to us from the pulpit, a thrill of anguish pervaded the congregation, which was evident from the death-like stillness. A hymn was read, but who could then sing? A subdued effort was at last made, and the services proceeded. Like bereaved children we mingled our prayers and tears, and on receiving the benediction, we went silently out, as in the pressure of some great public calamity, and some bitter, heartfelt sorrow. Thus, one week after the solemn public services in which he had been engaged, it pleased Almighty God to remove him from his work on earth to his rest in heaven. During his last illness, though often suffering intensely, he never forgot his interest in public affairs. The blessed Bible was first read to him, each morning, and then the news of the day. He had an eye for every thing; every movement of Government, every march of the troops, the aspect of Europe, and the Northern States, every thing civil and military, and all that belonged to God's Church upon earth—dying as he had lived, true to Virginia, true to the South, true to the Church, and true to the Lord his God.

Saturday Night—Spent to-day at the hospital. Heard of the shelling at Newbern, N.C., and of its fall.[42] My heart sickens at every acquisition of the

Federals. No further news from Arkansas. Yesterday evening I went to see the body of our dear Bishop; cut a piece of his hair; kissed his forehead, and took my last look at that revered face.

Monday Night—This morning I was at the funeral, at St. Paul's Church; the service was read by the Rev. J. P. McGuire and Rev. C. J. Gibson.[43] Bishop Johns made a most solemn address.[44] The procession, long and sad, then wended its way to Hollywood Cemetery.

15th—Our army has fallen back to the Rappahannock, thus giving up the splendid Valley and Piedmont country to the enemy.[45] [B]ut it almost breaks our hearts to think of it. Winchester was occupied last Wednesday! Lord, how long shall our enemies prosper? Give us grace to bear our trials.

24th—Our people continue to make every effort to repel the foe, who, like the locusts of Egypt, overrun our land, carrying the bitterest enmity and desolation wherever they go. Troops are passing through Richmond on their way to Goldsborough, N.C., where it is said that [Union Gen. Ambrose E.] Burnside is expected to meet them. Everybody is busy in supplying their wants as they pass through. On Sunday, just as the girls of one of the large seminaries were about to seat themselves at table, the principal of the school came in: "Young ladies," he said, "several extra trains have arrived, unexpectedly filled with troops. The committee appointed to attend them are totally unprepared. What can we do to help our hungry soldiers?" "Give them our dinner," cried every young voice at once. In five minutes baskets were filled and the table cleared. When the girls reached the cars, the street was thronged with ladies, gentlemen, children, servants, bearing waiters, dishes, trays, baskets filled with meats, bread, vegetables, etc. Every table in Richmond seemed to have sent its dinner to Broad Street. And our dear, dusty, hungry gray coats dined to their hearts' content, filled their haversacks, shouted "Richmond forever!" and went on their way rejoicing.

March 27—This has been a day of uneasiness to us all. General Jackson has had a fight at Kernstown, near Winchester. No particulars except that the enemy were repulsed, and our loss heavy.[46] Many that are so dear to us are in that "Stonewall Brigade;" and another day of suspense must pass before we can hear from them. Our Western army under Beauregard are fighting at Island No. 10, with what success we know not.[47] The enemy presses us on every side.

29th—After much anxiety, more authentic information from the "Valley" received this morning. We gave them a good fight, but the field was left in the enemy's hand. Poor, noble Winchester, to what degradation is she brought! Our dear W. B. C.[48] was shot through the hip; the wound painful, but not mortal; he was carried to Staunton, and his mother has gone to him. The rest of our own peculiar "boys" are safe, but many lives were lost. It is thought that a great crisis is at hand. The Peninsula is the place appointed by rumour for a great battle. The croakers[49] dread much from their numbers; my trust is in One who can save by many or by few.

April 7—Just returned from a little trip to the country in time to hear the morning news of a splendid victory yesterday, at Shiloh. No particulars received. Skirmishing near Yorktown reported; nothing definite.

9th—Our victory at Shiloh complete,[50] but General Albert Sidney Johnston was killed. The nation mourns him as one of our most accomplished officers. He fell while commanding in the thickest of the fight. It is an overwhelming loss to the Western army, and to the whole country. Beauregard pursued the enemy, but their General (Grant) having been reinforced very largely, our army had to retreat to Corinth, which they did in good order. This was done by order of General Johnston, should [Gen. Don Carlos] Buell reinforce Grant. They are now at Corinth, awaiting an attack from the combined forces. [Gen. Earl] Van Dorn reinforced Beauregard. We are anxiously awaiting the result.

10th—Spent yesterday in the hospital by the bedside of Nathan Newton, our little Alabamian.[51] I closed his eyes last night at ten o'clock, after an illness of six weeks. His body, by his own request, will be sent to his mother. Poor little boy! He was but fifteen, and should never have left his home. It was sad to pack his knapsack, with his little gray suit, and coloured shirts, so neatly stitched by his poor mother, of whom he so often spoke, calling to us in delirium, "Mother, mother," or, "Mother, come here." He so often called me mother, that I said to him one day, when his mind was clear, "Nathan, do I

look like your mother?" "No, ma'am, not a bit; nobody is like my mother."
The packing of his little knapsack reminds me of

The Jacket of Gray[52]

"Fold it carefully, lay it aside,
Tenderly touch it, look on it with pride,
For dear must it be to our hearts evermore,
The jacket of gray, our loved soldier-boy wore.

"Can we ever forget when he joined the brave band
Who rose in defence of our dear Southern land,
And in his bright youth hurried on to the fray—
How proudly he donned it, the jacket of gray?

"His fond mother blessed him, and looked up above,
Commending to Heaven the child of her love;
What anguish was hers, mortal tongues may not say,
When he passed from her sight in his jacket of gray.

"But his country had called him, she would not repine,
Though costly the sacrifice placed on its shrine;
Her heart's dearest hopes on the altar she lay,
When she sent out her boy in his jacket of gray.

"Months passed, and war's thunders rolled over the land,
Unsheathed was the sword, and lighted the brand;
We heard in the distance the sound of the fray,
And prayed for our boy in the jacket of gray.

"'Ah vain, all in vain,' were our prayers and our tears;
The glad shout of victory rang in our ears;
But our treasured one on the battle-field lay,
While the life blood oozed out on the jacket of gray.

"Fold it carefully, lay it aside,
Tenderly touch it, look on it with pride,

For dear must it be to our hearts evermore,
The jacket of gray our loved soldier-boy wore.

"His young comrades found him, and tenderly bore
The cold lifeless form to his home by the shore;
Oh, dark were our hearts on that terrible day
When we saw the dead boy in the jacket of gray.

"Ah, spotted and tattered, and stained now with gore,
Was the garment which once he so proudly wore;
We bitterly wept as we took it away,
And replaced with death's white robes the jacket of gray.

"We laid him to rest in his cold, narrow bed,
And 'graved on the marble we placed o'er his head,
As the proudest of tributes our sad hearts could pay,
He never disgraced the poor jacket of gray.

"Fold it carefully, lay it aside,
Tenderly touch it, look on it with pride,
For dear must it be to our hearts evermore,
The jacket of gray our loved soldier-boy wore."

11th—The "Virginia" went out again to-day.[53] The Federal Monitor would not meet her, but ran to Fortress Monroe, either for protection, or to tempt her under the heavy guns of the fortress; but she contented herself by taking three brigs and one schooner, and carrying them to Norfolk, with their cargoes. Soldiers are constantly passing through town. Every thing seems to be in preparation for the great battle which is anticipated on the Peninsula.

Fort Pulaski has surrendered to the enemy's gun-boats.[54] The garrison fought until several breaches were made. They then surrendered, and are now prisoners. Lord, have them in thy holy keeping!

15th—A panic prevails lest the enemy should get to Richmond. Many persons are leaving town. I can't believe that they will get here, though it seems to be their end and aim. My mind is much perturbed; we can only go on doing our duty, as quietly as we can.

20th—On Wednesday we saw eight thousand troops pass through town. We were anxious to see many who were among them. The sidewalks were thronged with ladies, many of them in tears. General C.[55] passed with his brigade, containing the 17th, with its familiar faces. Colonel H[erbert] and himself rode to the sidewalk for a shake of the hand, but the rest could only raise their hats in recognition. I knew the cavalry would pass through Franklin Street, and hurried there to see my dear W. B. N[ewton]. The order "Halt" was given just as he, at the head of his troop, was passing. I called him aloud. Amid the din and tumult of course he could not hear, but as he raised his cap to salute the ladies near him, his quick eye met mine; in an instant he was at my side: "My dear aunt, what are you doing here?" "I came to look for you; where are you going?" "Our orders extend to the steamers at the wharf," he replied; "but don't be uneasy, we are going to the right place." His face glowed with animation, and I meant to appear cheerful to him, but I found, after he was gone, that my face was bathed in tears. They all looked as if the world were bright before them, and we were feeling the appalling uncertainty of all things. A mother stood by,[56] straining her weeping eyes for the parting glance of her first-born; and so many others turned their sad, weary steps homewards, as their dear ones passed from their sight.

21st—The ladies are now engaged making sand-bags for the fortifications at Yorktown; every lecture-room in town crowded with them, sewing busily, hopefully, prayerfully. Thousands are wanted. No battle, but heavy skirmishing at Yorktown. Our friend, Capt. McKinney, has fallen at the head of a North Carolina regiment.[57] Fredericksburg has been abandoned to the enemy. Troops passing through towards that point. What does it all portend? We are intensely anxious; our conversation, while busily sewing at St. Paul's Lecture-Room, is only of war. We hear of so many horrors committed by the enemy in the Valley—houses searched and robbed, horses taken, sheep, cattle, etc., killed and carried off, servants deserting their homes, *churches desecrated.*[58]

27th—The country is shrouded in gloom because of the fall of New Orleans.[59] It was abandoned by General Lovell—necessarily, it is thought. Such an immense force was sent against the forts which protected it, that they could not be defended. The steamer *Mississippi,* which was nearly finished, had to be burnt.[60] We hoped so much from its protection to the Mississippi River.

Oh, it is so hard to see the enemy making such inroads into the heart of our country! It makes the chicken-hearted men and women despondent, but to the true and brave it gives a fresh stimulus for exertion. I met two young Kentuckians to-night who have come out from their homes, leaving family and fortunes behind, to help the South. After many difficulties, running the blockade across the Potomac, they reached Richmond yesterday, just as the news of the fall of New Orleans had overwhelmed the city. They are dreadfully disappointed by the tone of the persons they have met. They came burning with enthusiasm; and anything like depression is a shock to their excited feelings. One said to me that he thought he should return at once, as he had "left every thing which made home desirable to help Virginia, and found her ready to give up." All the blood in my system boiled in an instant. "Where, sir," said I, "have you seen Virginians ready to give up their cause?" "Why," he replied, "I have been lounging about the Exchange [Hotel] all day, and have heard the sentiments of the people." "Lounging about the Exchange! And do you suppose that Virginians worthy of the name are now seen loung-ing about the Exchange? There you see the idlers and shirkers of the whole Southern army. No true man under forty-five is to be found there. Virginia, sir, is in the camp. Go there, and find the true men of the South. There they have been for one year, bearing the hardships, and offering their lives, and losing life and limb for the South; it is mournful to say how many! There you will find the chivalry of the South; and if Virginia does not receive you with the shout of enthusiasm which you anticipated, it is because the fire burns steadily and deeply; the surface blaze has long ago passed away, I honour you, and the many noble young Kentuckians who have left their homes for the sake of our country, but it will not do for Kentucky to curl the lip of scorn at Virginia. Virginia blushes, and silently mourns over her recreant daughter, and rejoices over every son of her who has the disinterestedness to leave her and come to us in this hour of our bitter trial."

I do not believe that this young man really means, or wishes to return; he only feels disheartened by the gloom caused by our great national loss.

May 2d—The morning papers contain a most spirited letter by the Mayor of New Orleans,[61] in reply to the Federal commander who demanded the surrender of the city, and that the Confederate flag should be taken down. He refuses to do either, telling him that the city is *his* by *brute force*, but he will never surrender it.

Our young friend J. S. M.,[62] is here, very ill; I am assisting to nurse him. I feel most anxious about him; he and his four brothers are nobly defending their country. They have strong motives, personal as well as patriotic. Their venerable father and mother, and two young sisters, were forced to leave their comfortable home in Fairfax a year ago. The mother has sunk into the grave, an early sacrifice, while the father and sisters continue to be homeless. Their house has been burnt to the ground by Federal soldiers—furniture, clothing, important papers, all consumed. Sad as this story is, it is the history of so many families that it has ceased to call forth remark.

3d—It is distressing to see how many persons are leaving Richmond, apprehending that it is in danger; but it will not—I know it will not—fall. It is said that the President does not fear; he will send his family away, because he thinks it better for men, on whom the country's weal is so dependent, to be free from private anxiety. General Johnston is falling back from Yorktown, not intending to fight within range of the enemy's gun-boats. This makes us very anxious about Norfolk.

May 5th—Yesterday we had a blessed Sabbath, undisturbed by rumours; it is generally a day of startling reports set afloat by idlers. The Bishop preached and administered confirmation at St. Paul's. The President was a candidate for confirmation, but was detained by business.[63] It is such a blessing to have so many of our public men God-fearing, praying Christians!

7th—Our "peaceful" Sabbath here was one of fearful strife at Williamsburg.[64] We met and whipped the enemy. Oh, that we could drive them from our land forever! W. B. N[ewton] is reported "missing"—oh, that heart-breaking word! How short a time since that blessed glimpse of his bright face, as he passed through town, and now he is on his weary way to some Northern prison; at least we *hope so*. His poor wife and mother! Our young friend G. W. was killed![65] How many bright hopes were crushed in one instant by the fall of that boy! I thank God that he had no mother. General Johnston still falls back,[66] leaving the revered Alma Mater of our fathers to be desecrated, perhaps burned. A party of Yankees landed on Sunday at the White House.[67] That Pamunky country, so fertile, now teeming with grain almost ready for the sickle, is at their mercy; we can only hope that they have no object in destroying it, and that they will not do it wantonly. W[estwood] and

S[ummer] H[ill] and their dear inmates are painfully near them. Richmond, or the *croakers* of Richmond, have been in a panic for two days, because of the appearance of gun-boats on James River. I believe they will not get nearer than they are now. I sat up last night at the hospital with D. L.,[68] who is desperately ill—his mother in the Federal lines. My companion during the night was Colonel M.,[69] of Maryland. While listening to the ravings of delirium, two gentlemen came in, announcing heavy firing on the river. We had been painfully conscious of the firing before, but remembering that Drury's Bluff was considered impregnable, I felt much more anxious about the patient than about the enemy.[70] The gentlemen, however, were panic-stricken, and one of them seemed to think that "sunrise would find gun-boats at Rocketts."[71] Not believing it possible, I felt no alarm, but the apprehensions of others made me nervous and unhappy. At daybreak I saw loads of furniture passing by, showing that people were taking off their valuables.

12th—Just returned from a visit to S[ummer] H[ill]. The family full of patriotism and very bright. While there, W[illiam Newton]'s horse and servant came home. His family bore it well, considering imprisonment the least casualty that could have befallen him.[72] If Richmond is invested, that beautiful country will be in the hands of the enemy; the families (except the gentlemen) will remain at home to protect the property as best they may. They are now sending corn, bacon, etc., into Richmond for safety. None but the croakers believe for an instant that it will fall.

Two hours ago we heard of the destruction of the "Virginia" by our own people.[73] It is a dreadful shock to the community. We can only hope that it was wisely done. Poor Norfolk must be given up. I can write no more to-day.

13th—General Jackson is doing so gloriously in the Valley that we must not let the fate of the "Virginia" depress us too much.[74] On the 9th of May he telegraphed [Adjutant] General [Samuel] Cooper: "God blessed our arms with victory at McDowell yesterday." Nothing more has been given us officially, but private information is received that he is in hot pursuit down the Valley. The croakers roll their gloomy eyes and say, "Ah, General Jackson is so rash!" and a lady even assured me that we had every thing to fear from the campaign he was now beginning in the Valley. I would that every officer and soldier in the Southern army was crazed in the same way; how soon we would be free from despotism and invasion!

May 14—The anxiety of all classes for the safety of Richmond is now intense, though a strong faith in the goodness of God and the valour of our troops keeps us calm and hopeful. A gentleman, high in position, panic-struck, was heard to exclaim, yesterday: "Norfolk has fallen, Richmond will fall, Virginia is to be given up, and to-morrow I shall leave the city, an exile and a beggar." Others are equally despondent, and, as is too frequently the case in times of trouble, attribute all our disasters to the incompetency and faithlessness of those entrusted with the administration of public affairs. Even General Lee[75] does not escape animadversion, and the President is the subject of the most bitter maledictions. I have been shocked to hear that a counter-revolution, if not openly advocated, has been distinctly foreshadowed, as the only remedy for our ills. The public authorities of Richmond, greatly moved by the defenceless condition of the city, appointed a committee, and appropriated funds to aid in completing the obstructions at Drury's Bluff.[76] The Legislature also appointed a committee to wait upon the President and ascertain the progress of the work. A member of this committee, a near con-nection of mine,[77] has given me an account of their interview with Mr. Davis. He received them, as is his invariable custom, with marked cordiality and respect. The subject was opened by the chairman of the Senate Committee, who stated the object of the mission, and then made appropriate inquiries for information. The President proceeded to give a distinct narrative of the progress of the work, expressed his great desire for its early completion, and regretted that the natural difficulties arising from frequent freshets in the river, which the efforts of man could not overcome, had rendered the prog-ress of the work slow. He said he had just returned from a visit to the Bluff, accompanied by General Lee; and having heard complaints against the man in charge of the work, he had discharged him, and had appointed another, strongly recommended for efficiency.[78] That the flood was now subsiding, and he thought he could assure the committee that the obstruction of the river would be complete in twenty-four hours. At this point the door-bell rang, and General Lee was announced. "Ask General Lee in," said the President. The servant returned, saying that the General wished to see the President for a few moments in the ante-room. The President retired, met General Lee and the Secretary of the Navy [Stephen F. Mallory], and soon returned to the committee. The conversation being renewed, some further inquiry was made with regard to Drury's Bluff. The President replied: "I should have given you a very different answer to your question a few moments ago from that which I shall be compelled to give you now. Those traitors at Norfolk, I fear, have defeated our plans," "What traitors?" asked nearly every member of the committee at the same moment. He then proceeded to give a detail of the desertion of the captain and crew of a steamer engaged in transporting guns from Norfolk to Drury's Bluff, who had gone over to the enemy with vessel and cargo,[79] and full information as to the unfinished condition of the works. A member of the committee asked: "Can nothing be done to counteract these traitors?" The President replied: "Every thing will be done, I assure you, which can be done." The member continued: "But, Mr. President, what will be done?" The President politely declined to answer the question, saying there were some things that it was not proper to communicate. The member again pressed for the information, saying: "This is a confidential meeting, and, of course, nothing transpiring here will reach the public." The President, with a smile on his countenance, said: "Mr. ——, I think there was much wisdom in the remark of old John Brown at Harper's Ferry: 'A man who is not capable of keeping his own secrets is not fit to be trusted with the business of other people.'" There was no unpleasant feeling manifested in the committee, and the parting was kind and cordial on both sides; yet, next morning, it was rumoured on the streets that the President had been rude to the committee, and that the meeting had been extremely unpleasant. On the night of this meeting the river was obstructed by the sinking of the steamer *Patrick Henry,* and other vessels, in the channel.[80] This, it is supposed, was the plan agreed upon by Mr. Davis and General Lee in their short interview. Several days have passed since this interview, and I trust that all is now safe. How thankful I am that I knew nothing of this until the danger was passed!

The Legislature is in almost constant session during these dark days. It contains many gentlemen of great intelligence and of ardent zeal in the public cause.[81] The whole body is as true as steel, and its constant effort is to uphold the hands of the President, to fire the popular heart, and to bring out all the resources of Virginia in defence of the liberty and independence of the South. I am told that day after day, and night after night, "thoughts that breathe and words that burn"[82] are uttered in the hall, which, in other days, had often rung with the eloquence of the noblest statesmen, patriots, and orators of the land. These proceedings are all in secret session, and, for prudential reasons, are withheld from the public; but are they never to see the light? Is no one taking note of them? I trust so, indeed, that the civil history of Virginia, during this great struggle, may not be lost to posterity.[83]

15th—It is now ascertained beyond doubt that my nephew, W. B. N[ewton], reported "missing" at Williamsburg, is a prisoner in the enemy's hands. We are very anxious for his exchange, but there seems some difficulty in effecting it.[84] His father, accompanied by Colonel Robertson,[85] of the Fourth Virginia Cavalry, called to see the President a few nights ago, hoping to do something for him. The President had just returned from a long ride to inspect the fortifications. In answer to their card, he desired to see the gentlemen in his study, where he was reclining on a sofa, apparently much fatigued, while Mrs. Davis sat at a table engaged in some fine needle-work. The President immediately arose and received the gentlemen most courteously, introducing them to Mrs. D[avis]. Colonel R[obertson] stated the object of the visit, saying that Captain N[ewton] was one of the very best officers of his rank in the army, and that his services were almost indispensable to his regiment, and urged the President to use every effort to procure his exchange. His father seconded the request with the warmth natural to a parent under such circumstances. The President seemed deeply interested in the subject, and regretted that nothing could then be done, as there was a difficulty pending between the belligerents on the subject of exchange; as soon as that difficulty was removed he would, with pleasure, do all in his power to procure the exchange. Mrs. Davis listened with much interest to the conversation, and her feelings became warmly interested. She said that her husband was a father, and would feel deep sympathy; but if, in the pressure of public business, the subject should pass from his mind, she would certainly remind him of it. She made a very favourable impression on the minds of these gentlemen, who had never seen her before, by her ease of manner, agreeable conversation, and the kindness of heart which she manifested. After a most pleasant interview of an hour, the visitors arose to leave, but Mrs. Davis invited them with so much cordiality to remain and take a cup of tea with them, which, she said, was then coming up, that they could not decline. The servant brought in the tea-tray, accompanied by some light refreshment. Mrs. D[avis] poured out the tea for the company of four. The scene reminded them of the unpretending and genial hospitality daily witnessed in the families of Virginia.

18th—The 16th was the day appointed by the President for fasting and prayer. The churches here were filled, as I trust they were all over the land.

27th—General Jackson's career going on gloriously.[86] After defeating [Gen. Robert H.] Millroy, and [Gen. John C.] Fremont's advance in the Valley, and driving them back in confusion, so that nothing was to be feared from [their] threatened union with Banks, he pursued the enemy as far as Franklin, Pendleton County. Then returning, he marched on rapidly, captured Front Royal on the 23d, chasing the enemy through it at more than double-quick. Still pressing hard upon Banks, he gave him no rest night or day, piercing his main column while retreating from Strasburg to Winchester—the "rear part retreating towards Strasburg. On Sunday, 25th, the other part was routed at Winchester. At last accounts, Brigadier-General George H. St[e]uart[87] was pursing them with cavalry and artillery, and capturing many." I quote from the General's own telegram, dated Winchester, May 26th.[88] And now, notwithstanding our condition in Richmond, our hearts and voices are attuned to praise, and our paeans are more loud and bright in contrast to our late distressing trials.

29th—No official accounts from "Stonewall" and his glorious army, but private accounts are most cheering. In the mean time, the hospitals in and around Richmond are being cleaned, aired, etc., preparatory to the anticipated battles. Oh, it is sickening to know that these preparations are necessary! Every man who is able has gone to his regiment. Country people are sending in all manner of things—shirts, drawers, socks, etc., hams, flour, fresh vegetables, fruits, preserves—for the sick and wounded. It is wonderful how these things can be spared. I suppose, if the truth were known, that they cannot be spared, except that every man and woman is ready to give up every article which is not absolutely necessary; and I dare say that gentlemen's wardrobes, which were wont to be numbered by dozens, are now reduced to couples.

It is said that General Johnston, by an admirable series of manoeuvres, is managing to retreat from Williamsburg, all the time concealing the comparative weakness of his troops, and is retarding the advance of the enemy, until troops from other points can be concentrated here.

31st—The booming of cannon, at no very distant point, thrills us with apprehension. We know that a battle is going on. God help us! Now let every heart be raised to the God of battles.

Evening—General Johnston brought in wounded, not mortally, but painfully, in the shoulder.[89] Other wounded are being brought in. The fight progressing; but we are driving them.

Night—We have possession of the camp—the enemy's camp. The place is seven miles from Richmond. General Lee is ordered to take General Johnston's place. The fight may be renewed to-morrow.

June 1—The loss yesterday comparatively small.[90] General Johnston had managed his command with great success and ability until he received his wound. What a pity that he should have exposed himself! but we are blessed people to have such a man as General Lee to take his place. He (Gen. J.) is at the home of a gentleman on Church Hill, where he will have the kindest attention, and is free from the heat and dust of the city.[91]

2d—The battle continued yesterday near the field of the day before. We gained the day! For this victory we are most thankful. The enemy were repulsed with fearful loss; but our loss was great. The wounded were brought until a late hour last night, and to-day the hospitals have been crowded with ladies, offering their services to nurse, and the streets are filled with servants darting about, with waiters covered with snowy napkins, carrying refreshments of all kinds to the wounded. The roar of the cannon has ceased. Can we hope that the enemy will now retire? General Pettigrew is missing—is thought captured.[92] So many others "missing," never, never to be found! Oh, Lord, how many! How long are we to be a prey to the most heartless of foes? Thousands are slain, and yet we seem no nearer the end than when we began.

7th—Sad news from the Valley. The brave, gallant, dashing General Ashby has fallen![93] He was killed yesterday, in a vigorous attack made by the enemy on our rear-guard, at a point between Harrisonburg and Port Republic. The whole country will be shocked by the calamity, for it had a high appreciation of his noble character and achievements. General Jackson valued him very highly, as did both men and officers. His daring was wonderful, and wonderfully did he succeed in his dashing and heroic efforts. "His sagacity in penetrating into the designs of the enemy seemed almost intuitive."[94] It is so hard, in our weakness, to give up such men!

9th, Night—General Jackson is performing prodigies of valor in the Valley; he has met the forces of Fremont and Shields, and whipped *them in detail.* They fought at Cross Keys and Port Republic yesterday and to-day. I must preserve his last dispatch, it is so characteristic:

> "Through God's blessing, the enemy near Port Republic, was this day routed, with the loss of six pieces of artillery."
>
> "T. J. Jackson,
> "Major-General Commanding."[95]

And now we are awaiting the casualties from the Valley. This feeling of perpetual anxiety keeps us humble amid the flush of victory.[96] What news may not each mail bring us, of those as dear as our heart's blood? Each telegram that is brought into the hospital makes me blind with apprehension until it passes me, and other countenances denote the same anxiety; but we dare not say a word which may unnerve the patients; they are rejoicing amid their pain and anguish over our victories. Poor fellows! Dearly have they paid for them, with the loss of limb, and other wounds more painful still. They want to be cured that they may be on the field again. "Thank God," said a man, with his leg amputated, "that it was not my right arm, for then I could never have fought again; as soon as this stump is well I shall join Stuart's cavalry; I can ride with a wooden leg as well as a real one."

The "Young Napoleon" does not seem to be dispirited by his late reverses.[97] The *New York Herald* acknowledges defeat of the 31st, but says they recovered their loss next day; but the whole tone of that and other Northern papers proves that they *know* that their defeat was complete, though they will not acknowledge it. They are marshalling their forces for another "On to Richmond." O God, to Thee, to Thee alone, do we look for deliverance. Thou, who canst do all things, have mercy upon us and help us!

June 12—We are more successful in Virginia than elsewhere. The whole Mississippi River, except Vicksburg and its environs, is now in the hands of the enemy, and that place must surrender, though it holds out most nobly, amidst the most inveterate efforts to take it. Memphis has fallen! How my spirit chafes and grieves over our losses! O God, let us not be given over a "hissing and a reproach to our enemies."[98]

15th—General Stuart has just returned to camp after a most wonderful and successful raid.[99] He left Richmond two or three days ago with a portion of his command; went to Hanover Court-House, where he found a body of the enemy; repulsed them, killing and wounding several, and losing one gallant man, Captain Latane, of the Essex cavalry;[100] continuing his march by the "Old Church," he broke up their camp and burnt their stores; thence to Tunstall's Station on the York River Railroad; fired into the train, destroying a part of it, and taking some prisoners; thence to Pamunky River; found three transports loaded with provender, which they burned; filled their haversacks with West India fruit, which had been brought on for Federal consumption; then went on towards Charles City Court-House, encountering a train of wagons; took their horses, mules, and drivers, and burnt the wagons and contents; thence they went to a Yankee sutler's stand, took what they wanted, and burnt the rest; thence across the Chickahominy and on to Richmond; bringing 175 prisoners and a number of horses and mules. We are all full of excitement and delight, hoping that he discovered much about the Federal army which may be useful, but which, of course, is kept from the public; and I trust most fervently that our dear ones at S[ummer] H[ill] and W[estwood] may have been cheered by their presence, for they must have gone very near them, if not immediately by their gates—how the appearance of our men must have excited them! I wish I could see some member of the cavalry who could tell me all about it—where they went, and whom they saw. General Stuart must have gone, it is said, within a few miles, perhaps nearer, of his father-in-law, the Federal General Cooke.[101] I wonder what the old renegade Virginian thinks of his dashing son-in-law? If he has a spark of proper feeling left in his obdurate heart, he must be proud of him.

June 27th—Yesterday was a day of intense excitement in the city and its surroundings. Early in the morning it was whispered about that some great movement was on foot. Large numbers of troops were seen under arms, evidently waiting for orders to march against the enemy. A. P. Hill's Division occupied the range of hills near "Strawberry Hill,"[102] the cherished home of my childhood, overlooking the old "Meadow Bridge."

About three o'clock, the order *to move*, so long expected, was given.[103] The Division marched steadily and rapidly to the attack—the Fortieth Regiment, under command of my relative, Col. B.,[104] in which are so many of our dear boys, leading the advance. The enemy's pickets were just across the river, and the men supposed they were in heavy force of infantry and artillery, and that the passage of the bridge would be hazardous in the extreme; yet their courage did not falter. The gallant Fortieth, followed by Pegram's Battery,[105] rushed across the bridge at double-quick, and with exultant shouts drove the enemy's pickets from their posts. The enemy was driven rapidly down the river to Mechanicsville, where the battle raged long and fiercely. At nine o'clock all was quiet; the bloody struggle over for the day. Our victory is said to be glorious, but not complete. The fighting is even now renewed, for I hear the firing of heavy artillery. Last night our streets were thronged until a late hour to catch the last accounts from couriers and spectators return-ing from the field. A bulletin from the Assistant Surgeon of the Fortieth,[106] sent to his anxious father, assured me of the safety of some of those dear to me; but the sickening sight of the ambulances bringing in the wounded met my eye at every turn. The President, and many others, were on the surrounding hills during the fight, deeply interested spectators. The calm-ness of the people during the progress of the battle was marvellous. The balloons of the enemy hovering over the battle-field could be distinctly seen from the outskirts of the city, and the sound of musketry was distinctly heard. All were anxious, but none alarmed for the safety of the city. From the firing of the first gun till the close of the battle, every spot favourable for observation was crowded. The tops of the Exchange, the Ballard House, the Capitol, and almost every other tall house were covered with human beings; and after nightfall the commanding hills from the President's house to the Alms-House[107] were covered, like a vast amphitheatre, with men, women, and children, witnessing the grand display of fireworks—beautiful, yet awful—and sending death amid those whom our hearts hold so dear. I am told (for I did not witness) that it was a scene of unsurpassed magnificence. The brilliant light of bombs bursting in the air and passing to the ground, the innumerable lesser lights, emitted by thousands and thousands of muskets, together with the roar of artillery and the rattling of small-arms, constituted a scene terrifically grand and imposing. What spell has bound our people? Is their trust in God, and in the valour of our troops, so great that they are unmoved by these terrible demonstrations of our powerful foe? It would seem so, for when the battle was over the crowd dispersed and retired to their respective homes with the seeming tranquility of persons who had been witnessing a panorama of transactions in a far-off country, in which they felt no personal interest;[108] though they knew that their countrymen slept on their arms, only awaiting the dawn to renew the deadly conflict, on the success of which depended not only the fate of our capital, but of that splendid army, containing the material on which our happiness depends. Ah! many full, sorrowful hearts were at home, breathing out prayers for our success; or else were busy in the hospitals, administering to the wounded. Those on the hill-sides and house-tops were too nervous and anxious to stay at home—not that they were apprehensive for the city, but for the fate of those who were defending it, and their feeling was too deep for expression. The same feeling, perhaps, which makes me write so much this morning. But I must go to other duties.

Ten o'Clock at Night—Another day of great excitement in our beleaguered city. From early dawn the cannon has been roaring around us. Our success has been glorious! The citizens—gentlemen as well as ladies—have been fully occupied in the hospitals. Kent, Paine & Co.[109] have thrown open their spacious building for the use of the wounded. General C. of Texas,[110] aid[e] to General [John B.] Hood, came in from the field covered with dust, and slightly wounded; he represents the fight as terrible beyond example. The carnage is frightful. General Jackson has joined General Lee, and nearly the whole army on both sides were engaged. The enemy has retired before our troops to their strong works near Gaines's Mill. Brigade after brigade of our brave men were hurled against them, and repulsed in disorder. General Lee was heard to say to General Jackson, "The fighting is desperate; can our men stand it?" Jackson replied, "General, I know our boys—they will never give back."[111] In a short time a large part of our force was brought up in one grand attack, and then the enemy was utterly routed. General C[hambers] represents the valour of Hood and his brigade in the liveliest of colours, and attributes the grand success at the close of the day greatly to their extraordinary gallantry. The works were the strongest ever seen in this country, and General C[hambers] says that the armies of the world could not have driven our men from them.

Another bulletin from the young surgeon of the Fortieth.[112] That noble regiment has lost heavily—several of the "Potomac Rifles" among the slain—sons of old friends and acquaintances.[113] E. B.,[114] dreadfully wounded, has been brought in, and is tenderly nursed. Our own boys are mercifully spared. Visions of the battle-field have haunted me all day. Our loved ones, whether friends or strangers—all Southern soldiers are dear to us—lying dead and dying; the wounded in the hot sun, the dead being hastily buried. McClellan is said to be retreating. "Praise the Lord, O my soul!"

28th—The casualties among our friends, so far, not very numerous. My dear R. T. C[olston] is here, slightly wounded; he hopes to return to his command in a few days. Colonel Allen, of the Second Virginia, killed. Major Jones, of the same regiment, desperately wounded.[115] Wood McDonald killed.[116] But what touches me most nearly is the death of my young friend, Clarence Warwick, of this city.[117] Dearly have I loved that warm-hearted, high-minded, brave boy, since his early childhood. To-night I have been indulging sad memories of his earnest manner and affectionate tones, from his boyhood up; and now what must be the shock to his father and brothers, and to those tender sisters, when to-morrow the telegraph shall tell them of their loss! His cousin, Lieutenant-Colonel Warwick,[118] is desperately wounded. Oh, I pray that his life may be spared to his poor father and mother! He is so brave and skillful an officer that we cannot spare him, and how can they? The booming of cannon still heard distinctly, but the sound is more distant.

June 30—McClellan certainly retreating. We begin to breathe more freely; but he fights as he goes. Oh, that he may be surrounded before he gets to the gun-boats [on the James River]. Rumours are flying about that he is surrounded; but we do not believe it—only hope that he may be before he reaches the river. The city is sad, because of the dead and dying, but our hearts are filled with gratitude and love. The end is not yet—oh that it were!

Mecklenburg County, July 15—Mr. [McGuire] and myself summoned here a short time ago to see our daughter, who was very ill. Found her better—she is still improving.

Richmond is disenthralled—the only Yankees there are in the "Libby" and other prisons. McClellan and his "Grand Army," on the James River, near Westover, enjoying mosquitoes and bilious fevers. The weather is excessively hot. I dare say the Yankees find the "Sunny South" all that their most fervid imaginations ever depicted it, particularly on the marshes. The gun-boats are rushing up and down the river, shelling the trees on the banks, afraid to approach Drury's Bluff. The Northern papers and Congress are making every effort to find out to whom the fault of their late reverses is to be traced. Our people think that their whole army might have been captured but for the dilatoriness of some of our generals. General Magruder is relieved, and sent to take command in the West.[119]

21st—Mr. [McGuire] sick, but better to-day. This is the anniversary of the glorious battle of Manassas. Since that time we have had many reverses, but our victories, of late, have atoned for all, except the loss of life.

We have had another naval fight on the Mississippi, just north of Vicksburg. Our large gun-boat, *Arkansas,* ran into the Federal fleet of twelve or thirteen gun-boats and rams, and overcame them completely.[120] Vicksburg stands the bombardment with unflinching gallantry. No news from the Army of the Potomac. It is reported that General Jackson has gone to meet General Pope, who is on this side of the Blue Ridge [Mountains], marching, it is supposed, to join McClellan.[121]

Mr. [McGuire] takes a ride to-day; the first since his sickness. My heart is full of gratitude for public and private blessings.

23d—Letters and papers to-day. It is reported that Hindman has captured Curtis and whole command in Arkansas.[122] Delightful, if true. The army in Virginia, and our dear ones, well.

28th—The report of Hindman's having captured Curtis untrue; but our army is doing well in the West. Murfreesboro, in Tennessee, has been captured by Confederates—a brigade, two brigadiers, and other officers taken.[123] "Jack Morgan" is annoying and capturing the Kentucky Yankees.[124]

The true Southerners there must endure an almost unbearable thralldom!

A long letter from S. S.,[125] describing graphically their troubles when in Federal lines. Now they are breathing freely again. A number of servants from W[estwood] and S[ummer] H[ill] and indeed from the whole Pamunky River, went off with their Northern friends. I am sorry for them, taken from their comfortable homes to go they know not where, and to be treated they know not how. Our man Nat went, to whom I was very partial, because his mother was the maid and humble friend of my youth, and because I had brought him up. He was a comfort to us as a driver and hostler, but now that we have neither home, carriage, nor horses, it makes but little difference with us; but how, with his slow habits, he is to support himself, I can't imagine. The wish for freedom is natural, and if he prefers it, so far as I am concerned he is welcome to it. I shall be glad to hear that he is doing well. Mothers went off leaving children—in two instances infants. Lord have mercy upon these misguided creatures! I am so thankful that the scurf of the earth, of which the Federal army seems to be composed, has been driven away from Hanover. I would that "Clarke" [County] were as free.

July 29—No army news. In this quiet nook mail-day is looked forward to with the greatest anxiety, and the newspapers are read with avidity from beginning to end—embracing Southern rumours, official statements, army telegrams, Yankee extravagances, and the various *et ceteras*. The sick and wounded in the various hospitals are subjects for thought and action in every part of our State which is free to act for them; we all do what we can in our own little way; and surely if we have nothing but prayer to offer, great good must be effected. Yesterday evening, while walking out, a young woman with a baby in her arms passed us rapidly, weeping piteously, and with the wildest expressions of grief; we turned to follow her, but found that another woman was meeting her, whom we recognized as her mother; in another moment all was explained by her father, whom we met, slowly wending his way home-ward. He had been to the hospital at Danville[126] to see his son-in-law, whose name appeared among the wounded there. On reaching the place, he found that he had just been buried. On returning he met his daughter walking; in her impatience and anxiety about her husband, she could not sit still in the house; and in her ignorance, she supposed that her father would bring him home to be nursed. Poor thing! she is one of thousands. Oh that the enemy may be driven from our land, with a wholesome dread of encroaching upon our borders again! Our people are suffering too much; they cannot stand it. The family here suffers much anxiety, as each battle approaches, about their young son, the pride and darling of the household.[127] He is a lieutenant in the —— Regiment; but during the fight around Richmond, as his captain was unfit for duty, the first lieutenant killed in the first fight, the command of the company devolved on this dear, fair-haired boy, and many praises have they heard of his bravery during those terrible days. He writes most delightfully encouraging letters, and never seems to know that he is enduring hardships. His last letter, written on a stump near Charles City Court-House, whither they had followed the enemy, was most exultant; and brave young Christian as he is, he gives the glory to God. He exults in having helped to drive them, as it were, *pen them up* on the river; and though they are now desecrating the fair homes of our ancestors (Berkeley and Westover), yet, as they dare not unfurl their once proud banner on any other spot in Lower Virginia, and only there because protected by their gun-boats, he seems to think that the proud spirits of the Byrds and Harrisons may submit when they reflect that though their ancestral trees may shelter the direst of foes, yet their *ancestral* marshes are yielding their malaria and mosquitoes with an unstinting hand, and aiding unsparingly the sword of the South in relieving it of invaders. Dear B[enjamin], like so many Southern boys, he was summoned by the tocsin of war from the class-room to the camp. His career was most successful in one of the first literary institutions in the country, and if he lives he will return to his studies less of a scholar, but more of a man, in the highest sense of the word, than any collegiate course could have made him. But we can't look forward, for what horrors may come upon us before our independence is achieved it makes my heart ache to dwell upon.

August 4—The girls just returned from a visit to Mrs. A. of several days, which they enjoyed greatly.[128] Every thing there very bright and cheerful, except the hearts of the parents—they yearn for their sons on the field of danger! A battle is now expected between Jackson and Pope.

August 5—The papers of last night brought us no news, except that our troops are firing upon the enemy's gun-boats near Coggin's Point.[129] The result not known. A battle between Jackson and Pope still imminent. Major Bailey made a brilliant cavalry raid a few days since upon the enemy in Nicholas County,[130] in which he took the command of a lieutenant-colonel prisoners, burnt their stores, and brought off many horses, mules, and arms. Morgan continues his successful raids in the West. The enemy has abandoned the siege of Vicksburg at this time.

9th—We hear of a little cavalry fight at Orange Court-House, in which we drove off the enemy. General Pope continues to commit depredations in his district of operations. He seems to have taken Butler as his model, and even to exceed him in ferocity. Our President has just given most sensible orders for retaliation.[131]

The Misses N.[132] are spending the summer here. Their home in Clarke in possession of the enemy, together with their whole property, they are dividing their time among their friends. It is sad to see ladies of their age deprived of home comforts; but, like the rest of the refugees, they bear it very cheerfully. Born and reared at Westover, they are indignant in the highest degree that it should now be desecrated by McClellan's army. They are deeply mourning the death of their noble young cousin, Captain B. Harrison,[133] of Upper Brandon, who was killed at the head of his troop, in one of the battles near Richmond.

Lynchburg, August 20—Mr. [McGuire] and myself arrived here last night, after a most fatiguing trip, by Clarksville, Buffalo Springs, then to Wolf's Trap Station on the Danville [Rail]road, and on to the Southside Railroad. The cars were filled with soldiers on furlough. It was pleasant to see how cheerful they were. Poor fellows! it is wonderful when we consider what the next battle may bring forth. They were occupied discussing the late battle at Cedar Run,[134] between General Jackson and a portion of Pope's army, commanded by [Gen. Nathaniel P.] Banks. It was a very fierce fight, and many casualties on both sides; but we won the day—the Lord be praised! Lynchburg is full of hospitals, to which the ladies are very attentive; and they are said to be very well kept. I have been to a very large one to-day, in which our old home friends, Mrs. R.[135] and Miss E. M.,[136] are matrons. Every thing looked beautifully neat and comfortable. As a stranger, and having so much to do for my patient at home, I find I can do nothing for the soldiers, but knit for them all the time, and give them a kind word in passing. I never see one without feeling disposed to extend my hand, and say, "God bless you."

29th—The Richmond papers of yesterday mention two severe skirmishes on the Rappahannock within a week. The enemy are retreating through Culpeper Court-House, etc., and our men are driving them on. General Jackson has reached Warrenton. Burnside's army is said to be near Fredericksburg, and Pope retreating towards Manassas. The safe situation of this town makes it a city of refuge to many. Several of our old friends are here. Mr. and Mrs. D.,[137] of Alexandria, are just across the passage from us; the J[ohns]'s are keeping house, and Mrs. M. is boarding very near us. This evening our friends the S's arrived. None but persons similarly situated can know the heartfelt pleasure of meeting with home friends, and talking of home scenes—of going back, as we did this evening, to the dear old times when we met together in our own parlours, with none to make us afraid.

We see very little of Lynchburg society, but in this pleasant boarding-house, with *refugee society,* we want nothing more. The warmest feelings of my heart have been called forth, by meeting with one of the most intimate friends of my youth—now Mrs. Judge D.[138] We met the other day in the church-door, for the first time for many, many years. Time has done its work with us both, but we instantly recognized each other. Since that time, not a day has passed without some affectionate demonstration on her part towards us. At her beautiful home, more than a mile from town, I found her mother, my venerable and venerated friend, Mrs. Judge C.[139] still the elegant, accomplished lady, the cheerful, warm-hearted, Christian Virginia woman. At four-score, the fire kindles in her eye as she speaks of our wrongs. "What would your father and my husband have thought of these times," she said to me—"men who loved and revered the *Union,* who would have yielded up their lives to support the Constitution, in its purity, but who could never have given up their cherished doctrines of State rights, nor have yielded one jot or tittle of their independence to the aggressions of the North?" She glories in having sons and grandsons fighting for the South. Two of the latter have already fallen in the great cause; I trust that the rest may be spared to her.

I see that the Northern papers, though at first claiming a victory at "Cedar Run," now confess that they lost three thousand killed and wounded, two generals wounded, sundry colonels and other officers. The *Times* is severe upon Pope—thinks it extraordinary that, as he knew two days before that the battle must take place, he did not have a larger force at hand; and rather *"strange"* that he should have been within six miles of the battle-field, and did not reach it until the fight was nearly over! They say, as usual, that they were greatly outnumbered. Strange, that with their *myriads,* they should be so frequently outnumbered on the battle-field! It is certain that our loss there was comparatively very small; though we have to mourn General Winder of the glorious Stonewall Brigade, and about two hundred others, all valuable lives.[140]

August 30—A package arrived last night from our sisters, with my sister M's[141] diary, for my amusement. It was kept while our dear ones of W[estwood] and S[ummer] H[ill] were surrounded by McClellan's army. I shall use my leisure here in copying it, that our children's children may know all that our family suffered during this cruel war. During the six weeks that they were surrounded by the foe, we only heard from them through letters written to their husbands in Richmond. These letters were captured by the enemy, and published in a New York paper; and one was republished in the Richmond *Enquirer,* where we were most delighted to find it. In that way W. B. N[ewton], then incarcerated in the walls of Fort Delaware,[142] heard from his mother, wife, and children, for the first time since he was captured, in March.

Mrs. N[ewton]'s diary begins:

"*May 18th*—S[ummer] H[ill], Hanover County, Va. C. M.[143] and myself set off yesterday morning for church. At my brother's gate we met Dr. N,[144] who told us that there were rumours of the approach of the enemy from the White House. We then determined not to go to our own church, but in another direction, to the Presbyterian church. After waiting there until the hour for service had arrived, an elder came in and announced to us that the minister thought it prudent not to come, but to have the congregation dismissed at once, as the enemy was certainly approaching. We returned home in a most perturbed state, and found that my husband had just arrived, with several of our sons and nephews, to spend a day or two with us. In a short time a servant announced that he had seen the Yankees that morning at the "Old Church." Then there was no time to be lost; our gentlemen must go. We began our hurried preparations, and sent for the carriage and buggy. We were told that the driver had gone to the Yankees. After some discussion, one of the gentlemen determined to drive, and they were soon off. It was then eleven o'clock at night, and the blackness of darkness reigned over the earth. It was the most anxious night of my life. Surrounded by an implacable foe, our gentlemen all gone, we knew not how long we should be separated, or what might not happen before we met, and the want of confidence in our servants, which was now for the first time shaken, made us very nervous. This morning we went to W[estwood], and took leave of our sister, Mrs. C.,[145] and daughters. Her sons are in the army, and being a refugee, she says she must follow the army, and go where she can reach them if they are wounded. We found C[atherine] busily dividing her year's supply of bacon among the servants, that each may take care of his own. As the enemy never regards locks, she knows that her meat-house will be unsafe; we secreted two guns, which had been inadvertently left, and returned, feeling desolate, but thankful that our gentlemen were safely off.

"*22d*—Papers from Richmond to-day. We are not yet in the enemy's lines.

"*23d*—The enemy's pickets gradually encroaching upon us. A squad of their cavalry has been in the Hanover Town lane all day; five or six lancers, with their red streamers, rode slowly by our gate this morning. C[atherine] encountered them in her walk home, and had a conversation with an officer, Major Doyle,[146] who made many *professions of friendship!*

"*24th*—We were aroused this morning at an early hour, by the servants rushing in, exclaiming: 'The house is surrounded by Yankees, and they are coming into the house.' I rushed to the window, and there they were. An officer in the front porch, and a squad of cut-throat-looking fellows on the steps; while a number with their red streamers and lances, were dashing hither and thither; some at the stable, some at the kitchen, others around the servants' quarters and at the barn, while the lane was filled with them. Dr. T.[147] had spent the night with little L., who is ill with scarlet fever. I knocked at his door, and asked him to go down and see what the people wanted. We dressed as rapidly as possible. C. and M. had been up all night with L.,[148] and were soon ready to go down. They quickly returned, to say that the officer was Colonel Rush,[149] of Philadelphia, and demanded that my little son Edward should be sent down immediately. It was in vain that they told him that E[dward] was a mere child—he had evidently heard that he was a young man, and demanded his presence. The child was aroused from his sleep, and hastily dressed himself, but not quickly enough for our impatient Colonel, who walked to the staircase and began to ascend, when C[atherine] called to him, 'Colonel R[ush], do you mean to go to a lady's chamber before she is dressed? The boy is in his mother's room.' Somewhat abashed, he stepped back. I soon descended, accompanied by E[dward] N[ewton] and W. S.[150] There on the mat before me stood a live Yankee colonel, with an aid on either side. I approached; he pointed to W[alter] S[ydnor], saying, 'Is that Edward N[ewton]?' 'No,' said I; 'that is my grandson; this is Edward N[ewton].' He said, 'I want the boys to go with me.' Looking him full in the eye, I said, 'Sir, will you take these children prisoners?' His eye fell, and with many grimaces he replied, 'Oh, no; I only want to ask the boys a few questions.' He then took them across the lawn, I all the time watching them; asked them many questions, but finding that he could get nothing out of them, he sent them back, calling them 'little rebels,' etc. The Colonel had seen defiant looks enough while in the house, and did not return. He asked M[ary] to let him give her a remedy for scarlet fever, which Mrs. *Colonel* Huger had given him.[151] 'Mrs. *General* Huger you mean?' replied M[ary]. 'Thank you, I have perfect confidence in Dr. T[alley].' In the mean time his commissary went to the meat-house, demanded the key, and looking in, said, 'I want three hundred pounds of this bacon, and shall send for it this evening.' Another man went to the stable, took Dr. T[alley]'s horse, saddle, and bridle, and went off with them. The Colonel was immediately informed of it, *seemed* shocked, and said, 'Impossible;' but on ordering it to be brought back, it was soon returned. Presently the Quartermaster[152] rode up to the door, calling out, 'Mrs. N[ewton], three horses were in your stable last night, and they are not there now; the Colonel wishes their absence accounted for.' 'Perhaps, sir,' replied M[ary], 'they have been stolen, as the other was; but as you get your information from the servants, I refer you to them.' He rode off, and the whole party returned to their camp.

"*Monday, 26th*—A cry of 'Yankees,' this morning, sent us to the windows;[153] there we saw a regiment of Lancers, one of regulars, one of rifles, and another of zouaves, composed of the most dreadful-looking creatures I ever beheld, with red caps and trowsers; also two guns. They were on their way to the Wyoming bridge, which they destroyed, and then made a reconnaissance of the Court House road. On their return they called here, boasting that they had killed one of our men; they advised M[ary] to hang out a white flag to protect her houses, which she, of course, declined doing.

"*27th*—Last night I could not sleep, in consequence of a threat made by one of the Yankee soldiers in our kitchen. He said that 30,000 soldiers had been ordered to the Court-House to-day, to 'wipe out' our people. Were our people ignorant of this, and how should we let them know of it? These were questions that haunted me all night. Before day I formed my plan, and awakened S.[154] to consult her on the subject. It was this: to send W[alter] S[ydnor] to the Court-House, *as usual,* for our letters and papers. If the Yankee pickets stopped him, he could return; if he could reach our pickets, he could give the alarm. She agreed to it, and as soon as it was day we aroused the child, communicated to him our plan (for we dared not write); he entered into the spirit of it, and by light he was off. I got up and went down to the yard, for I could not sit still; but what was my consternation, after a short time had elapsed, to see at the gate, and all along the road, the hated red streamers of our enemy, going towards the Court-House! S[ally] and myself were miserable about W[alter]. M[ary] and C[atherine] gave us no comfort; they thought it very rash in us to send him—he would be captured, and 'Fax' (the horse) would certainly be taken. We told them that it was worth the risk to put our people on their guard; but, nevertheless, we were unhappy beyond expression. Presently a man with a wretched countenance, and, from his conversation, an abolitionist of the deepest dye, rode in to inquire if the artillery had passed along. My fears about W[alter] induced me to assume a bland countenance and manner, and I told him of having sent a little boy for the mail, and I wanted him to see that he came home safely; he said that the boy would not be allowed to pass, and promised, gruffly, to do what he could for him; but at the same time made such remarks as made our blood boil; but, remembering W[alter]'s danger, we made no reply. He said he was aid to General Warren.[155] Before he left our gate, what was our relief to see W[alter] ride in, escorted by fourteen lancers, he and his horse unmolested! The child had gone ahead of the Yankees, reached our picket, told his story, and a vidette had immediately been sent with the information to head-quarters. I then for the first time took my seat, with my heart full of gratitude for W[alter]'s safety, and feeling greatly relieved that I had done what I could. At three o'clock the firing commenced; it was very heavy for some hours; we knew they were fighting, and knew, too, that our force at the Court-House was not large. Oh, what anxious moments we have experienced this day! The firing has now ceased, and the Yankees are constantly straggling in, claiming a great victory; but we have learned to believe nothing they say.

"*28th*—Now our mail is broken up, and we feel that we are indeed in the hands of the enemy. Oh, how forsaken and forlorn we are! Yet we do what we can to cheer each other, and get on right well.

"*30th*—This morning two horsemen rode up, and seeing our cold looks, said, 'Ladies, do you take us for Yankees?' 'Of course we do—are you not Yankees?' 'Oh, no; we belong to the Augusta troop,[156] and want to hear something of the movements of the enemy.' We pointed to their pickets, and implored them to go at once. We, of course, filled their haversack, and they were scouting about the woods for some time. Oh, how our hearts go out towards our own people!

"*June 1st*—We heard very heavy firing all day yesterday, and again to-day. At one time the roar was so continuous that I almost fancied I heard the shouts of the combatants; the firing became less about twelve o'clock, and now (night) it has ceased entirely. Dr. N[elson] and Dr. T[alley] have been accused by the Yankees of having informed our people of their meditated attack the other day. They were cross-examined on the subject, and of course denied it positively. They were threatened very harshly, the Yankees contending that there was no one else in the neighbourhood that could have done it. Poor little W[alter] was not suspected at all—they little know what women and children can do.

"*7th*—We have been now surrounded by the enemy for two weeks, cut off from every relative except our two households. Our male relations, who are young enough, are all in the army, and we have no means of hearing one word from them. The roar of artillery we hear almost every day, but have no means of hearing the result. We see the picket-fires of the enemy every night, but have, so far, been less injured by them than we anticipated. They sometimes surround our houses, but have never yet searched them.

"*8th*—The *New York Herald* reports a bloody fight on the 31st of May and 1st of June. They acknowledge from 3,000 to 4,000 killed and wounded—give us credit for the victory on the first, but say they recovered on the second day what they lost on the first. I have no doubt, from their own account, that they were badly whipped; but how long shall this bloody work continue? Thousands and thousands of our men are slain, and we seem no nearer the end than at first.

"*9th*—Yankee wagons about all day, looking for corn and fodder. I am thankful to say that M[ary] has none for them, the flood of last year having destroyed W[illiam]'s corn crop. I feel to-day our short-sightedness; what they considered a calamity when the flood came, we feel now to be a blessing, as we are not able to furnish food for our foes. God forgive me for my feelings towards them; but when I see insolent fellows riding around and around our dwellings, seeking what they devour, every evil feeling of my heart is kindled against them and their whole nation. They, the murderers of our husbands, sons, fathers, thinking themselves at liberty to riot over our homesteads! They got their wagons filled from my brother's barn, and in return pretended to give a bond, which they know is not worth the paper on which it is written. One had the assurance to tell C[atherine Nelson Brockenbrough] that her husband would be paid if he took the oath of allegiance. She told him that he would not do that for all the corn in the Southern Confederacy. Within two or three days they have become very bold; they ride up and demand the key of the corn-house or meat-house, and if it is not immediately given, they break open the door and help themselves.

"*11th*—Yesterday evening we had another visit from the Lancers: they fed the horses at M[ary]'s barn, ripping off the planks that the corn might roll out. The door was opened by the overseer, but that was too slow a way for thieves and robbers. They encamped for the night in front of W[estwood]. C[atherine] was detained there yesterday by rain, and was not at home all day, and they took that opportunity for searching every thing. While they were filling the wagons at the barn, four officers went over every part of the house, even the drawers and trunks. They were moderate in their robberies, only taking some damask towels and napkins from the drawers, and a cooked ham and a plate of rolls from the pantry. These men wore the trappings of officers! While I write, I have six wagons in view at my brother's[157] barn, taking off his corn, and the choice spirits accompanying them are catching the sheep and carrying them off. This robbery now goes on every day. The worst part of our thralldom is, that we can hear nothing from our own army.

"*13th*—Good news at last. Four letters were received last night by way of Ashland. We learned that we certainly whipped the Yankees on the 31st of May and 1st of June, and that Jackson has had a most glorious campaign in the Valley. We are grieved to hear that the gallant Ashby has been killed, and trust that it is a mere rumour, and that God has spared his valuable life. My sons were not in the late fight, but are stationed at Strawberry Hill, the home of my childhood. Every thing is being stolen on these two places and elsewhere. A lieutenant on General Porter's[158] staff rode up this evening to ask M[ary] to sell him butter, fowls, eggs, etc. She told him that her poultry-yard had been robbed the night before by some of his men. He professed great horror, but had not gone fifty yards when we heard the report of a pistol, and this wonderfully proper lieutenant of a moment before had shot the hog of an old negro woman who lives here.

"*14th*—While quietly sitting on the porch yesterday evening, I saw a young man rapidly approaching the house, on foot; at first we took it for granted that he was a Yankee, but soon found from his dress that he was one of our soldiers, and from his excited manner that there was something unusual the matter. He was Lieutenant Latane,[159] of Stuart's Brigade. They had been fighting on the road from Hanover Court-House to the Old Church, and his brother, the captain of the Essex Troop, had been killed about two miles from W[estwood]. The mill-cart from W[estwood] soon after passed along, and he put his brother's body into it, and brought it to W[estwood]. There he found a Yankee picket stationed. C[atherine] immediately took the dead soldier into her care, promising to bury him as tenderly as if he were her brother; and having no horse left on the place (the enemy had taken them all), sent him here, by a private way, to elude the vigilance of the picket, to get M[ary]'s only remaining horse—for the poor fellow had given up his to a soldier whose horse had been killed. The horse was soon ready, and as soon as we saw him safely off, we went over to W[estwood] to assist in preparing the body for the burial. Oh, what a sad office! This dear young soldier, so precious to many hearts, now in the hands of sorrowing, sympathizing friends, yet, personally, strangers to him! He looked so young—not more than twenty years of age. He was shot in four places; one ball had entered the region of his heart and passed out at the back. We cut a large lock of his hair, as the only thing we could do for his mother. We have sent for Mr. Carraway[160] to perform the funeral services, and shall bury him by our dear Willie Phelps,[161] another victim to this unholy war.

"*15th*—Yesterday was the only day for three weeks that we have been free from the hated presence of Yankees. Aaron, whom we sent for Mr. C[arraway] was not allowed to pass the picket-post, so we took the body of our poor young captain and buried it ourselves in the S[ummer] H[ill] grave-yard, with no one to interrupt us. The girls covered his honoured grave with flowers. He and our precious W[illie] lie side by side, martyrs to a holy cause.

"We have heard nothing from General Stuart; he had 5,000 men and three guns. The pickets have disappeared from around us. The servant we sent for Mr. C[arraway] says that General S[tuart] burnt the encampment near the Old Church, on Saturday evening, killed many horses, and severely wounded a captain, who refused to surrender; the men scampered into the woods.[162] He represents the Yankees as very much infuriated, vowing vengeance upon our people, from which we hope that they have been badly used. We feel intensely anxious about our brigade.

"*16th*—Yesterday we sent letters to the Court-House to be mailed, presuming, as we had not seen an enemy for twenty-four hours, that the coast would be clear for awhile; but Bartlett rode into a detachment of them in Taliaferro's Lane. The poor old man, in his anxiety to save his letters, betrayed himself by putting his hand on his pocket. They were, of course, taken from him. [The letters I mentioned as having been published in the New York papers.—Mrs. McGuire] They are heartily welcome to mine; I hope the perusal will do them good, but C[atherine] is annoyed. It was the first letter she had written to her husband since the depredations at W[estwood] and she had expressed herself very freely.

"*June 17th*—The Yankees have returned upon us. They came this morning early, and caught J. W.'s[163] horse, which they took off. We can hear nothing of General S[tuart]. We presume he has returned to Richmond. We shall have to pay for it, I dare say, by being robbed, etc.; but if it has done good to the great cause, we do not mind personal loss. We are now honoured with a guard of twenty-five men—why, we are at a loss to conjecture, unless our intercepted letters may have convinced them that we are dangerous characters. We doubtless have the will to do them harm enough, but, surrounded and watched as we are, the power is wanting. Our guard is composed of regulars, who are much more decent men than the volunteers.

"C[atherine] commenced harvest yesterday, in a small way, but so many servants are gone to the Yankees, that much of the wheat must be lost, and the corn cannot be worked. The milkmaid amused herself at their remarks to them: '*Ladies,* why do you work for white people now? You are all free now,' etc., etc.

"*18th*—Our guard in full force to-day. It is so absurd to see the great fellows on their horses, armed from head to foot, with their faces turned towards us, standing at our yard-gate, guarding women and children, occasionally riding about on the gravel-walks, plucking roses, with which they decorate their horses' heads. A poor woman came to-day in a buggy, in pursuit of corn. She had been robbed by the enemy of every grain. This is the case with many others, particularly with soldiers' wives. I asked an officer to-day, what had become of General Stuart? He said he was a 'smart fellow,' and he 'guessed' he had returned to Richmond, but he 'ought to have paid a visit to his father-in-law, General Cooke, commanding the United States cavalry not many miles distant.'

"*20th*—Our guard withdrew to-day, and we walked to W[estwood], a privilege we had not enjoyed for many days. We received a Richmond *Dispatch* by *underground railroad*. General Stuart's raid was like a story on 'Arabian Nights Entertainments.'[164] He passed down from Hanover Court-House, behind the whole of McClellan's army, in many places so near as to hear the pickets, capturing and burning every thing which they could not take with them. They then crossed the Lower Chickahominy, and got back to camp before the enemy had recovered from their surprise; losing but one man, Captain Latane, whom we had the honour of burying. The man who shot him, a Federal officer, was immediately killed by a private in his (Captain L[atane]'s) company.[165] The raiders burned two transports at the White House. Destroyed any number of wagons, mules, stores, etc., and carried back 200 prisoners. The Yankees have been making vast preparations for surrounding them as they returned; but they were too wise to be caught in that trap. Their masked batteries will be of no avail this time. At New Kent Court-House our men refreshed themselves with all manner of good things, at the expense of the enemy, providing themselves with clothing, boots, etc., and taking the sleek proprietor of the establishment prisoner.

"*21st*—Yesterday we heard firing all day—heavy guns in the morning and musketry during the day, and heavy guns again in the evening. Oh, that we could know the result! This morning is as calm and beautiful as though all was peace on the earth. O God, with whom all things are possible, dispel the dark clouds that surround us, and permit us once more to return to our homes, and collect the scattered members of our flock around our family altar in peace and safety! Not a word from my husband or sons.

"*22d*—Dr. T[alley] called to-day to say that the firing we heard on Friday was from our guns shelling the enemy, to drive them lower down the Chicka-hominy. Letters, by underground railroad, from our dear William, at Fort Delaware. He complains of nothing but his anxiety to be exchanged, and the impossibility of hearing from home. C[atherine], at the same time, got a letter from my brother. He writes in good spirits about our affair. [Gen. Stonewall] Jackson's career is glorious[.] The sick and wounded are doing well; hospitals are in good order, and the ladies indefatigable in nursing. Surgeon-like, he tells more of the wounded than any thing else. Rev. Mr. C[arraway] came up to-day, and gave us some amusing incidents of Stuart's raid. As some of our men rode by Mr. B.'s[166] gate, several of them went in with Mr. B.'s sons for a few moments. A dead Yankee lay at the gate. Mrs. W. (Mrs. B.'s daughter) supposing he was only wounded, ran out with restoratives to his assistance. While standing there, two Yankees came up. Mrs. W. ordered them to surrender, which one did without the slightest hesitation, giving up his arms, which she immediately carried in to her younger brother, who was badly armed. The other escaped, but her prisoner went along with the crowd. Yankee wagons are again taking of corn from W[estwood]. The men are very impertinent to C[atherine].

"*24th*—Yankee scouts are very busy around us to-day. They watch this river, and are evidently fearing a flank movement against them. Wagons passing to Dr. N[elson]s for corn, guarded by Lancers, who are decidedly the worst speci-mens we have seen. Compared with them, the regulars are welcome guests. It is so strange that Colonel Rush, the son of a distinguished man,[167] whose mother belonged to one of the first families in Maryland, the first cousin of James M. Mason,[168] and Captain [Sidney] Mason of our navy, of Mrs. General [Samuel] Cooper and Mrs. S[idney] S[mith] Lee, should consent to come among his nearest of kin, at the head of ruffians like the Lancers, to despoil and destroy our country! I suppose that living in Philadelphia has hardened his heart against us, for the city of Brotherly Love is certainly more fierce towards us than any other. Boston cannot compare with it. This is mortifying, because many of us had friends in Philadelphia, whom we loved and admired. We hope and believe that the Quaker element there is at the foundation of their ill-will.

"*25th*—I got by chance a Philadelphia paper of the 20th. Very little bragging, but an earnest appeal to their men to be united, to forget that there will be any more presidential elections, and to let squabbling among themselves alone; that the critical time is at hand, etc.

"*Friday, 27th*—The roar of cannon and musketry has been incessant to-day; now as I sit in the yard it is terrific. I doubt not that a general engagement is going on. O God! be with us now; nerve the hearts and strengthen the arms of our men! Give wisdom and skill to the commanders, and grant us victory for thy great name's sake!

"*28th*—We have just heard of our success, and that Jackson and [Gen. Richard S.] Ewell have come from the Valley, and have flanked the enemy on the Chickahominy. Two of our troopers called in this morning.

"*July 1st*—Firing continues, but lower and lower down. No news from my dear boys. I wish, but dread, to hear.

"*2d*—My boys and nephew safe, God be praised! McClellan in full retreat. C[atherine] and M[ary] are sending off a wagon with ice, chickens, bread, eggs, vegetables, etc., to our hospital at Cold Harbor.

"*July 4th*—A beautiful, glorious day, and one which the Yankees expected confidently to spend triumphantly in Richmond. Last Fourth of July old General Scott expected to be there, to tread in triumph the fallen fortunes of our quondam friends, and to-day McClellan has been obliged to yield his visions of glory. 'Man proposes, but God disposes.'[169] Many of their companions in arms are there, in the Libby and other prisons, wounded in the hospitals, and dead in the swamps and marshes, or buried on the battle-fields while the 'Grand Army' and the 'Young Napoleon' are struggling desperately to get out of the bogs of the Chickahominy to the gunboats on James River. I sent the carriage to Richmond a day or two ago for Mr. N.,[170] but he writes that he is sending it backwards and forwards to the battle-fields for the wounded. It is a season of wide-spread distress; parties are going by constantly to seek their husbands, brothers, sons, about whose fate they are uncertain. Some old gentlemen passed yesterday, *walking* all the way from Lancaster County.[171] All the boats and bridges have been destroyed on the rivers, and conveyances can't be put across. Ladies are sent from river to river by those persons who have conveyances and horses left to them. Oh,

I trust that blood enough has been spilled now! Dr. S.[172] has just arrived; he has been twenty miles below Richmond. He says the Yankee dead still lie unburied in many places—our men are too much worn out to undertake to bury them. The Yankee hospitals, as well as our own, are all along the roads; their hospital flag is red; ours is orange. They have their own surgeons, and, of course, many delicacies that our men can't have. The Northern papers speak of this retreat of McClellan's as a 'strategic movement.' The bloody fights of eight days, the retreat of thirty miles, attended by immense loss of life, thousands of prisoners, many guns, stores of all kinds, etc., a 'strategic movement!' But our loss is heavy—so many valuable lives, and such suffering among the wounded. O God! interpose and stop this cruel war!"

I quote no further from Mrs. N[ewton]'s diary, as the next page was devoted to the visits of those dear ones whom God had preserved amid strife and danger. She mentions the return of our dear W. B. N[ewton] from Fort Delaware on the 5th of August, where he had been for several months. He asked but five days' furlough to be with his family, and then returned to his regiment (Fourth Cavalry). His reception by the company was most gratifying. As soon as he got to camp, it drew up in line, and requested him to come to the *front*, when the "Orderly" came up, leading a very handsome bay horse, elegantly equipped, which he presented to his "Captain," in the name of the company.[173]

Notes

1. Built in the early 1800s, Westwood was the home of John Brocken-brough. It adjoined Summer Hill, the 1803 mansion constructed by Mann Page III. Westwood is a two-story frame building and still in use. See *Old Homes of Hanover County, Virginia* (Hanover, Va.: Hanover County Historical Society, 1983), 60–62.

2. Two possibilities of identification exist for this figure. The more likely was Catherine Grim, listed in the 1860 Virginia Census—Frederick County as a fifty-seven-year-old housekeeper in Winchester. Another Catherine Grim appears in the 1860 Virginia Census—Shenandoah County as a twenty-seven-year-old day laborer in Mt. Jackson, south of Strasburg.

3. In 1860, Louis Richard Jones was admitted into the Methodist ministry at Winchester. Ben Ritter, Winchester, Va., to editor, March 25, 2005.

4. William Brockenbrough Phelps attended the University of Virginia

prior to his enlistment in Company C, First Kentucky. *Southern Historical Society Papers,* 33 (1905): 52. In the December 20 affair at Dranesville, the First Kentucky lost one killed and twenty-four wounded. United States War Department, *War of the Rebellion: Official Records of the Union and Confederate Armies* (Washington, D.C.: Government Printing Office, 1880–1901), series I, vol. 5, 494 (hereafter cited as *OR*).

5. Capt. James H. Jameson of the Eleventh Virginia was a native of Culpeper. He had been wounded at Dranesville and was on sick furlough with his wife and four children. Daniel E. Sutherland, *Seasons of War: The Ordeal of a Confederate Community, 1861–1865* (New York: Free Press, 1995), 78.

6. From Shakespeare's *All's Well That Ends Well.*

7. William Brockenbrough Newton, a captain in the Fourth Virginia Cavalry, was home on recruiting duty during January–February, 1862. Kenneth L. Stiles, *4th Virginia Cavalry* (Lynchburg, Va.: H. E. Howard, 1985), 128.

8. Dr. William Spencer Roane Brockenbrough and his wife, the former Catherine Page, then inhabited Westwood.

9. James McQueen McIntosh graduated last in the West Point Class of 1849. He resigned as captain of the First U.S. Cavalry in 1861 and became colonel of the Second Arkansas Mounted Rifles. In January 1862, McIntosh received promotion to brigadier general.

10. Just before Christmas 1861, McClellan fell ill with typhoid fever and did not return to duty until the first week in January. His wife was the former Ellen Marcy.

11. Salmon Portland Chase was Secretary of the Treasury in the Lincoln administration. The "Miss C" mentioned several lines down the page was Chase's second child, vivacious Catherine Jane "Kate" Chase.

12. Secretary of State William Henry Seward was the most powerful member of Lincoln's cabinet.

13. John Ellis Wool, born three years after Cornwallis's surrender at Yorktown, was the oldest officer to exercise active command on either side during the Civil War. At that time he was in charge of the Department of the East, which oversaw occupied territory such as the Fort Monroe area.

14. The *Jamestown* was then one of five small wooden gunboats comprising the James River Squadron. Early in March, the ironclad *Virginia* joined the force.

15. Mrs. McGuire was likely referring to the parsonage of the Second Presbyterian Church on Fifth Street in downtown Richmond. The Rev. Moses Drury Hoge was its first pastor and the most noted clergyman in the wartime capital.

16. Christopher Gustavus Memminger then served as Confederate Secretary of the Treasury.

17. Mrs. Herbert A. Claiborne was the former Katherine Cabell. After her husband's death, she married ex-Confederate general William Ruffin Cox. One writer stated of Mrs. Claiborne: "Few Richmond women of her generation held a more distinguished place in the city and in Virginia." Robert Beverly Munford Jr., *Richmond Homes and Memories* (Richmond, Va.: Garrett and Massie, 1936), 74.

18. Because of the crowded conditions in Richmond, most refugees experienced deep hardships. Often they walked the streets in search of lodging they could afford. Landlords charged exorbitant prices. This led to a practice called "room-keeping." Five or six families would rent a single house and then allot two to three rooms to each family. In some cases, a family might have to make do with a single room.

19. Once-prosperous refugees could not help but feel envy at those who had managed to keep the household intact. Two years after this diary entry, Mrs. McGuire was still wondering at the "wheel of fortune." Yet by then she openly resented people of wealth who would not share their good fortune with those in poorer circumstances. See diary entry for September 10, 1864.

20. Roanoke Island controlled the passage between Pamlico and Albemarle sounds on the North Carolina coast. The ten-mile strip of land was the key to Richmond's back door. In charge of the 3,000 Confederates and four artillery batteries there was Gen. Henry A. Wise. The former Virginia governor was no soldier and had been given that assignment in part to remove his carping personality from Virginia.

21. The Confederacy's principal defense on the Tennessee River, Fort Henry surrendered on February 6 after a heavy bombardment from Union warships.

22. Mrs. McGuire was referring to Willoughby Newton and John Bowyer Brockenbrough of Hanover County.

23. From Henry Wadsworth Longfellow's "Excelsior."

24. Founded in 1789, the Richmond Light Infantry Blues was a proud part of the Forty-sixth Virginia in General Wise's brigade. In command of the company was Capt. O. Jennings Wise, son of the general and editor of the *Richmond (Va.) Enquirer.* The February 8 action at Roanoke Island was costly for the Blues. It lost Captain Wise and another man dead, seven men wounded, and half of the company taken prisoner. "For the moment," a unit historian wrote, "the old Company ceased to be." John A. Cutchins, *A Famous Command: The Richmond Light Infantry Blues* (Richmond, Va.: Garrett and Massie, 1934), 112.

25. Robert Coles, a native of Philadelphia, Pa., was killed while leading his company of the Forty-sixth Virginia.

26. Hubert P. Lefebvre was headmaster of Mrs. Anna Maria Mead's school

for girls. His wife was Mary O. Lefebvre. Virginius Dabney, *Richmond: The Story of a City* (Garden City, N.Y.: Doubleday, 1976), 147; 1860 Virginia Census—James City County.

27. For public reaction to Captain Wise's death and funeral, see Sallie Brock Putnam, *Richmond during the War: Four Years of Personal Observation* (New York; G. W. Carleton, 1867), 98; Clifford Dowdey, *Experiment in Rebellion* (Garden City, N.Y.: Doubleday, 1946), 145–46.

28. Charles Todd Quintard was the Episcopal chaplain of the First Tennessee. For his activities in Richmond at this time, see Charles T. Quintard, *Doctor Quintard, Chaplain, C.S.A., and Second Bishop of Tennessee: The Memoir and Civil War Diary of Charles Todd Quintard,* ed. Sam Davis Elliott (Baton Rouge: Louisiana State University Press, 2003), 39–41.

29. Mrs. McGuire's concern was well-founded. Fort Donelson was the only major Confederate defense not only of the Cumberland River but also of the state capital of Nashville. At its fall, Grant reported the capture of "from 12,000 to 15,000 prisoners including Generals Buckner and Bushrod Johnson; also about 20,000 stand of arms, 48 pieces of artillery, 17 heavy guns, from 2,000 to 4,000 horses, and large quantities of commissary stores." *OR,* series I, vol. 7, 625.

30. A gloomier but more realistic picture of Davis's inauguration is in William C. Davis, *Jefferson Davis: The Man and His Hour* (New York: HarperCollins, 1991), 394.

31. Bishop John Johns had moved to Richmond in December 1861, and during the winter months "he preached regularly . . . and was engaged daily with increasing interest, in visiting the sick soldiers in our hospitals, ministering from cot to cot and assembling the convalescents for social worship." Sumner Wood, *The Virginia Bishop: A Yankee Hero of the Confederacy* (Richmond, Va.: Garrett and Massie, 1961), 43–44.

32. In 1818 Dr. John Brockenbrough had erected at Clay and Twelfth Streets the home that became the White House of the Confederacy. He was Judith McGuire's cousin.

33. A side-wheel steamer originally built for the coasting trade between New York and Charleston, *Nashville* became a Confederate transoceanic vessel. Early in 1862 the ship crossed the Atlantic (burning a Union schooner in the process) and successfully ran the blockade into Morehead City, N.C. This was such an embarrassment throughout the North that demands were loud for the dismissal of Secretary of the Navy Gideon Welles.

34. Bishop Johns wrote of his ailing colleague: "His advanced age, his infirmities at the time, and the inclement season, combined to render the journey

from Clarke [County] to Richmond very hazardous. But he was so impressed with the importance of the object, that he would not allow any personal inconvenience, or apparent risk, to prevent its accomplishment." John Johns, *A Memoir of the Life of the Right Rev. William Meade, D.D.* (Baltimore: Innes, 1867), 507.

35. The officer was Murray Mason, a naval commander who spent the war on duty in Richmond. (In 1868 Mrs. McGuire took the printed copy of her diary owned by her good friend Mrs. Margaret Dickins and identified in the margins many of the individuals she had originally cited by initials only. Hereafter, these additions will be cited as Dickins Copy.)

36. On March 8, 1862, the ironclad CSS *Virginia* attacked a Union fleet in Hampton Roads, Va. The *Virginia* destroyed two ships and ran three others aground. Yet the next morning, when the *Virginia* moved to finish the Union fleet, she encountered the USS *Monitor*. History's first battle between ironclad ships followed. Three hours of heavy combat produced a tactical draw.

37. Modern research seems to confirm that McIntosh made a foolhardy assault without orders or support. He was in front of his Second Arkansas Mounted Rifles when he was killed instantly. See William L. Shea and Earl J. Hess, *Pea Ridge: Civil War Campaign in the West* (Chapel Hill: University of North Carolina Press, 1992), 113–15.

38. McIntosh's wife was the former Judith Brockenbrough Phelps of Covington, Ky. Amy D. McDonald, Florida State University Library, to editor, April 23, 2004.

39. The remains of McIntosh were subsequently removed to the state cemetery in Austin, Tex.

40. McCulloch's death was far more costly to the Confederacy than that of McIntosh. A former Texas Ranger and compatriot of David Crockett, McCulloch disdained uniforms and wore a velvet suit in battle. A Union sharpshooter killed McCulloch early in the fighting at Pea Ridge.

41. The son of a member of George Washington's military staff, the Rt. Rev. William Meade was at the time the senior bishop in all of the Confederate dioceses. At his death in March 1862, the Bishop of North Carolina declared: "I have not known, no one of this generation, I believe, has known, a man superior to him in nobleness of nature, in the depth and power of religious principle, in determined zeal for what he believed truth and duty, in devotion to his Maker and his Redeemer." J. B. Cheshire, *The Church in the Confederate States* (New York: Longmans, 1912), 53.

42. On March 14, Union Gen. Ambrose E. Burnside and 11,000 troops ad-

vanced on the important old coastal community of New Bern, N.C., and seized it after a brief but spirited fight. This gave the Federals another serviceable base for inland expeditions.

43. Churchill J. Gibson was rector of Grace Episcopal Church in Richmond.

44. Bishop Johns's funeral oration is in Johns, *Meade*, 507–14.

45. Confederate forces in northern Virginia seemed too far from Richmond to permit swift adjustment if Gen. George McClellan's Army of the Potomac made a lunge toward the capital. On March 9, Confederate Gen. Joseph E. Johnston ordered his army to retire southward behind the Rappahannock River. Johnston would continue the withdrawal until he was on the peninsula east of Richmond.

46. On March 23, inadequate intelligence led Maj. Gen. "Stonewall" Jackson to attack a superior force at Kernstown. The Sunday afternoon battle produced the only tactical defeat Jackson suffered during his Civil War career.

47. Island No. 10 was located on the Mississippi River near the Kentucky-Tennessee border. There the river made a large S curve, and Confederates on the island could block Union shipping. On April 8, Union army and naval forces under Gen. John Pope captured the island, its 7,000 defenders, and 150 heavy guns. General Beauregard was not involved in the campaign.

48. Sgt. William B. Colston of the Second Virginia recovered from his hip wound but would be injured again at the battle of Fredericksburg.

49. "Croaker" was a popular term applied to one who was a chronic complainer and pessimist about the course of the Civil War.

50. Mrs. McGuire fell victim here to misinformation. After two days of fighting at Shiloh, which produced over 23,000 casualties, Gen. P.G.T. Beauregard retreated back to his base at Corinth, Miss. The smashing Union victory brought national fame to Union Gen. U. S. Grant.

51. Nathan Glass Newton was only fourteen at his February 1862 enlistment in his father's company of the Twenty-sixth Alabama. Ann Robinson King, Birmingham, Ala., to editor, March 26, 2004.

52. Caroline Augusta Ball was the author of this poem.

53. This report of the *Virginia*'s activities was untrue. On March 10, the vessel went into dry dock for four weeks of repairs and refitting. Raimondo Luraghi, *A History of the Confederate Navy* (Annapolis, Md.: Naval Institute Press, 1996), 148–50.

54. Fort Pulaski guarded the river entrance to Savannah, Ga., and was one of the most formidable coastal installations in America. Yet two days of bombardment (April 10–11) from U.S. Navy rifled artillery reduced the fort to rubble and closed Savannah as a blockade-running seaport.

55. Montgomery Dent Corse had been colonel of the Seventeenth Virginia, a regiment composed of companies from Alexandria and surrounding areas. At this time he commanded a brigade consisting of the First, Seventh, Eleventh, Seventeenth, and Twenty-fourth Virginia. Col. Arthur Herbert then commanded the Seventeenth Virginia.

56. Mrs. McGuire later identified this figure as Mrs. John A. Meredith. Dickins Copy. Wife of a Richmond circuit court judge, Sara A. Meredith was then in her mid-forties and the mother of five children. The oldest, William Bernard Meredith, was adjutant of Richardson's Virginia artillery battalion. 1860 Virginia Census—Henrico County; Robert E. L. Krick, *Staff Officers in Gray: A Biographical Register of the Staff Officers in the Army of Northern Virginia* (Chapel Hill: University of North Carolina Press, 2003), 220.

57. Col. Robert M. McKinney of the Fifteenth North Carolina was killed April 15, 1862, in an engagement at Lee's Mill, Va.

58. At the end of Jackson's Valley Campaign, a local citizen observed: "Meadows of clover are trodden into mud; the tossing plumes of the wheat-fields along the line of march are trodden down, as though a thousand reaping-machines have passed over and through them. Dead horses lie along the road, entirely overpowering the sweet scent of the clover-blossoms. . . . Fences are not, landmarks have vanished, and all is one common waste." Markinfield Addey, *"Stonewall Jackson": The Life and Military Career of Thomas Jonathan Jackson, Lieutenant-General in the Confederate Army* (New York: C. T. Evans, 1863), 92–93.

59. New Orleans was the South's largest city and key to the all-important Mississippi River. By April, most of the city's defenders had been sent to the front lines in Tennessee. The military commander at New Orleans, Gen. Mansfield Lovell, could do little more than watch as Union warships ran past two downriver forts and anchored at New Orleans's docks.

60. The ironclad CSS *Mississippi* was only days from completion when its executive officer, Lt. James I. Waddell, ordered the vessel put to the torch. A Confederate naval cadet considered the *Mississippi* worth a dozen *Merrimacks* to the South. Luraghi, *Confederate Navy*, 163.

61. To Flag Officer David G. Farragut's demand for the surrender of the city, Mayor John T. Monroe responded in part: "Our women and children can not escape your shells if it be your pleasure to murder them. . . . You wish to humble and disgrace us by an act against which our nature rebels. . . . We will stand your bombardment. . . . The civilized world will consign to indelible infamy the heart that will conceive the deed and the hand that will dare to consummate it." Three days later, with the threat of bombardment still imminent, Monroe

surrendered the city. Charles L. Dufour, *The Night the War Was Lost* (Garden City, N.Y.: Doubleday, 1960), 312–13, 329.

62. John Stevens Mason, a teacher, enlisted in the "Alexandria Riflemen" in April 1861, and became part of the Seventeenth Virginia. Mason's illness was not serious. He continued with the regiment until wounded at Second Manassas. Lee A. Wallace Jr., *17th Virginia Infantry* (Lynchburg, Va.: H. E. Howard, 1990), 127.

63. On the following day, May 6, the Rev. Charles Minnegerode baptized Jefferson Davis; and at a noon service, Bishop Johns confirmed his membership in the Episcopal faith. Ernest B. Furgurson, *Ashes of Glory: Richmond at War* (New York: Knopf, 1996), 129–30.

64. The Union army was advancing westward up the peninsula when, on May 5, the van collided with the rear of the retiring Confederate army at Williamsburg. An all-day fight in steady rain followed. Both forces suffered substantial losses. The Confederates resumed their retreat under cover of darkness.

65. Mrs. McGuire noted after the war that the soldier was George Wheeler. However, no Virginia Confederate by that name fought at Williamsburg.

66. Johnston commanded the Southern army to victory at Manassas in July 1861. Thereafter, wrote a critic, the general "had cherished his reputation like a champion reluctant to risk his title. In pursuing his cautious policy, he was true to his essentially defensive military nature." Dowdey, *Experiment in Rebellion*, 191.

67. White House, in New Kent County on the Pamunkey River, had been the site of George Washington's courtship of the widow Martha Custis. At the time of the Civil War, it was the plantation of Robert E. Lee's son, William Henry Fitzhugh Lee.

68. Henry Llewellen Dangerfield Lewis of Clarke County was then serving as a courier for Gen. Jeb Stuart. Lewis enjoyed a productive postwar career as insurance agent, farmer, and state senator. Dickins Copy; Robert J. Driver, *1st Virginia Cavalry* (Lynchburg, Va.: H. E. Howard, 1991), 199.

69. Lt. Col. John Prevost Marshall was then with the First Maryland. Owing to bad health, he did not survive the war.

70. Located eight miles downriver from Richmond, Drewry's (or Drury's) Bluff loomed ninety feet above the river and was a key to the defenses of the capital. Batteries of guns and river obstructions eventually made Drewry's Bluff a truly formidable installation.

71. A Richmond suburb, Rocketts lay to the east of the city on flat ground and contained a number of public wharves.

72. Captain Newton would be exchanged three months later and would return to duty with his cavalry regiment.

73. The CSS *Virginia* was too deep-drafted to get up the James River and not sufficiently seaworthy to escape to open water. On Sunday, May 12, when Norfolk fell under Federal control, Confederates scuttled the *Virginia*. Doing so eliminated the South's major challenge to the U.S. Navy.

74. Gen. Thomas J. Jackson was then in the opening phase of his 1862 Valley Campaign. On May 8, he defeated a Union force moving against him from the west at McDowell. After that, Jackson turned north to confront two other Union armies.

75. Lee had been an informal advisor to Davis from the preceding autumn until March 1862, when the president in effect named Lee his chief of staff. The Virginian continued to work hard at thankless tasks until June 1, when Davis appointed Lee to command the Confederacy's premier army.

76. Work on the Drewry's Bluff defenses did not begin until mid-March 1862, when it became obvious that a Union offensive was likely to start up the peninsula. Heavy rains slowed the hasty efforts of early May. Jefferson Davis, *The Papers of Jefferson Davis*, ed. Lynda L. Crist, Mary S. Dix, and Kenneth H. Williams (Baton Rouge: Louisiana State University Press, 1995), 8:107–8, 175, 178.

77. The "near connection" may well have been John White Brockenbrough. He was a distinguished jurist from Rockbridge County, and he served in the Provisional Confederate Congress. In 1865, as rector of the Board of Trustees of Washington College, Brockenbrough personally offered Lee the presidency of the impoverished school.

78. Maj. Walter H. Stevens had been in charge of the first efforts to fortify Drewry's Bluff. On May 14, Lee ordered Gen. William Mahone, the most experienced construction engineer then available, to proceed with his infantry brigade and take command of the defenses at the bluff.

79. Mrs. McGuire seems to have been the only known printed source for this treachery by a boat crew. The incident does not appear in the reports and correspondence of either Union or Confederate naval officials.

80. The CSS *Jamestown* was sunk in front of Drewry's Bluff to prevent all vessels but those of the lightest drafts from ascending the James. The *Patrick Henry* and smaller gunboats were above Drewry's Bluff.

81. If Mrs. McGuire was referring here to the Virginia General Assembly, she was truthful. Yet if her reference was to the Confederate Congress, that body did not deserve the diarist's praise. The Southern Congress achieved little in the Civil War. Personal jealousies, contentious personalities, an ongoing fight with President Davis, and sometimes blind insistence on state rights—all

performed in secret session—impaired the work and reputation of the national legislature.

82. From Thomas Gray's "The Progress of Poesy."

83. Many of the proceedings of the Confederate Congress are published in *OR*, series IV, vols. 1–3.

84. In 1861–1862, President Lincoln refused to initiate a prisoner exchange because it might be construed as official recognition of the Confederate States. Yet field commanders on both sides arranged many informal exchanges whereby one side released its prisoners and the other side exchanged a like number of men. The surplus on one side or the other was usually released on parole until formally exchanged.

85. Beverly Holcombe Robertson commanded the Fourth Virginia Cavalry before his June 1862 appointment to succeed Jackson's fallen cavalry chief, Turner Ashby.

86. Following the victory at McDowell, Jackson and his small force swept northward down the Shenandoah Valley and routed Gen. Nathaniel P. Banks's army at the May 25 battle of First Winchester.

87. Gen. George Hume Steuart commanded two regiments of cavalry under Jackson, but his conduct at Winchester left much to be desired. In Jackson's official report of the action, the commander accused Steuart of being an hour late in renewing pursuit of the Union army. "Had the cavalry played its part in the pursuit," a displeased Jackson stated, "but a small portion of Banks' army would have made its escape to the Potomac." James I. Robertson Jr., *Stonewall Jackson: The Man, the Soldier, the Legend* (New York: Macmillan, 1997), 399–401, 409; *OR*, series I, vol. 12, pt. 2, 706–7.

88. Jackson's telegram was a last-page item in the *Richmond (Va.) Dispatch*, May 27, 1862.

89. Johnston's wounds at Seven Pines included a musket ball in the shoulder, shell fragments in the chest and thigh, plus a hard fall from his horse. That night President Davis appointed Lee to command of the Army of Northern Virginia.

90. Heavy rains in the latter part of May had sent the Chickahominy River, which cut through the middle of the Union lines, out of its banks. All four bridges crossing the river in that area were washed away. Johnston reacted on May 31 by hurling two-thirds of his force against one of two Union corps at Seven Pines, south of the Chickahominy. Confusion, knee-deep water, and Union reinforcements beat back the feeble Confederate attacks. Southern losses were 6,134 men; Union casualties, 5,031 troops, in a two-day engagement that accomplished nothing tactically.

91. Johnston spent several months recuperating in a home at Broad and Twenty-eighth Streets on Church Hill in Richmond. Craig L. Symonds, *Joseph E. Johnston: A Civil War Biography* (New York: Norton, 1992), 175.

92. At Seven Pines, North Carolina's James Johnston Pettigrew was shot in the throat, shot again, and bayoneted before being taken prisoner. He was exchanged three months later and returned to duty.

93. Late in the afternoon of June 6, Gen. Turner Ashby was killed in a brief but spirited fight with Federals. A growing belief now is that Ashby was the victim of friendly fire.

94. Jackson's official report stated in part: "As a partisan officer I never knew his superior; his daring was proverbial . . . and his sagacity almost intuitive in divining the purposes and movements of the enemy." *OR*, series I, vol. 12, pt. 3, 712.

95. Thomas J. Jackson to Adj. Gen. Samuel Cooper, June 9, 1862, Adjutant General's Papers, Museum of the Confederacy, Richmond, Va.

96. Victories on the battlefield usually led to wild celebrations behind the lines. Yet that emotion often took a different form for women who learned heartbreakingly what the cost of victory was. Young Sallie Putnam wrote after Seven Pines: "The clouds were lifted and the skies brightened upon political prospects, but death held high carnival in our city." After the 1864 Battle of the Wilderness, another chronicler noted that the Confederate capital "was wild with joy and with woe as well." Putnam, *Richmond during the War*, 151; Myrta L. Avary, *A Virginia Girl in the Civil War, 1861–1865: Being a Record of the Actual Experiences of the Wife of a Confederate Officer* (New York: D. Appleton, 1903), 228.

97. Indeed, on June 2, McClellan had issued a congratulatory order to his army. "The events of every day prove your superiority; wherever you have met the enemy you have beaten him. . . . I ask of you one last crowning effort. . . . Soldiers! I will be with you in this battle, and share its dangers with you. Our confidence in each other is now founded upon the past." *The Civil War Papers of George B. McClellan*, ed. Stephen W. Sears (New York: Ticknor and Fields, 1989), 286.

98. "A curse, and an astonishment, and a hissing, and a reproach" is in Jeremiah 29:18.

99. Gen. "Jeb" Stuart's famous "Ride around McClellan" began on June 12 and lasted four days. Stuart captured 165 Federals and 260 horses. The one-hundred-mile journey also resulted in the destruction of millions of dollars worth of property while greatly elevating Southern morale.

100. A twenty-nine-year-old physician and plantation owner before the war,

William Latane had helped organize the "Essex Light Dragoons." It became part of the Ninth Virginia Cavalry. By April 1862, Latane was its captain. He was killed in a June 13 skirmish and buried at "Summer Hill" by Catherine Brockenbrough and Mary Newton. Mrs. McGuire's diary contains the first published account of the death and burial of Captain Latane. See "The Burial of Latane," *Southern Historical Society Papers* 24 (1896): 192–94; Howard Meriwether Lovett, "Tappahannock-on-the-Rappahannock," *Confederate Veteran* 33 (June 1925): 218; Mary Newton Stanard, *Richmond: Its People and Its Story* (Philadelphia: J. B. Lippincott, 1923), 192–93.

101. Philip St. George Cooke was a native of Leesburg, Va., a West Point graduate, and a soldier of high distinction. When civil war began, he renewed his allegiance to the Union—despite the fact that his son and son-in-law both became Confederate generals. "Jeb" Stuart reacted with cold fury to his father-in-law's decision. "He will regret it but once," Stuart declared, "and that will be continually." Emory M. Thomas, *Bold Dragoon: The Life of J. E. B. Stuart* (New York: Harper and Row, 1986), 95.

102. "Strawberry Hill" was a Brockenbrough summer estate between Richmond and Mechanicsville. It overlooked the Chickahominy River Valley.

103. Lee's great counteroffensive against the Union army is known as the Seven Days' Campaign. It began on June 26 with an ill-advised attack at Mechanicsville, northeast of Richmond. Gen. A. P. Hill's frontal assaults were beaten back with tragic ease. Confederate losses were almost 1,500 men, while Union casualties were fewer than 400 soldiers.

104. John Mercer Brockenbrough was colonel of the Fortieth Virginia. At Mechanicsville, the regiment suffered eight men killed and eighteen wounded. Robert E. L. Krick, *40th Virginia Infantry* (Lynchburg, Va.: H. E. Howard, 1985), 13.

105. William R. J. Pegram's "Purcell Battery" at Mechanicsville lost forty-seven of ninety men, half of its horses, and four of its six guns. James I. Robertson Jr., ed., "'The Boy Artillerist': Letters of Colonel William Pegram, C.S.A.," *Virginia Magazine of History and Biography* 98, no. 2 (April 1990): 225.

106. Hiram E. Cole was then twenty-two years old and served with John B. Newton as an assistant surgeon in the Fortieth Virginia.

107. The large brick building known as the Alms House stood on Hospital Street north of Shockoe Cemetery at the edge of Richmond. Davis's presidential residence was downtown. During most of the war, the Alms House was Hospital No. 1 in the Richmond medical network.

108. Here Mrs. McGuire displayed more bravado and stamina than many of her female compatriots. Twenty-five miles away, Mrs. Roger Pryor wrote of

the impossibility of describing "the terror and demoralization" of Petersburg women when Federals first opened fire on the city in 1864. She herself reached safety and "literally went all to pieces, trembling as though I had a chill." Sara A. R. Pryor, *Reminiscences of Peace and War* (New York: Macmillan, 1905), 280, 297.

109. Horace L. Kent, R. A. Paine, and William G. Paine ran a large mercantile and auctioneering business in Richmond.

110. Sixty-year-old Thomas Jefferson Chambers, a native of Culpeper County, Va., had been a lawyer in Kentucky and Alabama as well as a judge in Texas. In the Texas Revolution he was a general of reserves. Chambers served as a volunteer aide to Gen. John B. Hood during the Seven Days' Campaign. Krick, *Staff Officers in Gray*, 94.

111. When Jackson arrived at Gaines's Mill, the roar of battle was heavy. "Do you think your men can stand it?" Lee asked Jackson. A second or two of silence followed, then Jackson exclaimed: "They can stand almost anything! They can stand that!" Robertson, *Stonewall Jackson*, 481.

112. Twenty-four-year-old John Brockenbrough Newton was assistant surgeon of the Fortieth Virginia at the time. He later became Episcopal Bishop of Virginia. See Mary Newton Stanard, *John Brockenbrough Newton* (Richmond, 1924).

113. The bloodiest day of the Civil War for the Fortieth Virginia was at Gaines's Mill. By sundown, twenty-three men were dead and thirty-six wounded. Krick, *40th Virginia*, 13–14. The "Potomac Rifles," Company K of the regiment, consisted largely of Northumberland County men.

114. Edward Brockenbrough of Company B of the Fortieth Virginia was killed in action at Gaines's Mill. Ibid., 74.

115. The command structure of the Second Virginia took frightful losses at Gaines's Mill. Lt. Col. Raleigh Colston was wounded in the thigh. Col. James Walkinson Allen was shot through the head and killed, while a shell fragment blew away Maj. Francis Buckner Jones's knee and proved fatal.

116. Craig Woodrow McDonald, teacher and law student, joined the Thirteenth Virginia at war's outset. He became a captain and aide to Gen. Arnold Elzey. McDonald was killed at Gaines's Mill while leading reinforcements into the battle. David F. Riggs, *13th Virginia Infantry* (Lynchburg, Va.: H. E. Howard, 1988), 127.

117. Clarence Warwick had been a student at Episcopal High School prior to joining the Fourth Virginia Cavalry.

118. Bradfute Warwick was a mustached soldier of fortune from one of the better families of Virginia. He began his Confederate service as major of the

Fourth Texas—an assignment that nettled the Texans in the ranks. Yet Warwick had become one of the unit's most beloved officers when he fell mortally wounded at Gaines's Mill. Harold B. Simpson, *Gaines' Mill to Appomattox: Waco and McLennan County in Hood's Texas Brigade* (Waco: Texian Press, 1963), 52; *OR*, series I, vol. 11, pt. 2, 564.

119. In the latter stages of the Seven Days' Campaign, Gen. John Bankhead Magruder seemed to fall apart mentally. Persistent rumors of drunkenness circulated throughout Richmond. Magruder became the scapegoat for Confederate failures in the campaign. President Davis exiled him to the Trans-Mississippi Department.

120. On July 15, the new Confederate ironclad, *Arkansas,* attacked Union vessels in the Yazoo River north of Vicksburg. The ironclad made it to the safety of Vicksburg's batteries. It and three Union ships were damaged in the action.

121. With Lee stalemating McClellan on the peninsula, President Lincoln authorized the creation of a second Union army and sent it on an advance into north-central Virginia. Lee dispatched Jackson's forces to the rail junction of Gordonsville to watch this second threat, and to attack if practicable.

122. No battle of note occurred during this time in Arkansas between Confederate Gen. Thomas C. Hindman and Union Gen. Samuel R. Curtis.

123. Gen. Nathan Bedford Forrest's July 15 attack on the Union garrison at Murfreesboro resulted in the capture of 1,200 men, several pieces of artillery, and enormous amounts of supplies. No Union general was taken prisoner.

124. Col. John Hunt Morgan and his mounted "Kentucky Cavaliers" had just begun what would later be called the First Kentucky Campaign. The swashbuckling cavalryman would become the "Jeb Stuart of the West."

125. The wife of well-to-do Hanover County farmer William B. Sydnor is listed in the 1860 census only as "S. F." She was around fifty years old at the time of Mrs. McGuire's citation.

126. In the spring of 1862, Danville in southside Virginia became a medical center for sick and wounded soldiers. Most of the hospital buildings were converted tobacco warehouses.

127. Benjamin Harrison McGuire enlisted January 20, 1862, in the Twenty-second Virginia Infantry Battalion. He received promotion to lieutenant in late summer. On July 1, 1863, McGuire was killed at Gettysburg. Dickins Copy; Thomas M. Rankin, *22nd Battalion, Virginia Infantry* (Lynchburg, Va.: H. E. Howard, 1999), 92.

128. Mark Alexander was a well-to-do farmer in Mecklenburg County. He and his wife, Sally, had three sons, one of whom was a physician. Dickins Copy; 1860 Virginia Census—Mecklenburg County.

129. During August 4–5, Federals made a reconnaissance around Coggin's Point. No major action occurred.

130. Neither Maj. Robert Augustus Bailey nor his Twenty-second Virginia had launched any offensive moves in the south-central county of Nicholas, in what is now West Virginia. At the time, the regiment was recuperating from action in late May at Lewisburg.

131. After assuming command of the Union Army of Virginia, Gen. John Pope followed the bombastic nature of Gen. Benjamin F. Butler by issuing threats to the civilian population of Virginia. Rebel property was to be confiscated; local citizens who aided Confederates would be treated as spies and executed. The orders were never enforced, yet thereafter civilian property in the path of an invading army became a prime target of total war. For Davis's retaliatory directive, see *Papers of Jefferson Davis*, 8:310.

132. According to the 1860 Clarke County census, Abbie and Ann Rose Nelson were spinsters sixty- and fifty-five-years-old, respectively, and with moderate means. Their home was in the Millwood area.

133. Benjamin Harrison was captain of the "Charles City Light Dragoons" of the Third Virginia Cavalry when he was killed July 1 at Malvern Hill.

134. On August 9, Jackson attacked the lead corps of Pope's army at Cedar Mountain (or Slaughter Mountain, as it is sometimes called). Federals momentarily broke the Southern lines, but Jackson rushed reserves into action and forced the Union forces to retire from the field. Union casualties were 314, killed, 1,445 wounded, and 622 captured. Confederate losses were 223 killed, 1,060 wounded, and 31 missing. *OR*, series I, vol. 12, pt. 2, 139, 183–85.

135. Kate Mason Rowland was a highly respected member of Richmond society. She is best known for her volunteer nursing duties in local hospitals.

136. No one who ever met "the widely known" Emily Mason, one source stated, could forget the Richmond spinster's "patrician features and her wonderfully expressive black eyes—eyes distinctive of the Masons for many generations." Munford, *Richmond Homes*, 57–58.

137. Margaret Dinkins was a longtime Alexandria friend. It was in her copy of the printed McGuire diary that Mrs. McGuire identified a number of individuals previously cited by initials only.

138. Elizabeth Cabell Daniel was the wife of Judge William Daniel Jr. She named their Lynchburg home "Rivermont" because of its location high above the James River. That name now denotes a prominent section of the city.

139. Judge William H. Cabell's wife was the former Agnes Gamble. She died in 1863 at the age of eighty-three. Alexander Brown, *The Cabells and Their*

Kin: A Memorial Volume of History, Biography, and Genealogy (Richmond, Va.: Garrett and Massie, 1939), 271, 278.

140. Gen. Charles Sidney Winder, the third commander of the Stonewall Brigade, died from a shell wound at Cedar Mountain. Confederate killed, wounded, and missing at this battle numbered almost 1,400 men.

141. Mary Stevenson Brockenbrough, born in 1810, married Willoughby Newton of Hanover County. Brockenbrough Records, Museum of the Confederacy, Richmond, Va.

142. Fort Delaware, of the same design as Forts Sumter and Pulaski, stood on Pea Patch Island in the Delaware River downstream from Wilmington, Del. Its proximity to the war zone made it a principal compound for Southern soldiers captured in the East.

143. Catherine M. Brockenbrough was the wife of physician and well-to-do farmer William Spencer Roane Brockenbrough. They lived at Westwood.

144. Then in his late seventies, Dr. William Randolph Nelson resided at "Gold Hill" on River Road near the Newton estate. *Old Homes of Hanover County*, 46; 1860 Virginia Census—Hanover County.

145. Sarah Jane Brockenbrough Colston was the sister of Mrs. McGuire.

146. Capt. John A. Doyle then served in the Commissary of Subsistence Department of McClellan's army. See *OR*, series I, vol. 11, pt. 1, 173.

147. Dr. Ezekiel Starke Talley was then in his early sixties. He and his wife, M. F., had seven children. Included in the five boys were two who would die on the same day in battle.

148. Catherine and M. F. Aubrey Newton had been tending to five-year-old Lucy, their sister.

149. Richard H. Rush led the Sixth Pennsylvania Cavalry.

150. Fourteen-year-old Walter Sydnor was the third of five children of William B. and S. F. Sydnor. 1860 Virginia Census—Hanover County.

151. South Carolinian Benjamin Huger had graduated from West Point and was a colonel in the U.S. Army when civil war began. He became a major general in command of the Department of Norfolk for the first year of the struggle. Mrs. Huger, the former Elizabeth Celestine Pinckney, was his first cousin. Jeffrey L. Rhoades, *Scapegoat General: The Story of Major General Benjamin Huger, C.S.A.* (Hamden, Conn.: Archon Books, 1985), 4.

152. Quartermaster of the Sixth Pennsylvania Cavalry was Lt. Theodore M. Sage. Samuel P. Bates, *History of Pennsylvania Volunteers, 1861–5* (Harrisburg, Pa.: B. Singerly, 1869), 2:754.

153. In the third week of June, Federals made a reconnaissance into Hanover County to pinpoint the northern flank of the Confederate army. The Sixth

Pennsylvania Cavalry ("Rush's Lancers") was part of the contingent. For Rush's report of the expedition, see *OR*, series I, vol. 11, pt. 1, 667–68.

154. Sally A. Page Newton was the teenage daughter (and oldest of five children) of William and Mary Newton. 1860 Virginia Census—Hanover County.

155. Col. Gouverneur Kemble Warren of the Fifth New York was temporarily commanding a brigade at the time. Promotion to brigadier general came in September of that year.

156. The only mounted Augusta County soldiers then engaged on the peninsula were the "Valley Rangers" of the First Virginia Cavalry.

157. Thomas J. Page appears in the 1860 Hanover County census as a fifty-year-old farmer, married, without children, and having $27,300 in assets.

158. Brig. Gen. Fitz John Porter commanded the V Corps in the Army of the Potomac. His troops were then somewhat isolated by the swollen Chickahominy River slicing through the Federal lines.

159. John Latane abandoned studies at the University of Virginia to join his brother's cavalry company. Promoted to lieutenant in June 1862, he was mortally wounded in an 1864 action by friendly fire from his own men. Robert K. Krick, *9th Virginia Cavalry* (Lynchburg, Va.: H. E. Howard, 1982), 85.

160. George Carraway was rector of Immanuel and St. Paul's Churches in Hanover County.

161. Mrs. McGuire reported the death of William Phelps in her January 20, 1862, entry.

162. Reference here is to the June 12–13 skirmishes at Haws Shop and Old Church. Captain Latane was killed at the former engagement, with the officer who shot him falling wounded. Now that Stuart had obtained the information that Lee sought—the position of the Union right flank, Stuart determined to return to Richmond by riding around McClellan's massive army. See H. B. McClellan, *The Life and Campaigns of Major-General J. E. B. Stuart: Commander of the Cavalry of the Army of Northern Virginia* (Boston: Houghton Mifflin, 1885), 53–57.

163. "J. W." was the eldest of William S. R. Brockenbrough's four children. She was eleven years old at the time. 1860 Virginia Census—Hanover County.

164. *The Arabian Nights' Entertainments,* also called *A Thousand and One Nights,* is a collection of ancient Persian-Indian-Arabian tales first put together around the year 1450. The most famous of the stories is *Aladdin, or the Wonderful Lamp.*

165. Mrs. Newton was reporting rumor. Although Capt. William B. Royall of the Fifth U.S. Cavalry suffered "several saber wounds" and much loss of blood

in the Haws Shop fight, the injuries were not fatal. Royall ended the war a major in charge of the cavalry depot at Carlisle Barracks, Pa. *OR*, series I, vol. 11, pt. 1, 1021; *OR*, series I, vol. 11, pt. 2, 758.

166. George W. and B. B. Bassett lived close to Westwood, the Brockenbrough estate. The couple had seven children. In 1860 Ella Moore Bassett, the third daughter, married Lewis W. Washington of Jefferson County, Va. 1860 Virginia Census—Hanover County; *Hanover County Historical Society Bulletin* 1 (1969–1987): 41.

167. Benjamin Henry Rush was born in England while his father was American ambassador to the Court of St. James. His grandfather, Benjamin Rush, was signer of both the Declaration of Independence and the Constitution. Rush's Sixth Pennsylvania Cavalry proved to be one of the elite units in the Civil War, thanks to its colonel's meticulous detail and devotion to duty.

168. Member of a prominent Virginia family, James Murray Mason had a pre–Civil War career that included state legislator, constitutional convention member, congressman, and U.S. senator.

169. From Thomas a Kempis, "Imitation of Christ."

170. This reference is likely to Willoughby Newton, father of Capt. William B. Newton.

171. Lancaster County, situated where the Rappahannock River empties into Chesapeake Bay, would have been one hundred miles from Richmond on the roads of that day.

172. E. T. Shelton was then in his late twenties. He was married and had three children. 1860 Virginia Census—Hanover County.

173. This must have been a hasty ceremony. On the day (August 27) that Newton returned to duty, the Fourth Virginia Cavalry and other units seized Manassas Junction and then rode "over fences, across ravines, and through swamps" in pursuit of the retreating Union army. Stiles, *4th Virginia Cavalry*, 18, 128.

Selected Bibliography

Addey, Markinfield. *"Stonewall Jackson": The Life and Military Career of Thomas Jonathan Jackson, Lieutenant-General in the Confederate Army.* New York: C. T. Evans, 1863.

Avary, Myrta L. *A Virginia Girl in the Civil War, 1861–1865: Being a Record of the Actual Experiences of the Wife of a Confederate Officer.* New York: D. Appleton, 1903.

Bean, William G. *Stonewall's Man: Sandie Pendleton.* Chapel Hill: University of North Carolina Press, 1959.

Berkeley, Henry Robinson. *Four Years in the Confederate Artillery: The Diary of Private Henry Robinson Berkeley.* Edited by William Runge. Richmond: Virginia Historical Society, 1991.

Bill, Alfred Hoyt. *The Beleaguered City: Richmond, 1861–1865.* New York: Knopf, 1946.

Blair, William. *Virginia's Private War: Feeding Body and Soul in the Confederacy, 1861–1865.* New York: Oxford University Press, 1998.

Brewer, James H. *The Confederate Negro: Virginia's Craftsmen and Military Laborers, 1861–1865.* Durham, N.C.: Duke University Press, 1969.

Brown, Alexander. *The Cabells and Their Kin: A Memorial Volume of History, Biography, and Genealogy.* Richmond, Va.: Garrett and Massie, 1939.

Buck, Lucy. *Sad Earth, Sweet Heaven: The Diary of Lucy Buck during the War between the States, December 25, 1861–April 15, 1865.* 2nd ed. Edited by William P. Buck. Birmingham, Ala.: Buck Publishing, 1992.

Calcutt, Rebecca Barbour. *Richmond's Wartime Hospitals.* Gretna, La.: Pelican Publishing Company, 2005.

Caldwell, Susan. *"My Heart Is So Rebellious": The Caldwell Letters, 1861–1865.* Edited by J. Michael Welton. Warrenton, Va.: Fauquier National Bank, 1990.

Colt, Margaretta Barton. *Defend the Valley: A Shenandoah Family in the Civil War.* New York: Crown, 1994.

Cooper, William J., Jr. *Jefferson Davis, American.* New York: Knopf, 2000.

Cunningham, H. H. *Doctors in Gray: The Confederate Medical Service.* Baton Rouge: Louisiana State University Press, 1958.

Cutchins, John A. *A Famous Command: The Richmond Light Infantry Blues.* Richmond, Va.: Garrett and Massie, 1934.

Dabney, Virginius. *Richmond: The Story of a City.* Garden City, N.Y.: Doubleday, 1976.

Davis, Jefferson. *The Papers of Jefferson Davis.* Vol. 8. Edited by Lynda L. Crist, Mary S. Dix, and Kenneth H. Williams. Baton Rouge: Louisiana State University Press, 1995.

Davis, William C. *The Cause Lost: Myths and Realities of the Confederacy.* Lawrence: University Press of Kansas, 1996.

———. *Jefferson Davis: The Man and His Hour.* New York: HarperCollins, 1991.

Dew, Charles B. *Ironmaker to the Confederacy: Joseph R. Anderson and Tredegar Iron Works.* 2nd ed. Richmond: Library of Virginia, 1999.

Donald, David Herbert. *Lincoln.* New York: Simon and Schuster, 1995.

Dowdey, Clifford. *Experiment in Rebellion.* Garden City, N.Y.: Doubleday, 1946.

Driver, Robert J. *1st Virginia Cavalry.* Lynchburg, Va.: H. E. Howard, 1991.

Edmonds, Amanda Virginia. *Journals of Amanda Virginia Edmonds: Lass of the Mosby Confederacy, 1859–1867.* Edited by Nancy Chapplear Baird. Delaplane, Va.: N. C. Baird, 1984.

Faust, Drew Gilpin. *Mothers of Invention: Women of the Slaveholding South in the American Civil War.* Chapel Hill: University of North Carolina Press, 1996.

Frye, Dennis E. *2nd Virginia Infantry.* Lynchburg, Va.: H. E. Howard, 1984.

Furgurson, Ernest B. *Ashes of Glory: Richmond at War.* New York: Knopf, 1996.

Gallagher, Gary W., ed. *The Richmond Campaign of 1862: The Peninsula and the Seven Days.* Chapel Hill: University of North Carolina Press, 2000.

Green, Carol C. *Chimborazo: The Confederacy's Largest Hospital.* Knoxville: University of Tennessee Press, 2004.

Grimsley, Mark. *The Hard Hand of War: Union Military Policy toward Southern Civilians, 1861–1865.* Cambridge and New York: Cambridge University Press, 1995.

Guerrant, Edward O. *Bluegrass Confederate: The Headquarters Diary of Edward O. Guerrant.* Edited by William C. Davis and Meredith L. Swentor. Baton Rouge: Louisiana State University Press, 1999.

Hennessy, John J. *Return to Bull Run: The Campaign and Battle of Second Manassas.* New York: Simon and Schuster, 1993.

Hess, Earl J. *Banners to the Breeze: The Kentucky Campaign, Corinth, and Stones River.* Lincoln: University of Nebraska Press, 2000.

Holzer, Harold, and Mark E. Neely Jr. *Mine Eyes Have Seen the Glory: The Civil War in Art.* New York: Orion Books, 1993.

Johnston, Angus J. *Virginia Railroads in the Civil War.* Chapel Hill: University of North Carolina Press, 1961.

Krick, Robert E. L. *40th Virginia Infantry.* Lynchburg, Va.: H. E. Howard, 1985.

———. *Staff Officers in Gray: A Biographical Register of the Staff Officers in the*

Army of Northern Virginia. Chapel Hill: University of North Carolina Press, 2003.

Krick, Robert K. *Conquering the Valley: Stonewall Jackson at Port Republic.* New York: William Morrow, 1996.

———. *9th Virginia Cavalry.* Lynchburg, Va.: H. E. Howard, 1982.

———. *Stonewall Jackson at Cedar Mountain.* Chapel Hill: University of North Carolina Press, 1990.

Lee, Robert E. *Recollections and Letters of General Robert E. Lee.* New York: Doubleday, 1907.

———. *The Wartime Papers of R. E. Lee.* Edited by Clifford Dowdey. Boston: Little, Brown, 1961.

Luraghi, Raimondo. *A History of the Confederate Navy.* Annapolis, Md.: Naval Institute Press, 1996.

Marvel, William. *The Battles for Saltville: Southwest Virginia in the Civil War.* Lynchburg, Va.: H. E. Howard, 1992.

McClellan, George B. *The Civil War Papers of George B. McClellan: Selected Correspondence, 1860–1865.* Edited by Stephen W. Sears. New York: Ticknor and Fields, 1989.

McClellan, H. B. *The Life and Campaigns of Major-General J. E. B. Stuart: Commander of the Cavalry of the Army of Northern Virginia.* Boston: Houghton Mifflin, 1885.

McKnight, Brian D. *Contested Borderland: The Civil War in Appalachian Kentucky and Virginia.* Lexington: University Press of Kentucky, 2006.

McPherson, James M. *Battle Cry of Freedom: The Civil War Era.* New York: Oxford University Press, 1988.

Munford, Robert Beverly, Jr. *Richmond Homes and Memories.* Richmond, Va.: Garrett and Massie, 1936.

Neely, Mark E., Jr., Harold Holzer, and Gabor S. Boritt. *The Confederate Image: Prints of the Lost Cause.* Chapel Hill: University of North Carolina Press, 1987.

———. *The Union Image: Popular Prints of the Civil War North.* Chapel Hill: University of North Carolina Press, 2000.

O'Reilly, Francis Augustin. *The Fredericksburg Campaign: Winter War on the Rappahannock.* Baton Rouge: Louisiana State University Press, 2003.

Osborne, Randall, and Jeffrey Weaver. *The Virginia State Rangers and State Line.* Lynchburg, Va.: H. E. Howard, 1994.

Parks, Joseph Howard. *General Edmund Kirby Smith, C.S.A.* Baton Rouge: Louisiana State University Press, 1954.

Parrish, T. Michael, and Robert M. Willingham. *Confederate Imprints: A Bibliogra-*

phy of Southern Publications from Secession to Surrender. Austin, Tex.: Jenkins Publishing, ca. 1984.

Pember, Phoebe Yates. *A Southern Woman's Story: Life in Confederate Richmond.* Edited by Bell Irvin Wiley. Jackson, Tenn.: McCowat-Mercer Press, 1959.

Perdue, Charles L., Jr., Thomas E. Barden, and Robert K. Phillips, eds. *Weevils in the Wheat: Interviews with Virginia Ex-Slaves.* Charlottesville: University Press of Virginia, 1976.

Pryor, Sara A. R. *Reminiscences of Peace and War.* New York: Macmillan, 1905.

Putnam, Sallie Brock. *Richmond during the War: Four Years of Personal Observation.* New York: G. W. Carleton, 1867.

Quintard, Charles T. *Doctor Quintard, Chaplain, C.S.A., and Second Bishop of Tennessee: The Memoir and Civil War Diary of Charles Todd Quintard.* Edited by Sam Davis Elliott. Baton Rouge: Louisiana State University Press, 2003.

Rable, George C. *Fredericksburg! Fredericksburg!* Chapel Hill: University of North Carolina Press, 2002.

Rankin, Thomas M. *22nd Battalion, Virginia Infantry.* Lynchburg, Va.: H. E. Howard, 1999.

Rhoades, Jeffrey L. *Scapegoat General: The Story of Major General Benjamin Huger, C.S.A.* Hamden, Conn.: Archon Books, 1985.

Riggs, David F. *13th Virginia Infantry.* Lynchburg, Va.: H. E. Howard, 1988.

Robertson, James I., Jr., ed. *Stonewall Jackson: The Man, the Soldier, the Legend.* New York: Macmillan, 1997.

Salmon, John S. *The Official Virginia Civil War Battlefield Guide.* Mechanicsburg, Pa.: Stackpole Books, 2001.

Schultz, Jane E. *Women at the Front: Hospital Workers in Civil War America.* Chapel Hill: University of North Carolina Press, 2004.

Sears, Stephen W. *To the Gates of Richmond: The Peninsula Campaign.* New York: Ticknor and Fields, 1992.

Shea, William L., and Earl J. Hess. *Pea Ridge: Civil War Campaign in the West.* Chapel Hill: University of North Carolina Press, 1992.

Simkins, Francis Butler, and James Welch Patton. *The Women of the Confederacy.* Richmond, Va.: Garrett and Massie, 1936.

Simpson, Harold B. *Gaines' Mill to Appomattox: Waco and McLennan County in Hood's Texas Brigade.* Waco: Texian Press, 1963.

Stanard, Mary Newton. *Richmond: Its People and Its Story.* Philadelphia: J. B. Lippincott, 1923.

Stiles, Kenneth L. *4th Virginia Cavalry.* Lynchburg, Va.: H. E. Howard, 1985.

Sutherland, Daniel E. *Seasons of War: The Ordeal of a Confederate Community, 1861–1865.* New York: Free Press, 1995.

Symonds, Craig L. *Joseph E. Johnston: A Civil War Biography.* New York: Norton, 1992.

Thomas, Emory M. *Bold Dragoon: The Life of J.E. B. Stuart.* New York: Harper and Row, 1986.

———. *Robert E. Lee: A Biography.* New York: Norton, 1995.

United States Surgeon General's Office. *The Medical and Surgical History of the War of the Rebellion.* 6 vols. Washington, D.C.: Government Printing Office, 1870–88.

United States War Department. *War of the Rebellion: A Compilation of Official Records of the Union and Confederate Armies.* 128 vols. Washington, D.C.: Government Printing Office, 1880–1901.

Vandiver, Frank E. *Ploughshares into Swords: Josiah Gorgas and Confederate Ordnance.* Austin: University of Texas Press, 1952.

Virginia. *Messages of the Governor of Virginia, and Accompanying Documents.* Richmond, Va., 1864.

———. *Proceedings of the Virginia State Convention of 1861.* 4 vols. Richmond: Virginia State Library, 1965.

Wallace, Lee A., Jr. *17th Virginia Infantry.* Lynchburg, Va.: H. E. Howard, 1990.

Weaver, Jeffrey. *The Civil War in Buchanan and Wise Counties: Bushwhackers' Paradise.* Lynchburg, Va.: H. E. Howard, 1994.

Wiley, Bell Irvin. *Embattled Confederates: An Illustrated History of Southerners at War.* New York: Harper and Row, 1964.

Wills, Brian Steel. *The War Hits Home: The Civil War in Southeastern Virginia.* Charlottesville: University Press of Virginia, 2001.

Wilson, Harold S. *Confederate Industry: Manufacturers and Quartermasters in the Civil War.* Jackson: University Press of Mississippi, 2002.

Index